MEXICO CITY AND VICINITY

To San Luis Potosí
Querétaro
To Guadalajara
To Morelia
Actopan
Pachuca
Tulancingo
Tula
To Poza Rica
TEXAS
Tepotzotlán
Teotihuacán
Otumba
Chapingo
MEXICO CITY
Texcoco
To Jalapa
San José de Purúa
Ixtapalapa
Tlaxcala
VALLE DE BRAVO
Chalco
Tlalmanalco
Huejotzingo
To Orizaba
Toluca
Metepec
Amecameca
Ixtaccíhuatl
(Snow
Volcanoes)
Tenango
Popocatepetl
PUEBLA
Tenancingo
Malinalco
Tepoztlán
Ixtapan de la Sal
PYRAMID OF
XOCHICALCO
Cuernavaca
Atlixco
Cuautla
GRUTAS DE
CACAHUAMILPA
Las Estacas
Izúcar de
Matamoros
Taxco
To
Iguala
L. Tequesquitengo
To Acatlán

Del Rio
(UNITED STATES)
dras
gras
Nuevo
Laredo
Laredo
Rio Grande
Brownsville
TAS DE GARCÍA
MONTERREY
Matamoros
tillo

Gulf of Mexico

Ciudad
Victoria
EL SALTO
Luis
osí
Ciudad
Valles
lores Hidalgo
S. M. de Allende
Querétaro
e de Santiago
riria
Cuitzeo
elia
MEXICO CITY
Toluca
Cholula
Cuernavaca
PUEBLA
Taxco
Matamoros
Iguala
Acatlán
ilpancingo

Tampico
Tuxpan
Poza Rica
Papantla
Pachuca
El Tajín
Cuetzalán
Jalapa
Tlaxcala
Veracruz
Córdoba
Orizaba

Gulf of Campeche

Mérida
MAYAPÁN
UXMAL
CHICHÉN ITZÁ
KABAH
LABNA
SAYIL
TULUM
Campeche
Isla
Mujeres
Cozumel I.

Yucatan

Peninsula

Ciudad del Carmen
La Venta
Lake
Términos
BRITISH
HONDURAS

Coatzacoalcos
Villahermosa
PALENQUE
Isthmus of **Tehuantepec**
Oaxaca
MITLA
Tuxtla Gutiérrez
Juchitán
San Cristóbal de
las Casas
YAXCHILÁN
BONAMPAK
Comitán
MONTE ALBÁN
PAN AMERICAN
HIGHWAY
Tehuantepec
GUATEMALA
Ciudad
Cuauhtémoc

Acapulco

Gulf of
Tehuantepec
Tapachula

N
W E
S

Don Pitcher

THE MEXICO TRAVELER

Books by SELDEN RODMAN

Verse

DEATH OF THE HERO
THE AMAZING YEAR
THE REVOLUTIONISTS
THE AIRMEN
LAWRENCE: THE LAST CRUSADE
MORTAL TRIUMPH AND OTHER POEMS

Art

THE FRESCOES OF OROZCO
THE INSIDERS
CONVERSATIONS WITH ARTISTS
THE EYE OF MAN
PORTRAIT OF THE ARTIST AS AN AMERICAN
RENAISSANCE IN HAITI
HORACE PIPPIN: A NEGRO ARTIST IN AMERICA

Music

THE HEART OF BEETHOVEN

History and Travel

MEXICAN JOURNAL: THE CONQUERORS CONQUERED
HAITI: THE BLACK REPUBLIC
QUISQUEYA: A HISTORY OF THE DOMINICAN REPUBLIC
THE ROAD TO PANAMA
THE GUATEMALA TRAVELER
THE PERU TRAVELER
THE CARIBBEAN
THE MEXICO TRAVELER

Anthologies

ONE HUNDRED MODERN POEMS
ONE HUNDRED AMERICAN POEMS
WAR AND THE POET (with Richard Eberhart)
THE POETRY OF FLIGHT
A NEW ANTHOLOGY OF MODERN POETRY

Quetzalcoatl

Drawing by José Clemente Orozco. Museum of Modern Art, New York. Gift of Clemente Orozco.

THE
MEXICO
TRAVELER

A Concise History and Guide

by SELDEN RODMAN

MEREDITH PRESS / New York

First Edition

Library of Congress Catalog Card Number: 69–19047

MANUFACTURED IN THE UNITED STATES OF AMERICA FOR MEREDITH PRESS

VAN REES PRESS • NEW YORK

To

LUCAS JOHNSON, JONATHAN ROSE
and DIANA COLUMBUS

ACKNOWLEDGMENTS

D URING my first trip to Mexico, a journalistic assignment in
1937, I received help from Dr. Ramón Beteta, then Under Secretary
of Foreign Affairs in the Cárdenas government; Solamón de la Selva,
Director of the Information Bureau of the National Revolutionary
Party (now the Party of Revolutionary Institutions, PRI); the late
Josephus Daniels, our Ambassador to Mexico at that time; the late
Diego Rivera and his second wife, the late Frida Kahlo.

During the six months I spent in Mexico in 1956–57, visiting almost
every part of the country, so many Mexicans were of help to me
that it would be impossible to list them all. My debt to most of them
is mentioned in the record of that visit, *Mexican Journal*; but I would
like especially to cite here again the special insights I received from
such friends as the late Miguel Covarrubias, Octavio Paz and Carlos
Fuentes, David Alfaro Siqueiros and the late José Vasconcelos,
Mathias Goeritz and Juan O'Gorman, the late Alfonso Reyes and
the late Dr. Atl, Rufino Tamayo, Alberto Ruz Llullier, and Antonio
Souza and among my compatriots Donald Demarest, Maia Wojcie-
chowska, Margaret Jessup, Giles Greville Healey, and the late Alma
Reed.

During a brief visit in 1960 in connection with the Mexican Government's exhibit of my collection of paintings at the San Carlos
Academy, my hosts were Arnold and Esmeralda Belkin, and my
friends and traveling companions José Luis Cuevas, Francisco Icaza
and his wife Concha de Icaza, Antonio Gonzáles de León and my
daughter Oriana.

The four months I spent in Mexico in 1963 working on a study
of Orozco's frescoes were made profitable and enjoyable by such

friends as Ignácio Díaz-Morales, Artémio Sepúlveda, Robert Brady, and my wife Carole.

During the six months in 1967–68 when I was in Mexico working specifically on the present book, friends and traveling companions who were most helpful included, in addition to my wife and many of those already mentioned, Diana Columbus, Lucas and Helen Johnson, Jonathan and Mona Rose, Stephen Banker, Michael and Sandy-Lee Macoby, Manuel Parra, Felix Candela, Donald Cordry, Malcolm Butler of the American Embassy, Vernard Lanphier and Culver E. Gidden, American Consuls in San Luis Potosí and Morelia, respectively, Clark and Marian Blyth, Herbert Hofmann-Ysenbourg and Maxwell Gordon. Without the help of Ernest Silverman of the Mexican National Tourist Council in New York, and of Miguel Guajardo and his assistant Rene Ruiz Cervantes at the Consejo Nacionál de Turismo (headed by Lic. Miguel Alemán) in Mexico City, my extensive travel by air during this period would not have been possible; and to Herbert Williamson, publications manager of Volkswagen of America, Inc., and Rene Espinosa Olvera, Public Relations Manager of Volkswagen de México, S.A., I am similarly indebted for facilitating my rapid transit of the roads.

PREFACE

"IN MEXICO," India's Prime Minister Nehru once remarked to Mexico's muralist Siqueiros, "artists are more important than politicians." [1]

The observation is true in a symbolic sense. One comes to Mexico to admire its eighth-century sculpture, its seventeenth-century churches, its twentieth-century murals, or to be renewed by association with the beauty, hospitality and friendship of a people not far removed from the traditional virtues of the soil. One does not come to Mexico to learn from its political institutions, the independence of its newspapers, the incorruptibility of its petty officialdom, or the cleanliness of its sanitary facilities—which is not to say that the present government of Mexico is not in many ways admirable, and superior in its tolerance and stability to others in Latin America, but that it is the product of a history far more subject than our own to interferences from the outside—interferences in which we frequently participated. To relate the history without placing a great deal of emphasis on the cultures that determined it would be as shortsighted as to describe the landscape and arts without reference to the events that depended on the one and shaped the other.

The history of Mexico, to borrow Apollinaire's phrase, has been grave, noble and tragic. Only superficially has it been frivolous, corrupt and brutal. Sensationalism feeds upon the ignobilities. We are reminded more often of the blood sacrifices of the Aztecs than of Netzahualcoyotl's poetry or the gentleness of the Zapotecs. The

[1] Quoted in the author's *Mexican Journal: The Conquerors Conquered*, New York, The Devin-Adair Co., 1958. (Paperback edition published by University of Southern Illinois Press in 1965.)

ix

conquistadors' cruelty makes better copy than the Franciscans' compassion. Sor Juana's militant feminism and Tresguerras' command of all the arts are less obvious products of New Spain than those *retablos* overloaded with gold leaf—which we ascribe too easily to the Church's indifference to the poverty of its flock. The sublimity of Padre Hidalgo and Padre Morelos in the fierce struggle for independence from Spain is beyond our horizon. The American invaders of 1847 were well aware of the venality of Mexico's rulers, at that nadir in their prey's history, and took as much advantage as they could of Santa Anna's duplicity; but understandably they were less impressed by the self-sacrifice of Chapultepec's cadets. Manet found Juarez' incorruptibility less romantic material for his brush than the foreign puppet Maximilian's fortitude before the firing squad at the Hill of Bells. A sunset glow of "law and order," under which American and British imperialism were able to do with Mexico as they pleased, still suffuses the police state of Porfirio Díaz. The Revolution of 1910 is not seen as a popular riposte to that age of savage repression, nor in terms of the martyrdom of Francisco Madero, nor even as primitive response to land hunger and feudal despotism on the part of such heroes as Zapata and Villa, but as simple banditry and bloodletting. And Cárdenas, perhaps the most selfless, constructive ruler any nation ever had, is remembered among us (if he is remembered at all) as an unprincipled adversary of American business, or the recipient of Stalin's tainted Peace Prize.

There is no history so dramatic in its confrontations, and to visualize these one must travel in Mexico. Conversely, unless one is ready to settle for Tijuana, Acapulco and Taxco, Mexico's history is the key to its landscape. The blind Prescott, with a poet's divination, could comprehend the magnitude of Cortés' feat, but for ordinary mortals the ascent from tropical Veracruz to the capital by way of the snow volcanoes is essential. The towering mountains and desert wastes of the north are no more than towering mountains and desert wastes unless one suffers with the stragglers of Zachary Taylor's and Santa Anna's armies, or thrills to the matchless daring of Francisco Villa swimming the Rio Grande with his eight companions to begin the reconquest of Mexico. The capital's mammoth Zócalo may seem the emptiest of squares unless the inner eye can people it with Cuauhtémoc's legions driving the Spaniards to their *Noche Triste*, Winfield Scott raising the Stars and Stripes to the plaudits of the future commanders of the American Civil War, the valorous Madero riding into it to his fate, and Cárdenas defying the

American plunderers with the chickens and wedding rings of peasant Mexico. Guanajuato is the most picturesque of cities, but to enter the Alhóndiga's gate mindful of Pípila bearing his gravestone with the *tumulto* of Hidalgo behind him is to see it in another light. To study Orozco's three mighty cycles in fresco at Guadalajara without any knowledge of the devastating events the artist had witnessed two decades before he painted them has to be as fractional an experience as contemplating the Sistine Chapel without any knowledge of Christianity in the Italian Renaissance.

Visitors will be charmed or repelled by the Mexican character according to their temperaments.

The stereotype of the Mexican as a lazy peon dozing under his sombrero, debilitated by tropical ailments but quite ready to knife you for your purse if you turn your back, was firmly established when Flandrau visited Mexico in 1905. That perceptive American saw violence as no more prevalent than in the United States but more noticeable because always "pictorial" and "dramatic"—as "in a painting that tells a story." He thought it "not surprising that a population perpetually in the throes of intestinal disorder should be somewhat lacking in energy," and added: "When one lives among them one marvels, not like the tourist of a week, that they are dirty, but that under the circumstances they are as clean as they are; not that so many of them are continually sick, but that any of them are ever well; not that they love to get drunk, but that they can bear to remain sober." He was describing misery under the Díaz dictatorship, but he was not pessimistic about the future. "Children rarely cry; their capacity for amusing themselves with nothing is without limit. Had I the ordering of this strange, unhappy world, I think all children would be born Mexican and remain so until they were fifteen." The indolence, he predicted, would quickly give way before education—and a "less emotional" diet.[2]

The equally perceptive Octavio Paz, writing *after* the Revolution, that "fiesta of bullets," sees *machismo* (exaggerated maleness) as the principal flaw in the Mexican character. "The verb *chingar*—malign and agile and playful like a caged animal—creates many expressions that turn our world into a caged jungle: There are tigers in business, eagles in schools, lions among our friends. A bribe is called a *mordida* (bite). Bureaucrats gnaw their 'bones' (public employment). . . . The only thing of value is manliness, personal strength, a capability for imposing oneself upon others." *Machismo*, in Paz's view, is a defense

---

[2] Charles Macomb Flandrau in *Viva Mexico!* Reprinted by Harper & Brothers, n.d.

mechanism. "We are taught from childhood to accept defeat with dignity." Stoics like Cuauhtémoc and Juárez are the characteristic Mexican heroes. "Resignation is one of our most popular virtues." This in turn fosters the love of form for its own sake, the worship of juridical flummery, and that readiness to dissimulate which is a carry-over from colonial times: "Pretend it never happened, *señor*," says the mestizo; or to the query, "Who is there?" the impassive Indian, blending into the landscape, answers, "No one, *señor*. I am." Paz, who is writing for intellectuals, and *as one* without always being aware of it, contrasts his Mexican stereotype with the American one:

> The solitude of the Mexican, under the great stone night of the high plateau that is still inhabited by insatiable gods, is very different from that of the North American, who wanders in an abstract world of machines, fellow citizens, and moral precepts.... The Mexican ... has forgotten the word that ties him to all those forces through which life manifests itself. Therefore he shouts or keeps silent, stabs or prays, or falls asleep for a hundred years.... To us a realist is always a pessimist ... the North American wants to use reality rather than to know it.[3]

Nothing puzzles this pragmatic American in Mexico more than the worship of the law, which Paz touches upon but does not explore: "Avenida Lic. Benito Juárez" ... "Calle Lic. Miguel Alemán" ... It could be called the Licenciado Cult. To call an American street "Avenue Lawyer Lincoln" would be considered the ultimate insult to the memory of a man who rose above the profession he regarded with good-humored contempt. But in Mexico the fact that Juárez and Alemán *as Presidents* changed the face of Mexico counts for nothing beside the fact that they held law degrees. A *licenciado* is a man who is accustomed to dicker and make deals, a man who arranges the scale of the *mordidas*. Criticism of the *mordida* is met with the response, "It doesn't look like corruption because it's what the lawyers do!"

Since Flandrau's time, and even since 1950, when Paz wrote his unsparing critique of his country's soul, Mexico has changed greatly. Fifty percent of the people are still peasants, but in contrast to pre-Revolutionary times most of them either own small plots or share the common lands (*ejidos*), which all post-Revolutionary govern-

---

[3] Octavio Paz, *The Labyrinth of Solitude: Life and Thought in Mexico.* Translated by Lysander Kemp. New York, Grove Press, 1962.

ments have protected and enlarged. In consequence, the sullen passivity of the Indian, inherited from centuries of serfdom on the haciendas, is dying out; and along with it the defensive *machismo* of the mestizo caught traditionally between his resentment of the arrogant Creole and his fear of being pushed back among the "stupid" aboriginals.[4]

[4] According to a survey based on almost all the adults in a mestizo village, rather than merely a sample, "only 11 percent of the men have the extreme traits of *machismo,* and another 30 percent express these traits to a lesser degree. In turn, *machismo* is correlated with two more deeply rooted character factors: intense dependence on the mother and the authoritarian-exploitative syndrome." (Quoted from Michael Macoby's "On Mexican National Character," *Annals of American Academy of Political and Social Science,* March, 1967.) But the tendency to be mislead into believing that the fading persistence of these attitudes constitute the Mexican character is irresistible with a type of intellectual visitor to Mexico.

The tendency began with D. H. Lawrence: "...It is a country where men despise sex, and live for it.... In Mexico, at night, each little distance isolates itself absolutely, like a man in a black cloak turning his back.... The whole village was in that state of curious, reptile apprehension which comes over dark people.... The Indian understands soul, which is of the blood. But spirit which is superior, and is the quality of our civilization, this, in the mass, he darkly and barbarically repudiates.... When you mix European and American Indian, you mix different blood races, and you produce the half-breed, a calamity..." (*The Plumed Serpent,* 1926; Vintage paperback, 1955.)

Another brilliant novelist, Graham Greene, mines his neuroses as relentlessly at the expense of Mexico: "...There's something horribly immature about their cheerfulness; no sense of human responsibility; it is all one with the pistol-shot violence.... I have never been in a country where you are more aware all the time of hate. Friendship there is skin-deep—a protective gesture. That notion of greeting that you see everywhere upon the street, the hands outstretched to press the other's arms, the semi-embrace—what is it but the motion of pinioning to keep the other man from his gun? ... Cynicism, a distrust of men's motives, is the accepted ideology." (*The Lawless Roads,* 1939; Heinemann's Uniform Edition, 1955.)

And now, in 1968, comes John Lincoln's *One Man's Mexico* (Harcourt Brace), which Greene calls understandably "the best book on Mexico written this century," singing the same song. To Lincoln the countryside is menacing with "...drunken Indians who fall in love with [your] white skin until, imagining an insult, they move their hands to their *machetes.*... It seemed typical of the perversity of Mexico that a dove should prefer to sit on the ground and coo rather than in a tree.... Most people in Mexico carry a gun..." etc. It's not that any three of these gifted writers are bad reporters (except Lincoln in the last statement) but that they all generalize from personal idiosyncrasies—sexual, religious, social. Lincoln's descriptions of the cannibalistic Seris, the territorial Mayas, the capital's policemen and convicts, and of his states of mind while taking peyote and hallucinogenic mushrooms, are fine; but since they are almost exclusively what he is looking for in Mexico, they give him no right to say that every individual Mexican is a split personality "withdrawn at one moment into an almost subhuman torpor" and at the next "roused for no seemingly adequate reason to a sudden act of brutish violence or uncalculating humanity."

But just because during the thirty-year span during which I have traveled

Mexico has its problems—what country hasn't? Few would deny that since the Revolution of 1910, which was expected to bring equality, the rich have become richer and the poor poorer: many more millionaires, many more slum dwellers. Yet at the same time a middle class has come into being, the dominant class politically; and its government has become sensitive, if not always effectively responsive, to the demands of *all* classes.

The rapid rate of increase in the population, with the overcrowded cities receiving the overflow, is not a peculiarly Mexican problem, but it is a problem quite capable of canceling out all the progress registered in other sectors, and the one problem Mexico is doing little or nothing to tackle.

Socially, there is the problem of the family in which the father is a promiscuous patriarch (or dropout) and the mother brings up the children without support. Oscar Lewis [5] has shown that it is endemic to all classes. The father in his peasant family doesn't want his children to marry because young couples now move away to the city. The wife of the peasant who has already left the land speaks of her husband with contempt. The slum-born husband is "painfully aware of the lack of control over his wife." The lower-middle-class man on the way up spends his spare time shuttling between the three separate families he maintains in three districts of the capital. The *nouveau riche* wife angrily breaks the needle while giving her husband a male hormone injection because she knows its only purpose is to make him "more of a man with his sweetheart." But Lewis, while not allowing that these are dramatized cases, does concede that the younger generation in all five of his families "enjoys greater stability and a longer period of childhood than did their parents—and can look forward to more schooling."

The problem is perennial and Hispanic; but education, the key to all Mexico's problems, has yet to face up to it. There are more schools, colleges, and literate people than ever before; but by and large the student is not taught to think for himself, be critical of his own culture, or learn anything of practical value. The quality of higher education is especially low, and inaccessible to most of the youth.

---

to every part of Mexico I have never been taunted with my (unconcealed) pride in being an American, never arrested, and never failed to encounter help far in excess of common courtesy when in distress, *I do not assume that chauvinism, police brutality, and indifference to suffering do not exist in Mexico as they exist everywhere else.*

[5] *Five Families: Mexican Case Studies in the Culture of Poverty.* New York, Basic Books, 1959.

The assets? They are tremendous, and this book is about them. Take the history again. Has ever a people been so plagued with foreign aggressors and commercial despoilers? They call Mexicans xenophobic! Imagine the temper of the American people if their colonial masters had stayed for three hundred years, appropriating all the movable wealth, and training a civil service and clergy to prey upon the victims. And on top of that an invasion from a more powerful neighbor who seized half the country. And then a European invasion that gutted what was left. And then a legalized looting by all the nations of everything that still had value on the land and under it. No ... The miracle is that Mexicans *welcome* Spaniards, French, British, Americans to their country and even go out of their way to be nice to them. Looking at the country more positively, how many countries can boast heroes like Morelos, Juárez, Madero, Cárdenas? These leaders were not only brave and idealistic; they were almost uniquely untainted by acquisitiveness or the desire to perpetuate themselves in power.

As for the physical endowment of Mexico, it is testimony enough that so many people come just to see it that tourism dwarfs any other industry. They come not merely to enjoy the incomparable art and architecture of antiquity, the unrivaled ecclesiastical treasures, the grandeur of snowcapped mountains, the mystery of jungles and primitive villages, the benison of beaches, but to mingle with a people whose inner grace is a revelation barely comprehended but always sensed. The essence of it is expressed by an illiterate peasant woman fifty years old:

> Love is very sacred, because without love there would not be the world we would have if we loved each other, because even though there is friendship it is not enough. One must love. Beginning with love of parents, of sweethearts, love of a husband, love of children, love of a good friendship; even to raise an animal one must love. It is incomparable because people even commit suicide if they do not know how to love. The love of a father is eternal. One retains the love of friends even when they are absent. Love of God one must have also, for God sends us love in the form of understanding.[6]

[6] Quoted in Michael Macoby's "Love and Authority: A Study of Mexican Villagers." *The Atlantic*, 1964.

CONTENTS

Contents

Part I
HISTORY

1

INDIAN MEXICO AND THE SPANISH CONQUEST
(c. 1500 B.C.–A.D. 1521)

NEVER in history have two great civilizations collided with as little foreknowledge and as cataclysmic an impact as in Mexico. The Persian assault upon Greece, followed shortly by the Hellenic counteroffensive that swept over North Africa and to the western provinces of India, was by comparison a family affair; the Mediterranean soldiery knew where they were going, and the invaded kingdoms, with comparable cultures of their own, knew what to expect. The Roman conquest of western Europe was little more than an expansion of civilization's frontiers among tribes beginning to emerge from the Stone Age. The tribal chieftain Genghis Khan never brought the Orient's marginal nomads as far as Europe or the Middle East, and the great civilizations of the Orient itself remained relatively intact until modern times. Only in Peru did a civilization as exotic and intricately organized as Mexico's confront Europe's as blindly and succumb as quickly; but the military empire of the Incas had created no arts of its own to match the military Aztecs', and its advanced socialism could be destroyed without leaving a trace upon the transplanted hierarchies of Spain. Only in Mexico have the Indians of this hemisphere survived tenaciously enough to make their rich heritage a part of the modern state.

Origins

Where did the Indians of the connected North and South American continents come from? The supposition that they migrated from Asia by way of the "land bridge" in the Bering Strait has never been seriously challenged. Man's nearest relative, the anthropoid ape, is not indigenous to the Western Hemisphere; nor have any bones of Paleolithic man, or of any of the other predecessors of *Homo sapiens*, been unearthed here. A few non-Mongoloid skulls have been found, suggesting the possibility that an archaic people preceded the first wave of Asiatic migrants and were then assimilated, but there is no proof that they were an indigenous people. Tepexpan Man, the earliest skeleton discovered in Mexico, hardly predates 9000 B.C. and the migrations from Asia are presumed to have come about that time. Some three thousand years later, tubers and seeds began to be planted systematically, and the way was prepared for the cultivation of corn (maize), squash, beans, chili pepper and cotton, on which the earliest civilizations rested.

Ties with the Asiatic homeland, however, were never wholly broken. Recently in Ecuador a team headed by Emilio Estrada, working with Clifford Evans and Betty Meggers of the Smithsonian Institution, found unpainted pottery carbon-dated 2500 B.C. with incised decorations, precisely like that being made in Japan at the same period. A unique ritual complex hitherto unknown in the New World (to quote Evans) "makes its appearance: neck rests, models of houses with saddle roofs and columns, realistic figurines with legs folded one above the other, novel golf-tee earplugs, and pendants in stone and pottery fashioned in the form of a tusk." It was already established that occasional trans-Pacific voyages by raft or canoe had taken place in both directions by way of the Polynesian archipelago. The Polynesian settlement of Easter Island in the fourteenth century was only the last of such transfusions. Long before Thor Heyerdahl's westward drift on the *Kon Tiki* from Peru to the Tuamotu Islands (an eastward voyage against the prevailing winds and currents would require navigational skill), there was indirect evidence of a two-way circulation. "The sweet potato, a plant of admitted American origin, was found by the earliest European explorers under cultivation in Polynesia, and had been long known there by its Peruvian name *kumara*." [1] Mason points

[1] J. Alden Mason, *The Ancient Civilizations of Peru*, rev. ed. Baltimore, Maryland, Penguin Books, Inc., 1964.

out also the similarities between Peruvian and Chinese panpipes, the use of betel nuts and coca as narcotics (both releasing the alkaloid by mixing the quid with lime), and the close resemblances of bark cloth and weaving (tie-dye) techniques.

Pre-Aztec Civilizations

Partly because the Indian races never developed a system of phonetic writing, and partly because a handful of enlightened friars had to fight with the conquerors to preserve what little of the oral historical tradition could be salvaged, our knowledge of the early civilizations is based almost entirely on their arts. Archaeology, until the twentieth century, was not a science; until the nineteenth it didn't exist at all. But in recent decades, thanks to the archaeologists, artists and art historians, our knowledge of pre-Columbian cultures has become very great. Especially in Mexico and Central America, teams of American, British and Mexican experts have expanded the narrow horizon revealed by such pioneer savants as John Lloyd Stephens, Brasseur de Bourbourg, Alfred Percival Maudslay and Teobert Maler into a comprehensive picture of successive cultures, rising and falling, cross-fertilizing each other, and all contributing to the well-documented and larger (but not in every respect higher) culture of the Aztecs. Sylvanus Morley, Herbert Spinden, J. Eric S. Thompson, Manuel Gamio and Alfonso Caso are names as deservedly celebrated as their predecessors'. And Mexican artists, notably Miguel Covarrubias and Diego Rivera, have contributed to making us aware that *as art* pre-Columbian sculpture, painting and ceramics rank with any in the world.

One of the oddities of pre-Columbian civilization—a circumstance that, along with the failure to invent gunpowder and to domesticate the horse, contributed to the Conquest—was that the uses of the wheel were not discovered. There was no potter's wheel. Yet at Zacatenco near Mexico City beautifully modeled bowls and long-necked jars have been found dating from as early as 2000 B.C. From here also come the first of the small clay figurines used in a fertility cult. Since so many of these have been found in graves, it has been speculated that they may also have served as symbolic substitutes for human sacrifice. They reached their highest level at Tlatilco ("Where things are hidden"), a rich lode in Mexico City just off the main highway to Cuernavaca, which was discovered by accident in the late forties when a brick yard was being enlarged.

Related to this "archaic" period are the cultures of the so-called "village artists." Their ceramic figurines and larger molded figures have been found in great numbers in the modern Pacific Coast states of Jalisco, Colima and Nayarit. Each of the three has a distinctive style, easily recognizable. Jalisco's village artists, the earliest and least concerned with religion, made fairly large figures, sensuous and slant-eyed, with a "slip" of creamy white or red. Colima's artists burnished their red clay before firing it; their chubby dogs and expressionless conch players are suavely sophisticated. Nayarit, seemingly more archaic, is the most earthy and popular of Mexican styles. Its stubby warriors brandish their spears or nurse their wounds in a style verging on caricature that has been compared to Dubuffet's *art brut* for its obsession with "ugliness." Nayarit group sculptures include dozens of miniature actors demonstrating their skills in the ball court, flying about poles (*voladores*), or participating in funeral rites. The rare, almost life-size figures, seen to best advantage in Diego Rivera's Anahuacali Museum (see p. 217), are in the same reddish-gray ceramic flecked with black, and are as fiercely expressive.

The earliest of the great "horizon" cultures of Mexico, and the most recently identified, is known as Olmec. It flourished along the Gulf Coast from Tres Zapotes to La Venta and even perhaps as far south and east as Uaxactún in the Petén jungle of Guatemala. At La Venta, an island in the mangrove swamps southeast of Veracruz, its earliest temple city was found. Dating from 800–300 B.C., it was contemporaneous with Chavín de Huantar, the site of Peru's mother culture. Here were discovered some of the colossal "negroid" heads up to nine feet high and weighing as much as fifteen tons; they were quarried sixty miles inland and dragged through the jungles to their swampy site. But La Venta was perhaps the last Olmec stronghold. Olmec craftsmen sought employment in other kingdoms. Their sensitive work in jade, cut with bone drills, incised with fine lines and polished with powdered stone, is found as far west as Oaxaca and as far southeast as Uaxactún. When the small supply of jade was exhausted, the Olmecs worked stone, inlaying it in wood. The jadeite celts found along the Mezcala River in Guerrero, so highly prized by modern collectors for their abstract treatment of the human form, are probably Olmec, at least by influence.

As we enter the period contemporaneous with the first millennium of the Christian era, the "mother culture" of the mysterious Olmecs begins to be diffused among three wide-ranging theocracies that dominated Middle America culturally almost down to the Conquest. The "empire" of Teotihuacán, with its center not far to the north of the present Mexican capital, is believed to have originated several centuries before Christ. It reached its peak (according to Alfonso Caso) in A.D. 300–500; but through the more warlike Toltecs, who conquered it several centuries later, it continued to influence every other culture, stylistically and perhaps religiously. Even more persistent, though more isolated in the Oaxaca Valley, the Zapotec culture of Monte Albán had its first phase in the Olmec period and its final (fifth) in the so-called "Mixtec renaissance" of A.D. 1400 which produced the temple at Mitla near Oaxaca and the magnificent jewels found by Caso in Tomb 7 at Monte Albán. The third great culture of the Classic period, the Maya, spread over the lowland jungles of the Atlantic slope from Copán in Honduras, through Guatemala, to Palenque in Mexican Chiapas; it had its own late-flowering period in the Yucatán Peninsula in association with the Toltecs, who had migrated there from their homeland in central Mexico. Two lesser cultures, the Huastec in north-central Mexico and the Totonac on the Gulf Coast, flourished during the late-Classic period, producing marvelous sculptural styles of their own but not affecting the mainstream.

Known to the archaeologist for its pervasive impact upon Middle America, Teotihuacán is familiar to the Mexican traveler through its huge pyramids of the Sun and the Moon thirty-one miles northeast of the capital. The very name of this great civilization is unknown—the Aztecs, who knew less about it than we do, gave the site the name we know it by, "Place of the Gods." Presumably the pyramids were covered with rubble and shrubs in 1521, when Bernal Díaz del Castillo and Cortés' other warriors stumbled by them on the way to their greatest defeat, for the observant Díaz doesn't mention them. Larger than the Pyramid of Cheops in Egypt, the Temple of the Sun is 210 feet high, covers 55,000 square yards and its adobe bricks faced with stone are estimated to weigh 2,980,000 tons. The people who built it—and the enormous city that surrounded it—are presumed to have destroyed what they could and moved on about A.D. 658. Some four centuries later the Toltecs moved in, made the larger pyramid a shrine to their gods Quetzalcoatl and Tlaloc, and carved the effigies of those gods that now decorate it. Since the original city—the first true city in the Americas—had no walls, it is presumed that its builders were either unwarlike or had no significant foes. All about, examples of this people's four styles have been excavated; but the storytelling frescoes—one showing the rain-god's "paradise" with happy celebrants swimming, diving, and playing ball —date from the Toltec period.

Unlike Teotihuacán, Monte Albán, the Zapotec shrine on a hilltop outside of Oaxaca, was a ceremonial city, where this ancient civilization had its last rejuvenation under the Mixtecs just before the Conquest. Monte Albán's hieroglyphic writings, its calendar, its numerals, and its observatory antedate the Mayas, [2] to whom these intellectual feats are usually ascribed; and the art of these ancestors of the present Zapotecs, if less flamboyant and subtle than that of the Mayas, gives indication of a healthier, less caste-ridden, culture. No weapons were found in the Monte Albán tombs, nor is there evidence of human sacrifice.

The Mayas, by contrast, were both warlike and sacrifice-minded. But there is no denying that their culture—which reached its apogee in the so-called Classic period (c. A.D. 600–900)—reached heights of aesthetic and intellectual achievement unsurpassed in pre-Columbian America. Mexico is fortunate in having three Maya sites where the arts climaxed. All are in the State of Chiapas, bordering Guatemala. At Palenque, brought to the world's attention by John Lloyd Stephens' expedition of 1845, sculpture in lime-stucco reached an unparalleled degree of refinement. At Yaxchilán, discovered a few years later by A. P. Maudslay, the jungle still covers a wealth of stone monuments. At Bonampak, discovered by Giles Greville Healey in 1946, three chambers, entirely painted in fresco with unprecedented dramatic realism, revealed the Classic Mayas of A.D. 731–889 to be warriors who mutilated their captives, as well as masters of music, the dance, and fantastic costume. (See pp. 232–233.) Morley, Thompson, and other Maya archaeologists had already paid tribute to the intellectual achievements of this time-obsessed theocracy. Compared to the vigesimal system of the Mayas, the decimal one of the Romans was unwieldy. Long before Christ, the Mayas had invented and used the concept of zero. Employing a dot to connote 1, a bar for 5, and various "head" glyphs for larger periods of time, they were able to compute inconceivably vast stretches. A stela at Quiriguá in Guatemala, according to Thompson, refers to a date *four hundred million years ago*. "One can never assume the obvious," Thompson adds, "when dealing with the Maya, who excelled in the impractical but failed in the practical."

The "Maya renaissance" can be studied, without museums, at the Mexican sites of Uxmal and Chichén Itzá in Yucatán. The grandest

---

[2] They antedate the Olmecs, too, according to Ignacio Bernal, a Mexican archaeologist who has made notable discoveries in the Oaxaca Valley. See his "The Olmec Presence in Oaxaca," *Mexico Quarterly Review*, Vol. 3, No. 1, 1968.

pre-Columbian architecture in the Americas is at the former site, faced with cut stone embedded in cement. At Chichén Itzá the Mayas lived on through their conquerors, the Toltecs—gloriously. (See pp. 241–243.)

The peripheral Maya-related Huastec and Totonac cultures are seen to best advantage in the museums, especially in the National Museum of Anthropology and Archaeology in Mexico City. The Totonacs of the Gulf Coast were a uniquely happy people, if one may judge by their sculpture; they glorified children on swings and caught every evanescent aspect of smiling and laughing.

Toltec Interlude

The major deviations from the Maya norm at Chichén Itzá—the colonnaded halls of warriors, the skull rack, the effigies of eagles, jaguars, and feathered serpents, even the reclining Chac Mool whose enigmatic posture so intrigued Henry Moore—are Toltec.

More is known about the Toltecs than of any of the pre-Aztec peoples. They have a *history*. Much, but not all that we know about it, comes from the "Books of Chilam Balam," a series of seventeenth- and eighteenth-century manuscripts transcribing what had been handed down by word of mouth or transcription from original codices burned by Bishop Diego de Landa in the 1562 auto-da-fé in Yucatán. From these legendary chronicles, and from Bishop Landa's own invaluable memoirs, comes a large part of our knowledge of both the Maya and Toltec cultures.

The Toltecs migrated into the Valley of Mexico from the north some time in the tenth century A.D. Led by Mixcoatl, "Cloud Serpent," the first hero in pre-Columbian history whose name has come down to us, they built their capital at Culhuacán on the lake in which Tenochtitlán (Mexico City) was later established by the Aztecs. In 947 Mixcoatl was assassinated by a rival and his corpse was hidden. His orphaned heir, Ce Acatl "One Reed" Topiltzin, became priest of the Plumed Serpent, Quetzalcoatl, and assumed the name of that minor deity being worshiped at Xochicalco to the southwest. Finding his father's bones, the priest-prince assumed the throne and in the year 980 built Tula, the site of which is still well preserved fifty miles north of Mexico City. (See p. 210.) Quetzalcoatl ruled only nineteen years, but the Toltecs credited him with all the virtues—even with inventing corn and astronomy. But by preaching a mild religion in which only snakes and butterflies were sacrificed, he antagonized the priests of the rival Tezcatlipoca

"Smoking Mirror," a bloodthirsty deity whom the Aztecs were later to include in their pantheon, and he was driven out. First he went to Cholula—where the mighty Toltec pyramid of Quetzalcoatl still stands—and then to the Gulf Coast and Yucatán, where he is reputed to have died, but not before prophesying his *return* as a peaceful redeemer.[3]

Quetzalcoatl is the great culture hero of ancient Mexico and—if his actual existence is assumed—the first and one of the noblest figures in Mexican history. Orozco, who painted him at Dartmouth and made so many unforgettable drawings of his imperious image, envisaged him as a Jehovah or Hebrew prophet figure with wildly swirling white hair, riding his raft to Yucatán. Like the Greek Prometheus, he brought fire to man. He also restored the bones of past generations with his own blood. As a man of peace, forced out by militarism and human sacrifice, the Aztecs worshiped Quetzalcoatl as a kind of "hedge" against their extremism in both these activities; and when Cortés arrived, Moctezuma was psychologically disarmed by his suspicion that this could be the "white" god who had promised to return and end the reign of his defilers. The Toltec-Mayas in Yucatán, however, had identified Quetzalcoatl with their own conquering hero, Kukulcán, and in the *Popol Vuh*, the Sacred Book of the Quiché-Mayas, he is presented as a jealous god who demanded sacrifices until finally turned to stone.

The Empire of the Aztecs

Like the Romans, who conquered the known world of their time, ruling it harshly but effectively, the Aztecs were great adaptors of other peoples' ideas. In the chaos that followed the fall of Tula, they adapted the military efficiency of the Toltecs and made that peoples' fearsome Tezcatlipoca a colleague of their own fearsome tutelary deity, Huitzilopochtli, the sun god. Their pantheon, in fact, like the Romans', was hospitable to every conquered divinity; and from the conquered they also took styles of art and ornaments of dress, poetry and astronomy, weapons and games. From the jungle Mayas they took rubber and mantles of plaited tropical plumes; from the Totonacs their embroidery (but not their smiles); and from the Mixtecs of Oaxaca their golden bangles.

Like the Macedonians, who also conquered a world, the Aztecs

[3] I follow the sequence of André Emmerich, whose *Art Before Columbus* (Simon and Schuster, 1963) is as noteworthy for its historical clarity as for its aesthetic sensitivity.

began humbly. As a small band of mercenaries on the northern frontier of civilization, they attached themselves to the army of the Grand Chichimec whose grandfather, Xólotl, had destroyed Tula of the Toltecs in 1224. Ruling until 1363, this Chichimec warrior established his capital at Texcoco, twenty-nine miles east of present-day Mexico City, on one of the shallow, brackish lakes that then lay at the center of the Valley of Mexico. The Chichimec kingdom prospered for a century, holding sway over the whole Valley (Anáhuac). Its most brilliant, but perhaps not its strongest, ruler was the poet-philosopher Netzahualcoyotl who held sway until his death in 1472. As a poet, Netzahualcoyotl's verses were more elegiac than martial:

> The fleeting vanities of this world are like the green willow
> Which the sharp edge of the ax cuts down and the wind
>   uproots...

As a philosopher the King of Texcoco, revering the memory of Quetzalcoatl, opted for a single benign and invisible deity—"the god of the immediate vicinity . . . that one through whom all live" [4]—an enlightened attempt to impose unity on the reigning theocratic chaos that inevitably antagonized the powerful priesthoods of all Mexico. Under Netzahualcoyotl's weak son, Texcoco's growing detachment turned to decadence and the power base shifted to Aztec Tenochtitlán.

The Aztecs had been slowly consolidating their position on the islands of the neighboring lake for two centuries. In 1248 they occupied the hill that is now Chapultepec in the capital. But by the time their first king, Acamapichtli, was invested, they had moved to another island, the site of Mexico City's present central plaza, the Zócalo, guided thither according to legend by the omen of an eagle with a serpent in its beak that had alighted on a nopal cactus. Tradition gives this date as 1325. King Izcoatl, third in line from the founder of the dynasty, cleverly allied himself with the stronger rulers of Texcoco and Tacuba and soon dominated this triple alliance that ruled the whole valley by 1428. His successor, Moctezuma I, conquered the Totonacs to ensure a supply of food following a great drought, thus inaugurating the policy of Aztec imperialism. His son Axayacatl brought the arts to their summit and extended the empire to Oaxaca and beyond, leaving only the Tlaxcalan and Tarascan tribes unconquered in central Mexico. Axayacatl's two successors completed the great pyramid of Tenochtitlán with its twin shrines to Tezcatlipoca and Huitzilopochtli; but to supply these hungry gods with sacrificial victims, the Aztecs alienated the subjected and tributary peoples. This was the dangerously unstable situation of the huge empire when the deeply religious and refined Moctezuma II succeeded to the throne in 1502, little knowing that in less than two decades Indian Mexico would be overwhelmed by Spain.

Aztec Civilization

Religion was the dominant preoccupation of the Aztecs. And like everything else in the loosely federated empire, it was in a state of flux at the time of the Conquest. An attempt was being made to consolidate the myriad tribal and borrowed deities, and their functions, into a manageable few. Caso, whose definition of the major divinities I follow here, is at pains to place the ritual of human sacrifice—which had become an obsession by 1519 and was practiced on a vast scale—in some sort of historical perspective:

> Human sacrifice was not performed for the purpose of harming the sacrificed, nor was cruelty or vengeance its objective. It was something more than that. . . . The victim was considered a messenger to the gods, bearing the supplications of the Aztec people; witness the rite of sacrifice in the month of Toxcatl, in which the youth who represented Tezcatlipoca was treated and revered as if he himself were a god.
>
> Human sacrifice among the Aztecs, however repugnant it may be to us, was nothing more than many such aberrations which assume a religious guise in the history of mankind, and which, based upon false premises considered valid, can lead quite logically to the most terrible consequences. Burning heretics in this life to save them from the everlasting fires of hell, destroying individuals of a supposedly inferior race to keep them from contaminating the Aryan, and the like, are examples of similar practices found frequently in the history of ideologies and religions.[5]

[5] Caso, *op. cit.*

For all that, the Aztec holocausts represented a degeneration from the older pre-Columbian religions, and the methods of killing were cruel enough to fill even the cruel Spaniards with a horror not always hypocritical. Stretching the victim face-up over a rounded stone and tearing out his heart was the standard procedure; but riddling the victim with arrows so that his blood would drip slowly to induce Tlaloc to bring rain, or flaying him alive so that the priest of Xipe might dance in the warm skin were other methods employed.

The two principal gods to whom the sacrificed were offered by the Aztecs were Huitzilopochtli and Tezcatlipoca. Huitzilopochtli, who had "chosen" the Aztecs to be his people, and who does not appear to have been worshiped by any other people, "represented" the sun. If properly supplied with his nectar (human blood) he would see that the sun rose each morning; otherwise the gods of darkness would destroy him, and with him, the world. But Huitzilopochtli, "Hummingbird on the Left," a name that has never been explained to my knowledge, was also the god of war. His mother, Coatlicue, whose monstrous image is to be seen in the National Museum, represented the earth. Tonatiuh, the actual personification of the sun, seems to have played a more passive role. The so-called Calendar Stone, found under the Zócalo and now also exhibited in the National Museum, is Tonatiuh's portrait.

Tezcatlipoca, who shared with Huitzilopochtli the twin shrine atop the Aztec sacrificial pyramid (destroyed by Cortés, and replaced later by the Cathedral on the Zócalo) was inherited from the Toltecs. His name means "Smoking Mirror," and this symbol, worn at the temple, also replaces one of his feet, torn off by a monster in mythical combat. Tezcatlipoca was both the creator and the god of darkness. Black was therefore his favorite color, though he sometimes disguised himself in the skin of a jaguar.

Tlaloc, the rain god, and Quetzalcoatl, whose migratory history and disturbing prophecy have already been mentioned, were the other two principal divinities in the Aztecs' crowded pantheon. Tlaloc is the oldest of the pre-Columbian gods, older even than Quetzalcoatl; the Olmecs invoked him, and so did the people of Teotihuacán. The Mayas called him Chac and the Totonacs called him Tajím, but his beneficent function was always the same, to water the corn; and his displeasure if neglected was predictable: floods, droughts, hail, ice and lightning. In some images Tlaloc seems to be wearing eyeglasses and a moustache; in others (Teotihuacán) his unlovely face resembles a gas mask.

The Aztec century was a cycle of fifty-two years. The last day of the cycle was called One Reed. On this night it was customary for the priests to lead a procession to a hill near Ixtapalapa outside the city to see if the star Aldebaran passed in its course. It was ordained that if anything went wrong, the sun would never rise again and the world would come to an end. The legendary white god Quetzalcoatl had also said that he would return from overseas in a One Reed year to reestablish his rule. Nothing had happened in 1363, 1415, or 1467. The next One Reed year was 1519. . . .

When they were not sacrificing or preparing for doom, the Aztecs were an enterprising people, proud of their magnificent island city with its humming markets and manufactures, even given to gaiety [6] Xochipilli, the god of flowers, patron of dancing and love, is depicted cross-legged in stone at the National Museum, wearing butterflies, and at least *trying* to smile. His worship centered about the suburb of Xochimilco, then as now a floating garden. Before they became an empire, the Aztecs had ingeniously made up for their paucity of arable land by anchoring floats heaped with mud in their island harbors and letting long-rooted plants turn the well-fertilized water into food.

> The god of corn is born
> In Tamoanchán,
> In the place where there are flowers
> The god "One Flower,"
> The god of corn is born
> In the place where there is water and moisture,
> Where the sons of man are made,
> In beautiful Michoacán. [7]

Then, as now, the people of high, dry Anáhuac looked to lake-plenti-ful Michoacán as the earthly paradise.

The song was in Nahuatl, the *lingua franca* of Indian Mexico. The Aztecs made it so. The Otomis, Huastecs, Totonacs, Tarascans, Zapotecs, Mayas, went on speaking their own languages, but those who wished to trade with the master race (who controlled the trade by now), or have their tribute reduced, or find work carving stone

[6] Jacques Soustelle (*The Daily Life of the Aztecs*, Penguin, 1965) estimates Tenochtitlán's population to have been between 500,000 and 1,000,000 at the time of the Conquest.

[7] Fragment of a hymn to Centeotl, the corn god, quoted in Caso, *op. cit.* Soustelle translates the last line, "There where they fish for jade fishes"—interchangeable with "Michoacán" for anyone who has visited Lake Patzcuaro.

or doing featherwork in the metropolis, learned Nahuatl. Some of our common words—tomato, chocolate, chicle, chili, cacao, and coyote—are Nahuatl. It is a subtle language, as courtly in its suffixes as Japanese. And it was used by the poets and storytellers of the second Moctezuma's affluent court, as it had been in Texcoco during Netzahualcoyotl's old age, to glorify a philosophy of liberal enlightenment quite at variance with the military imperialism which was supplying slaves and sacrificial victims to the Aztecs by the hundreds of thousands. One story, preserved by the scholarly Franciscans a few decades later, tells of the Emperor's carelessly picking an ear of corn while journeying in the countryside and being rebuked by the peasant it belonged to for violating his own law of theft; Moctezuma was reputed to have been so impressed that he gave the peasant his imperial mantle and made him mayor of Xochimilco.

But no one can be sure whether liberalism or imperialism, Quetzalcoatl or Huitzilopochtli, would eventually have gained the upper hand. As it was, Aztec liberalism only made Spanish imperialism's task easier.

The rulers were disarmed by their sense of guilt. The ruled, presided over by such a multiplicity of sinful gods, were absolved of any need for feeling responsible for their actions. "Only the Gods," says Octavio Paz, "were free, and only they had the power to choose. The Aztec was as little responsible for his actions as for his death." [8]

There were many other instabilities in the Aztec house. The old class structure was breaking down. Some of the amenities of civilization, to be sure, were beginning to be enjoyed. Law and order prevailed as it hadn't in the violent old days. Women were admitted to the priesthood. Merchants, a rising bourgeoisie, were starting to share power with the military. Hospitals had been built. Witchcraft was on the wane. A plentiful supply of fresh water was brought by aqueduct from Chapultepec, and when that spring ran dry, from much farther away. Sanitation was rudimentary, yet epidemics were unknown. But the masses of the people, the peasants, lived as they had always lived, poorly, and the administrative machine in Tenochtitlán was heavy with red tape, unwieldy "files" of papyrus, legal disputes months and years unresolved. "Official morality extolled the frugality of former ages, just as vainly as it had done in the last days of the Roman republic, and sumptuary laws struggled in vain

---

[8] *The Labyrinth of Solitude, Life and Thought in Mexico.* Translated by Lysander Kemp. New York, Grove Press, 1962.

against the ostentation of luxury." [9] Above all, the confederation's outlying districts were ripe for rebellion, and its unconquered enclaves, the Tlaxcalans to the east and the Tarascans to the west, were but waiting cautiously for the first sign of rebellion in the provinces or disintegration at the center to fall upon their mighty enemies.

All during the decade that preceded 1519, there were alarming rumors from the east coast. Indians fleeing the genocide already underway in Hispaniola and Cuba may have drifted ashore on the Gulf Coast and made known their anguish. The Maya-Toltecs of Campeche and Yucatán in 1517 reported sighting two huge ships and boasted of an encounter with a landing party of white warriors whom they had routed, but few believed them. The following year, however, there were rumors of more ships, four this time, and of landings in Tabasco and Veracruz, parts of the confederation more directly subject to the Aztec ruler. Moctezuma dispatched messengers to invite the strangers to visit him, but when the messengers arrived, the strangers had sailed away. Was Quetzalcoatl about to return?

Cortés Comes to Mexico

It would be fascinating to know what Hernándo Cortés was doing and thinking during the seven years (1504–11) when he lived the life of a country gentleman on his hacienda in Hispaniola; and during the eight years (1511–1519) when he drifted west to the next "frontier" in Cuba, interspersing his duties as a landlord with a little legal work and a lot of wenching. As in Extremadura, Spain, where he had been born in 1485—fifteen years before Pizarro, who was an old man when he conquered Peru—Cortés held aloof from great events almost as though saving his genius for the decisive moment. He had dropped out of Salamanca University without waiting for his law degree, and had passed up an opportunity to participate with the great captains of France and Spain in the siege of Naples. He did join Diego Velásquez in the conquest of Cuba, but since the peaceable Arawaks put up even less resistance there than they had when Columbus massacred them in Hispaniola, that was anything but a preparatory campaign. The two most adventurous and talked-about events of the decade—the voyages of Hernández de Córdoba and of Juan de Grijalva to the coast of Mexico—Cortés elected not to join.

[9] Soustelle, *op. cit.*

Córdoba, excited by rumors of "gold to the north" brought back by the survivors of Balboa's epoch-making trip to Darien, set sail in two ships from Santiago de Cuba in February of 1517. Since nothing but jungles and savages had been encountered off the coast of Panama, they took a western course. It was only 150 miles to the northern cape of the Yucatán Peninsula, which they sighted shortly. The young Bernal Díaz del Castillo, who would live to write his great history of the Conquest in Guatemala in his nineties, was with Córdoba and described what they found: buildings of stone, warriors (the Toltec-Mayas) in quilted armor with gold ornaments, and hostility. The Spaniards were welcomed ashore— and then ambushed; only their firearms saved them. Continuing south, they reached the site of the present city of Campeche, where they found frescoed temples and altars with fresh blood. They were also astonished and rather alarmed to hear the word "Castilan" pronounced repeatedly. But near the Champotón River they rashly spent the night ashore and found themselves surrounded by Mayas who outnumbered them two hundred to one. They fled, leaving fifty dead on the beach. Back in Cuba, Córdoba died of his wounds.

Grijalva's expedition was hardly more successful. This time Velás-quez dispatched four ships and 250 *castillanos*. He directed them to continue southwest along the coast, and to make a settlement as a base for future parties. Again Bernal Díaz went along, and this time Pedro de Alvarado as well. A storm drove them past the tip of Yucatán, so that they sought refuge between Cozumel Island and the eastern shore of the peninsula. They caught a glimpse of Tulum (see pp. 244–245), which Grijalva described as a city "larger than Seville," and then, reversing their course, they finally made it to Champotón, the scene of Córdoba's discomfort. Pressing on, they made a landfall at Tabasco, where they bartered glass beads for gold. Off the present town of Alvarado (which Pedro named for himself), they caught a glimpse of the highest mountain in Mexico, Orizaba (18,700 feet), marveling at its snowy summit in the tropical heat of June. The interpreters were now useless, as the inhabitants spoke Nahuatl; but the party managed near Veracruz to make another rich haul—gold jewelry worth 16,000 pieces of eight, which the Indians were glad to exchange for what they took to be jade. On the island in Veracruz harbor, which he called San Juan de Ulúa, Grijalva found the bodies of two boys who had just had their hearts ripped out. Deciding that a settlement would fare badly, Grijalva returned to Cuba. Without knowing it, he had twice been in contact with spies from Moctezuma's court.

Cortés was now ready to make his move. He let it be known that this third voyage would be no explorer's or trader's junket; the object would be to conquer Mexico, and anyone who came along would share in the spoils. He recruited the bravest men—Pedro de Alvarado and his brothers, Gonzalo de Sandoval, Juan de Escalante, Francisco de Montejo, Alonso Puertocarrero, Christóbal de Olid, and of course Bernal Díaz. Only Pánfilo de Narváez held back. To finance the expedition—he had agreed with Velásquez to pay two thirds of the cost—Cortés raised eight thousand gold pieces by mortgaging his estate. There would be eleven ships this time, carrying 653 men—508 swordsmen, 100 sailors, 32 crossbowmen and 13 musketeers—as well as 14 cannon and 16 horses. (There had been no horses with the earlier expeditions, but Cortés weighed the difficulties against the psychological effect that cavalry was bound to have upon the superstitious Aztecs.) Too late Governor Velásquez, sensing that Cortés would be hard to control, regretted that he had not assumed command himself and tried to countermand his agreement. But in mid-February, 1519, the fleet sailed out of Havana, and a few days later Cortés landed at Tabasco and decisively defeated a local army of 10,000 Indians.

The March to Tenochtitlán

From the outset, Cortés had no intention of turning over the spoils of victory to Diego Velásquez. Though as a young man of nineteen in Hispaniola he had once turned down an offer of an *encomienda* (estate) with the haughty words, "I came for gold, not to till the soil like a peasant," his ambitions now vaulted far beyond monetary gain. Alexander the Great had become his professed model, and glory—the romantic glory of a medieval knight—was his major motivation. He was and would remain a devout Catholic and a loyal subject of his king, but he planned to conquer Mexico for God, for Spain, and for himself—not necessarily in that order. He had already in Tabasco shown his hand, he would not put up with amateurism; Alvarado was sharply rebuked and forced to give up loot that he had taken. "We will never pacify this country by robbing the Indians." He had also made a capture of incalculable value. Among twenty highborn women seized and given to the captains as consorts was an Azteca whom the Spanish called Doña Marina. Bernal Díaz calls her Malinche, and as such she is known to history. She spoke both Maya and Nahuatl and quickly mastered Spanish; she was a skillful negotiator as well as interpreter and became devoted to

Cortés. Communication with her was established through Jerónimo de Aguilár, a Spaniard who had been shipwrecked seven years before during one of the Darien expeditions and held captive in Tulum; [10] Cortés had been lucky enough to find the escaped prisoner on the beach.

Cortés' fleet approached San Juan de Ulúa on Maundy Thursday, 1519, two months after its departure. The Spaniards landed on Good Friday and celebrated Mass. The "Captain" (as Bernal calls him) already knew enough about his objective, the Aztec capital, to realize that it could not be taken by frontal assault. In the first place, it lay 250 miles away (and almost a mile high) on approaches that included jungle, mountains, desert, volcanoes and many peoples of doubtful disposition. In the second, Tenochtitlán's situation in the middle of a lake, connected to the mainland only by narrow causeways miles long, made it an almost impregnable fortress. In the third, there was the Aztec army, the largest and best equipped in Mexico, to reckon with. Moctezuma would have to be maneuvered into welcoming him, and without substantial allies this would probably be impossible. Cortés was already in the country of the Totonacs, long since subjugated by the Aztecs, and with plenty of grievances.

The strategy began auspiciously with Cortés' putting on a big show for the benefit of Moctezuma's ambassadors. The cannon were loaded and fired, while the cavalry raced up and down the beach with brandished lances, exhibiting their control over the fearsome "monsters." Scribes made quick sketches of the scene on sheets of henequen. A worm-eaten carved chair and a red silk cap were formally presented as gifts for the Emperor, and when one of the ambassadors asked for a steel helmet, Cortés requested that it be returned filled with gold dust. It was duly returned, some weeks later, along with a treasure in emeralds and superbly wrought gold ornaments—more than enough to cover the costs of the campaign. But Cortés wisely dispatched most of it directly to Charles V in the company of two of his trusted captains; and made doubly sure that he would not be troubled by the disgruntled Velásquez at his rear by running the remaining ten ships in his fleet aground in Veracruz harbor. Revolt against Cortés would no longer be an option. There would be only one direction available to his company: forward.

Meanwhile Cortés had moved his camp north along the coast to Cempoala, where the Totonac cacique (chief) was cleverly maneu-

[10] This accounted for the word "Castilan," which Córdoba's men had heard the Indian repeat.

vered into becoming his ally. When the chief complained bitterly over the presence of tax gatherers who had just arrived from Tenochtitlán demanding an increase in the tribute and sacrificial victims, Cortés suggested that they be seized. The Totonacs seized them happily; and Cortés secretly released them, advising them to flee to Moctezuma and tell him that he (Cortés) had done him this favor and was on his way! The Totonacs were now firmly under Cortés' control, and he felt sure enough of this to destroy their idols and begin their conversion to Christianity. He also regularized his position vis-á-vis the Spanish monarch by formally establishing a colony at Veracruz and having himself "elected" by plebiscite to its civil and military command. Cuba, of course, was not mentioned. The treasure on its way already far outweighed anything the King of Spain had received from Cuba, and there was the promise of far more to come. On August 16, Cortés departed for Tlaxcala, with 400 Totonac warriors and noblemen bringing up his rear.

The way to Tlaxcala led through the present provincial capital of Jalapa, then past the Cofre de Perote to Xocotlán and into the territory of the only Nahuatl-speaking people who still resisted Moctezuma. To make an ally of the warlike highlanders was necessary and looked easy, but proved otherwise. First the Tlaxcalans refused an alliance, and then they gave battle. Probably the Tlaxcalans thought that the Aztecs were using the Totonacs to attack them from the rear. Or perhaps they were merely testing Cortés, to see whether his vaunted invincibility and divinity were fraudulent. The Tlaxcalan army numbered 50,000. If it had attacked by night, or had had a unified command, or had not been intent upon taking prisoners for sacrifice, it might have overwhelmed the Spaniards. As it was, "all the plain was swarming with warriors, and there we were, four hundred in their midst," [11] as Bernal Díaz puts it. The little band stood firm. The Tlaxcalans charged repeatedly, lost heavily, and then retreated! The Spaniards were badly battered, and they had lost forty-five of their soldiers. There was talk of falling back, but Cortés pointed out that the Totonacs would take them for cowards and destroy them; besides, there were no ships. Seventeen days later, a delegation from the defeated Tlaxcalans announced that a "mistake" had been made, that they were now ready to join Cortés in an attack on the Aztec capital sixty miles away.

The main road led through the sacred city of Cholula, with its

[11] Bernal Díaz del Castillo, *The Discovery and Conquest of Mexico*. Translated by A. P. Maudslay. New York, Farrar, Straus and Cudahy, 1956.

360 teocallis (temples) and the great Toltec pyramid. Moctezuma exercised considerable control here, and he dispatched an army to wait in the gullies outside the city. The Cholulans appeared to be friendly and welcomed Cortés into their city, but the Tlaxcalan army was not admitted. What followed is still debated. From Malinche and others, Cortés received intelligence of an Aztec plot to ambush him. Some historians think that there was no plot; that Cortés either panicked or decided deliberately to terrorize Moctezuma. In any event, the Spaniards invited the Cholulan chieftains to an audience to discuss their departure, and when they arrived, fell upon them. The six thousand Tlaxcalans were alerted, entered the city, and completed the massacre. That Moctezuma did not take umbrage at this gross affront to his authority seems to bear out the theory of those who hold that the Aztec ruler believed he was being pursued by an avenging god. "To suppose that Moctezuma's mind wavered at this time is not to understand the grounds of his belief in Cortés' identity. That after recognizing him as Quetzalcoatl and passively acquiescing in his march inland, he now designed to trap and kill him as if he were a mortal, is irreconcilable with the nature of the prophecy that told of Quetzalcoatl's second coming: an astrological calculation translated into mythological terms." [12]

The truth is more likely that Moctezuma was confused. He tried many ways to arrest Cortés' progress, all of them halfhearted. Had he met him head-on at the beach, Cortés would have been destroyed. Now he apologized, through another embassy, for the Cholulans' churlishness, and invited the conquistador to visit him in Tenochtitlán. The Tlaxcalans offered Cortés a guard of ten thousand soldiers, but he accepted only a thousand porters. The frightened Totonacs returned to Cempoala. Unaccompanied, the Spaniards continued on, leaving their allies behind to be called upon if need be; it was not Cortés' strategy to seize the Aztec capital by force. On November 1, camp was pitched at twelve thousand feet in the saddle between the two great snow volcanoes overlooking Tenochtitlán.

Since Popocatepetl, the (then) active volcano, was held in great dread by the Indians, Cortés increased the aura of invincible divinity with which he was beginning to be regarded by having one of his captains, Diego de Ordás, climb it. "From this summit," Bernal Díaz says, "could be seen the great city of Mexico, and the whole of the lake, and all the towns which were built in it." From the saddle, Díaz adds, two roads led to the capital, one by Chalco, the other by

[12] Maurice Collins, *Cortés and Montezuma*. New York, Harcourt, Brace, & World, Inc., 1955.

Tlalmanalco,[13] and the Spaniards took the one by Chalco. Descending into the plain, they approached the causeway of Cuitlahuac separating the lake of Chalco from Xochimilco and had their first close view of the Aztec metropolis. Bernal Díaz' celebrated description of what they saw and their reception must be quoted in full:

> During the morning, we arrived at a broad Causeway and continued our march toward Iztapalapa, and when we saw so many cities and villages built in the water and other great towns on dry land and that straight and level Causeway going towards Mexico, we were amazed and said that it was like the enchantments they tell of in the legend of Amadis, on account of the great towers and cues and buildings rising from the water, and all built of masonry. And some of our soldiers even asked whether the things that we saw were not a dream. It is not to be wondered at that I here write it down in this manner, for there is so much to think over that I do not know how to describe it, seeing things as we did that had never been heard of or seen before, not even dreamed about.
>
> Thus, we arrived near Iztapalapa, to behold the splendour of the other Caciques who came out to meet us, who were the Lord of the town named Cuitlahuac, and the Lord of Culuacan, both of them near relations of Montezuma. And then when we entered the city of Iztapalapa, the appearance of the palaces in which they lodged us! How spacious and well built they were, of beautiful stone work and cedar wood, and the wood of other sweet scented trees, with great rooms and courts, wonderful to behold, covered with awnings of cotton cloth.
>
> When we had looked well at all of this, we went to the orchard and garden, which was such a wonderful thing to see and walk in, that I was never tired of looking at the diversity of the trees, and noting the scent which each one had, and the paths full of roses and flowers, and the many fruit trees and native roses, and the pond of fresh water.

[13] This is incorrect, since Chalco and Tlalmanalco, then as now, are on the same road; Cortés in his Second Letter to Charles V says they went by way of Amecameca—after meeting another embassy from Moctezuma who made a last attempt to persuade them to desist. (*Hernándo Cortés Five Letters 1519–1526*. Translated by J. Bayard Morris. London: George Routledge & Sons. 1928.)

There was another thing to observe, that great canoes were able to pass into the garden from the lake through an opening that had been made so that there was no need for their occupants to land. And all was cemented and very splendid with many kinds of stone [monuments] with pictures on them, which gave much to think about. Then the birds of many kinds and breeds which came into the pond. I say again that I stood looking at it and thought that never in the world would there be discovered other lands such as these, for at that time there was no Peru, nor any thought of it. Of all these wonders that I then beheld to-day all is overthrown and lost, nothing left standing.[14]

The first movement of the great drama was now approaching a crescendo. Moctezuma sent out his brother Cuitlahuac, the king of Ixtapalapa, and Cacamatzin, the King of Texcoco, to greet the bold invader. Wouldn't he prefer to wait just outside the city? He would not. Moctezuma himself was now born down the causeway in a golden litter canopied with feathers. Robed in gold and emeralds and proceeded by slaves who swept the earth, scattered flowers and scented the air with flasks of perfume, the Emperor politely greeted Cortés on his charger. Cortés dismounted and presented the king with a necklace of pearls, receiving in return a golden garland of shellfish. Then Moctezuma turned and reentered his city. Cortés and the Spaniards followed him. The date was November 8, 1519.

Moctezuma's Death and La Noche Triste

To understand the tragic second movement of the drama it is necessary to picture the terrible anxiety that gripped both camps. Consider first the Spaniards' dilemma. On the surface all was calm and bright. Without firing a shot, they had entered the Aztec capital and were lodged in a palace next to the Emperor's on the square facing the pyramid (Cortés described the plaza as twice the size of Salamanca's and Bernal Díaz compared it to Constantinople). They were being fed by an army of slaves, like kings. All about them the great city that resembled Venice with its canals and bridges and towers hummed like a discreet watch.[15] Its aromas of chocolate and

---

[14] Bernal Díaz, *op. cit.*

[15] Visitors to Indian vilages today, especially in Guatemala, where things have hardly changed, are invariably as impressed by the almost soundless murmur of the busy markets as Bernal Díaz was.

pimiento, of tobacco smoke and copal incense, though unfamiliar, were reassuring. The thin air was bracing. The water was pure. On the other hand, what could have been more disquieting than to have no lines of communication at all to one's familiar world? And to be quite in the dark about why one had been admitted freely, and about what to expect next? There were all kinds of sinister portents. Every morning priests splattered the white walls with the blood of living quails. From the zoo across the square came the roaring of jaguars. And every morning the steps to the dark shrine of the war god ran with the blood of newly slaughtered victims as the big drum sounded. Cortés in his second interview with the monarch had suggested that the sacrifices stop and that the ancestral gods be replaced with the Spaniards' religion, but this advice had not been well received. The common soldiers were beginning to grumble: When would the gold they had come for be seized and divided among them?

The pressure on Cortés came to a head when news arrived that the settlement at Veracruz had been attacked and the garrison commander, Juan de Escalante, killed. Moctezuma turned away in disgust when the head of one of the Spaniards was presented to him, but the prestige of the Spaniards had suffered a damaging blow. Those who suspected that the Aztec emperor was cunningly probing for their weaknesses demanded that he be seized as a hostage. Cortés reluctantly acceded. Moctezuma was seen in tears being escorted to his father's palace. Quiet descended over the cowed city. The Spanish soldiers mounted the teocalli, overturned the images of Huitzilopochtli and Tezcatlipoca, whitewashed the blood-spattered walls, and erected an altar to the Virgin. Cuitlahuatzin and Cacamatzin and the King of Coyoacán were arrested and forced to swear allegiance to Charles V. The vast Aztec treasure was distributed among the invited guests, Moctezuma mordantly remarking: "Pardon the insignificance of these presents, but I have nothing more. You have already taken everything." [16]

Outside the capital, meanwhile, trouble was coming from two directions. As May of 1520 approached, Cortés was playing for time. He was waiting for reinforcements, and he had no way of knowing that his embassy to Charles V was stalled in Madrid: The Spanish monarch was much too wily to recognize Cortés' claims over the Cuban Governor's until it was clear which of them would prevail.

---

[16] Quoted in Jean Descola, *The Conquistadors.* Translated by Malcolm Barnes. New York, The Viking Press, Inc., 1957.

Diego Velásquez had many friends at court, and he was now well enough convinced of Cortés' treachery to throw his own power into the balance. In May Moctezuma brought the news to Cortés that a fleet of eighteen vessels bearing more than twice as many soldiers and horses as Cortés commanded had dropped anchor at San Juan de Ulúa. Cortés was elated until he recognized the crude portrait of Pánfilo de Narváez. Immediately he resolved to split his small force. Putting Alvarado in command of eighty men to stand guard over Moctezuma and the treasure, he took his remaining seventy effectives and left to round up the two hundred-odd members of his band who had been left outside the capital to scout the approaches to Tenochtitlán. With these, and the remainder of the garrison at Veracruz, now commanded by the able and trustworthy Gonzales de Sandoval, he would have almost half as many warriors as Pánfilo de Narváez—more than enough, he figured, to dispose of an opponent with no experience in the field and softened up by the easy life of the sugar plantations. He knew, too, that the young prince, Cuauhtémoc, son of Moctezuma's predecessor, Ahuitzotl, was organizing an Aztec rebellion against him at Tlatelolco north of the city. There was no time to lose.

Cortés' lightning attack upon Pánfilo de Narváez' army was his masterpiece. It began with his interception of the messengers Narváez had sent to Sandoval; he entertained them lavishly, showed them the treasure that would be theirs, and sent them back to Narváez in such a state of exhilaration that they began to subvert the latter's soldiery. A messenger to Narváez, secretly distributing bars of gold, further undermined the invading force's resolve.

Picking up his scouts and joining forces with Sandoval's forty men, who had sought refuge among the friendly Totonacs, Cortés now fell upon Narváez in Cempoala by night and during a downpour. He directed one advance party to seize the cannon in the temple complex where the army was encamped, and another under Sandoval to seize their commander. Narváez, after losing an eye to a pike thrust, was captured. With their own guns now turned on them (and visions of gold no doubt affecting their ardor), the order to surrender in the name of the Spanish Emperor was all that was needed. "You must consider this a great feat, this victory, Señor Captain Cortés," Bernal Díaz quotes Narváez as exclaiming. Cortés' disdainful reply, that it was "one of the least important things he had done in New Spain," was not relayed to Diego Velásquez in Cuba directly, for all the ships were seized and all the soldiers were placed under Cortés' command for a swift return to Tenochtitlán.

Cortés was stunned by what confronted him when he arrived in the Aztec capital. The news had already trickled out that Alvarado and his eighty men had gone beserk during the festival of Tezcatlipoca in May, sallying out of their palace and slaying as many as possible of the dancers (whom they suspected of being an advance guard of Cuauhtémoc's forces). Cortés and his 1,300 soldiers, 96 horses, and augmented artillery crossed the unguarded and shorter causeway of Tacuba into the capital on June 24. The city was strangely quiet. Brushing aside Moctezuma, who came to greet him, Cortés upbraided Alvarado furiously for disobeying orders. But there was little time for recriminations; Alvarado's valor would be needed. Cuauhtémoc already controlled the markets on the lake shore and was cutting off the Spaniards' food supply. Moctezuma suggested releasing Cuitlahuac from bondage to negotiate—and Cuitlahuac promptly joined the rebels, who declared him acting sovereign. The following day, June 25, the Tacuba causeway was cut. Cortés tried two sorties and in both was repulsed with heavy losses. He then requested the captive King to speak to the besieging host and persuade them that the Spaniards only wanted to evacuate the capital. In his robes Moctezuma spoke to the Aztec soldiery. Some informed him, in tears, that he was no longer their ruler; there was no intention of allowing Cortés to escape alive. Even as he was replying to this, the Spanish soldiers who were guarding Moctezuma lowered their shields, and he was struck in the head by a stone. When Moctezuma died, a few days later, "Cortés wept for him and so did all of us captains and soldiers," Bernal Díaz reports. "There was not one of us who had known him intimately that did not lament him as if he were our father."

So, ambivalent to the end, the tragic sovereign of the Aztecs entered into history. As a man, he had been kind and generous; Bernal Díaz obviously found his personality more sympathetic and admirable than Cortés'. As a ruler, he was indecisive and bumbling. But in his defense it may be said that he was the victim of his religion, which he perhaps took more seriously than his militant cousins. The best evidence that he considered Cortés to be Quetzalcoatl is contained in the welcoming address which Father Sahagún quotes in Nahuatl: "All these days I have been watching for you, waiting to see you appear from your hidden place among the clouds and mist. For the kings, my ancestors, told me that you would return to sit on your mat, your stool. Now it has come true!"

Cortés' position in the besieged capital was now desperate. The day following the Emperor's death was spent building a portable bridge. The plan was to carry it ahead of the vanguard to span the broken sections of one of the causeways and thus fight a way out. The night of the sortie the soldiers loaded themselves with the gold ingots into which Cortés had melted down the Aztec treasure, and crept toward the Tacuba causeway. An alarm was sounded, and the heavily laden soldiers were attacked by swarms of warriors in canoes. The portable bridge was destroyed, but passage was made over the bodies of the Spanish dead and wounded, or by swimming. Alvarado is reported to have made the last breach in the causeway by pole-vaulting on his lance. The great treasure was jettisoned. All the guns were lost. Half the army was dead or had been captured for sacrifice. Under a cypress on the hill of Los Remedios, *El Árbol de la Noche Triste,* Cortés wept for his slain comrades.

Cuitlahuac was the victor, but he failed to follow up his advantage; and in a few days Cuitlahuac died of smallpox, a disease brought to Mexico by a Negro soldier from Cuba; there was then no defense against it.

The Destruction of the Aztec Empire

Cuauhtémoc, the Falling Eagle, had now become the eleventh (and last) Aztec king. He was a brave and resourceful leader, and he began by equipping a huge army to intercept Cortés' stragglers before they reached their allies in Tlaxcala. The battle took place on July 8, 1520, at Otumba, not far from the pyramid of Teotihuacán. If, as Prescott [17] has it, the number of the Indians exceeded 200,000 at Otumba and Cortés' tired and wounded remnant was less than 500, *entirely without firearms,* then the Spaniards were not unreasonable afterward to have claimed divine intervention! Cuauhtémoc perhaps erred in entrusting the command of the Aztecs in this engagement to one Cihuacoatl, for it was Cortés' singling out of this chieftain, when the Spaniards were surrounded and about to be overwhelmed by sheer numbers, that proved the turning point. At any rate, Cihuacoatl's death and the raising of his captured standard seems to have dispirited the host, for they suddenly began to fall back and the Spaniards counterattacked, finally escaping across the border into the kingdom of their allies.

Cortés took heart now, and at once enlisted the Tlaxcalans in a tremendous ship-building operation. Porters descended to the Gulf and returned with every salvageable part of the scuttled fleet. Brig-

[17] William Hickling Prescott, *History of the Conquest of Mexico.* New York, Modern Library, 1936.

antines with shallow draft were built. Cortés meanwhile secured his rear by enlisting the Tlaxcalans to wipe out the Aztec garrisons in the Totonac country. He was also fortunate in being able to seize the ships and soldiers Velásquez kept sending to reinforce Pánfilo de Narváez; the Cuban Governor still knew nothing about that hapless soldier's defeat. A trading vessel, loaded with munitions, was bought outright with remnants of the Aztec gold. By the time he was ready to begin the assault, Cortés had five hundred well-armed men under his command again and an auxiliary force of 10,000 Tlaxcalans. It was Cuauhtémoc's gravest handicap that the Tlaxcalans hated the Aztecs more than they feared the Spaniards.

The Spanish army drew up before Texcoco in the last days of 1520. Texcoco, the first bridgehead, fell in May. Cortés' army now had swelled to some nine hundred and the Tlaxcalans to a hundred thousand. Cortés saw that his forces were still too weak to take Tenochtitlán by assault. His brigantines could prevent the enemy from attacking his men on the causeways by canoe in daytime, but at night Cuauhtémoc's soldiers could cut the causeways again. To break the stalemate, Cortés decided to reduce the island fortress by blockade. He began this phase by destroying the aqueduct from Chapultepec. The Aztecs were without fresh drinking water, and soon they were reduced to eating their Tlaxcalan captives, and finally lizards and leathern shields. The siege lasted seventy-five days. Fifty thousand Aztecs perished from disease and starvation, and the few who had the strength left to try to escape were drowned. On August 13, the city capitulated. Cuauhtémoc was seized trying to get away and begged Cortés to kill him. The empire of the Aztecs was finished. "Never in the world had a people suffered so much," Bernal Díaz wrote.

For four years the miserable survivors were put to work systematically destroying the temples, statuary and homes of their people—and rebuilding in its place under the lashes of their conquerors a Spanish capital complete with a cathedral, palaces, and new aqueducts and causeways.

Cortés himself was appointed Governor and Captain-General of New Spain by Charles V in October of 1522. But thereafter his fortunes fared poorly. The Spanish monarch had no intention of allowing the great general's power to rival his own. He sent out treasurers, accountants and inspectors to curb Cortés' jurisdiction. After three years of administration, Cortés led a punitive expedition as far south as Honduras against one of his insubordinate captains. It lasted over a year and entailed hardships far surpassing the earlier campaigns. Then there was a trip to Spain to repair his political fences, and a period of ten years managing his vast estates and leading an exploratory expedition to Baja California off the Pacific coast of Mexico. Back in Spain in 1540, Cortés found his great past eclipsed by Pizarro's conquest of Peru, which was bringing a treasure greater than Mexico's to the Emperor's court. He accompanied an expedition to Algiers, where he accomplished nothing but the loss of Moctezuma's emeralds which he had still with him. At Castilleja de la Cuesta, Bernal Díaz relates, "Our Lord was pleased to take from him this toilsome life on December 2, 1547."

Cuauhtémoc, whose resurrection as a Mexican hero was still centuries away, was first tortured to reveal the hiding place of the Aztec treasure which had ceased to exist, and then hanged on the march to Honduras lest he inspire another rebellion.

2

THE COLONY AND THE
INDEPENDENCE (1522–1824)

EXACTLY three hundred years were to elapse between the fall of Tenochtitlán and the expulsion of the Spanish colonial administration from Mexico City—three hundred years of Indian subjugation and Spanish misrule. The ideologues of modern Mexico frequently cast Cortés and the Church in the roles of villains responsible for initiating that state of affairs; but in fact it was Cortés, alone among the Spaniards in America, who impressed upon Charles V the need for conciliating the conquered races; and it was the mendicant orders in the sixteenth century in Mexico who saved the Indians from annihilation and preserved their traditions and arts, thus making possible the racially integrated culture of today.

Had events followed logically from an extraordinary scene that took place outside the stricken city in 1524, progress to that goal might have been uninterrupted. Cortés had requested that the Spanish monarch send to the New World not bishops and prelates who would squander their resources in riotous living, but godly men from the religious fraternities; and when the Franciscans in their tattered garments, headed by Martín de Valéncia, arrived barefoot at the capital, Cortés had publicly kissed Fray Martín's feet and had himself scourged for his sins in the presence of the astonished Indians.

Unfortunately, neither Cortés nor Charles V were consistent in their policy of reconciliation, and the temper of the times would probably have defeated such a policy even had it been adhered to. Spain had only been unified for a few decades, and when the Moors were expelled from the Iberian Peninsula, the Jews were expelled with them, thus eliminating whatever religious tolerance had existed in Spain in the Middle Ages. Only in the early part of the long reign of Charles V (1516–56) had there been an interregnum of liberalism. The ideas of Erasmus were freely discussed, the philosophy of the scholastics challenged, and the concept of the self-determination of nations evolved. The first grammar of a modern language was published, and the first dictionary; Dürer, Titian, and Rubens came to Madrid and the arts flourished. So did the natural sciences. But the Renaissance in Spain was doomed, and along with it the progressivism of such Renaissance spirits as Cortés. Charles V in his old age retired to a monastery, leaving religious reforms to the fanatics at the Council of Trent, and politics to his sons and grandsons, the reactionary Philips (1556–1665).

As for Cortés, who had written the Emperor that servitude must not be the lot of the Indians with their "superior capacities," he ended by accepting the colonists' demand that they be forced to till the vast estates (his own included) under the vicious system of *repartimientos* (land grants); and he, who had stood sponsor to Cuauhtémoc's conversion and baptism, ended up by hanging him.

Completion of the Conquest

Reaction was in full sway as the Spanish power now overran the rest of Mexico. In 1521 Sandoval completed the subjugation of Veracruz and Tabasco, burning alive one of the recalcitrant caciques. Alvarado, on his way to the ruthless extermination of the peoples of Guatemala, subdued the Mixtecs and Zapotecs and founded the city of Oaxaca; Cortés admonished Alvarado for his senseless massacres, but as before in Tenochtitlán, Alvarado was beyond his control. Cortés' instructions were similarly flouted by Cristóbal de Olid in Michoacán, Colima and Jalisco, where nothing but plunder was accomplished. Sandoval, sent to suppress a rebellion in Pánuco to the north of the capital, this time burned alive four hundred of the Indians; and his successor, Nuño de Guzmán, went a step further by selling the inhabitants into slavery to the planters of Hispaniola and Cuba. Entrusted briefly with the government of Mexico, under the first *audiencia* (high court of justice) sent to limit Cortés' power, Guzmán terrorized the whole country, branded the Indians, permitted the rape of their women, humiliated the protesting Fathers, sealed the ports, and finally—after Bishop Zumárraga had smuggled an account of his crimes out of Mexico in a barrel of oil—retreated to the kingdom of the Tarascans in Michoacán, where he completed Olid's alienation of that friendly people. A second *audiencia*, headed by an upright bishop, arrived in 1530 and attempted to repair the damage.

While this reform administration and Antonio de Mendoza, the first viceroy, who arrived in 1535, were seeking to restore some order, and Cortés had retired in disgust to his palace in Cuernavaca to raise sugar and sheep, the sack of Mexico continued far to the south and north. In Yucatán the Francisco de Montejos, father and son, were finding the Mayas intractable. The elder Montejo was finally forced to retire from the peninsula in 1535, leaving not a Spaniard in occupancy; the wounded natives would commit suicide rather than serve their tormentors. The younger Montejo—at a cost in lives greater than the conquests of the Aztec and Inca empires combined, and by burning and mutilating on a stupendous scale—took hold in Mérida at last; but parts of the peninsula remained unsubdued, and the Itzá priesthood held out on an island in the Petén jungle until 1697. "Even though they were finally crushed by superior force," Parkes writes, "the Mayas preserved their spiritual independence; they refused to speak Spanish, the vocabulary of which was considerably smaller than that of their own language, so that their masters were compelled to learn Maya; and as late as the nineteenth century they were still rebelling against the domination of the whites." [1] Even in the twentieth, as we shall see, the people of Mérida have been the first to assert their independence.

The silver mines of northern Mexico attracted the Spaniards more than its river valleys and pasture lands. The rich strike at Zacatecas in 1546 and the almost equally fabulous lode uncovered at nearby Guanajuato in the next decade increased the wealth of Spain sevenfold. Heavily guarded mule trains clogged the road to the capital and on down to Veracruz, and in the capital the palatial homes of the silver barons began to rise. The conquest of the vast northern area, extending in the west into California and in the north and east into Arizona, New Mexico and Texas, was conducted with much less vigor. Here, as in Yucatán, pockets of Indian nationalism flared up and survived. The Pacific states of Michoacán and Jalisco, where Guzmán did his worst, have always held aloof from the federal leadership. (The so-called Mixton War of 1541, in which Alvarado perished, almost put an end to the European occupation.) The Huichol tribe in the mountains of Nayarit retains its Indian religion,

[1] Henry Bamford Parkes, *A History of Mexico*, Boston, Houghton Mifflin Company, 1938, 1950.

customs and dress still. The Yaquis of Sonora were the best soldiers of the Revolution of 1910 because they still believed themselves to be fighting Spanish imperialism.

The Colonial Power Structure

This city (Mexico) is the seat of an Archbishop, and of a Viceroy, who commonly is some great nobleman of Spain, whose power is to make laws and ordinances, to give directions, and determine controversies, unless it be in such great causes which are thought fit to be referred to the Council of Spain. . . . Most of the governors about the country being the Viceroy's creatures, placed by him, do contribute great gifts and bribes for their preferment. So likewise do all the rest whose right or wrong proceedings depend upon the Viceroy's clemency and mercy in judging the daily appeals of justice which come unto him. The King of Spain allows him out of his Exchequer a hundred thousand ducats yearly whilst he governs. His time is only five years, but commonly with his bribes to the courtiers of Spain, and the Counsellors to the Estate of the Indies he gets a prorogation of five years more, and sometimes of ten. . . .

Besides the Viceroy there are commonly six judges and a King's Attorney. . . . These may unite together to oppose the Viceroy in any unlawful and unjustifiable action, as some have done, and have smarted for it. Yet commonly they dare not, so that he doth what he listeth, and it is enough for him to say, "*Stat pro ratione voluntas.*" This power joined with covetousness in the Viceroy, and three score thousand ducats yearly joined with pride in the Archbishop, was like to be the ruin of that city in the year 1624 when the Count of Gelves was Viceroy.[2]

The Dominican friar-turned-Protestant, who called himself "The English American," was not the most unprejudiced of observers when it came to exposing the licentiousness of the priests; but he was the first foreign visitor to New Spain to set down his impressions, and for the most part they were accurate. Gelves, who was about to have his palace set on fire in a dispute with the Archbishop,

[2] *Thomas Gage's Travels in the New York,* edited and with an Introduction by J. Eric S. Thompson. Norman, Oklahoma, University of Oklahoma Press, 1958.

was, Gage adds, "... one of the best viceroys and governors that ever the Court of Spain sent to America" and "... there had never been so many thieves and malefactors hanged up as in his time." There were several better viceroys *before* Gelves, Gage might have added; but after him there were none. The fact of the matter was that by 1624 Spain itself had become hopelessly lax and corrupt, and no further effort was made (until much too late) to implement the laws by which Cortés, Charles V, and Bishop Bartolomé de las Casas had hoped to establish a prosperous colony with a degree of self-government and equity.

Las Casas, whose long life was devoted to saving the Indians, had been converted to this noble cause as a young priest in Hispaniola, where he had witnessed the Spanish campaigns under Columbus that ended with the annihilation of the native population. In Guatemala he had gained Alvarado's reluctant assent to subdue the rebellious northern province with the Cross alone, and had been so successful in converting the Mayas to Christianity that the area is known as the Verapaz to this day. In Spain his propaganda was instrumental in the enactment of the New Laws of 1542. Under this legislation, all *encomiendas* (as the *repartimientos*, binding the Indians as serfs to the landlords' land, were now known) were to cease in the next generation, public servants and clerics to surrender them immediately; slavery would be abolished; and all laws must be published in the Indian tongues as well as in Spanish.

When these laws were announced by the Viceroy in Peru, the landlords slew the Viceroy, and that was the end of it. In Mexico, six hundred colonists left by the next boat, and others declared they would kill their wives and children before submitting them to such "shame." The Viceroy, the envoy sent to enforce the law, even the friars (who didn't want to turn their native charges over to the cruel *corregidores*), pleaded with the Emperor to repeal the New Laws, and he did. Thenceforth, until the Independence, the Indians remained a race apart. The Spaniards, who had shown none of the racial bigotry of the Anglo-Saxon colonizers in the beginning, started talking about color as a proof of inferiority. The Indians, for their part, came to regard white men as their enemies. Slavery was eventually abolished, but they remained enslaved: as wage slaves in the silver mines and on the haciendas (which had replaced the *encomiendas*), enslaved by their debts to the masters and by their enforced ignorance, which left them no defense against legal chicanery. And as their communal lands (*ejidos*) in the fertile valleys were little by little taken away from them, they retreated into the inaccessible mountains—those that could get away. By the end of the century, the Indian population of Mexico is believed to have declined from eleven million to little more than two million.

Under the first Viceroy, Antonio de Mendoza, and his successor, Luis de Velasco, the rule of Spain had been patriarchal if not benign. The *ejidos* were protected, wages and hours in the mines were controlled; Archbishop Zumárraga in the capital and Bishop Quiroga in Michoacán began to educate the Indians, and an Indian college at Tlatelolco flourished briefly. But as Spain itself degenerated, so did the viceroys. Instead of protecting the weak and curbing the rapacious, they became wholly involved in maintaining their power vis-à-vis the Mexican-born Creoles and leaving their term of office with as much wealth as possible.

A primitive press was established in 1539, and a mint turned out the millions of silver dollars that became common currency throughout the Americas and in Asia as well for a time. But industry and commerce, far from being smiled upon by the mother country, were discouraged. Except for the products of the mines, it was to Spain's interest to supply everything else. Luxuries and most other manufactured goods were imported from Spain. The whole of Mexico's trade in the Atlantic was forced to pass through Cádiz and Seville, and the ships carrying it, getting precious little protection from the unseaworthy Spanish fleet, were at the mercy of British freebooters and pirates. In the Pacific, *one galleon a year* was permitted to pass between Acapulco and Manila. Without commerce or industry, Mexico soon became a country of self-sufficient feudal plantations.

The owners of these haciendas, the Creoles, were themselves an inferior class, ruled over and looked down upon by the despotic bureaucracy of Spanish officialdom, the hated *gachupines* (spur-wearers).

The *gachupines*, sometimes called *peninsulares* from their origin in the Iberian Peninsula, occupied the positions of political and clerical power, from the viceroyalty and the archbishopric on down. The Creoles hated them, especially for their airs, and in hating them began to develop a vestige of national feeling. They would have done so earlier had they not been able to exercise a sense of social and racial superiority of their own over a third class, the mestizos. A mixture of the races, mestizos were proud of not being Indians, but were rejected socially by the white Creoles. They worked in the mines and plantations, formed the lowest class in towns that had no Indians, and by the end of the eighteenth century had begun to outnumber the Creoles.

The *cabildo* (or *ayuntamiento*), a town council elected by the adult white property owners, was the only instrument of government in New Spain with a democratic potential. In the beginning it exercised its privilege of communicating directly with the King, bypassing the Viceroy's provincial governors (*adelantados*) and municipal officials (*corregidores*), but soon the latter gained control and the town councilors were reduced to regulating such functions as police, sanitary facilities, local justice and taxes. Until the time was ripe for rebellion, the *cabildos* remained subservient to the Spanish bureaucracy, their aggressiveness considerably blunted by the practice of selling offices, which had commenced under Philip II. This practice, and the *mordida,* under which public officials were encouraged to take action only when bribed to do so, soon became standard throughout Latin America. Paternalism, under which it was taken for granted that the government should regulate anything and everything, similarly became the norm, and this "inspired the people to devise ways to defeat the all-powerful state through passive resistance, mendacity, corruption, hypocrisy, and the famous Spanish dictum, *Obedezco pero no cumplo,* "I obey but do not carry out" [3]—another characteristic of the relations between rulers and the ruled that survives throughout Spanish America.

The Friars and the Church

From the time when rudimentary chapels were erected in Tenochtitlán where the sacrificial temple had towered, and atop the great pyramid of Quetzalcoatl in the holy city of Cholula, churches with bell towers and tiled domes came to dominate every settlement in central and southern Mexico. No less than twelve thousand of them were built in the Colonial period, and they still give the landscape its crowning color and the towns their architectural distinction. The early "fortress monasteries" like Tlalmanalco, Yuriria, Actopán and Atotonilco, built by the mendicant orders in Gothic-Renaissance styles, are unique. Four of the later churches—the Sacristy of the Cathedral in Mexico City, the Jesuit Seminary of San Martín at Tepotzotlan, Santa Clara in Querétaro and Santa Prisca at Taxco—have been ranked among the eight Baroque masterpieces of the world.

The little band of Franciscan, Dominican and Augustinian monks

[3] John Edwin Fagg, *Latin America: A General History*. New York, The Macmillan Company, 1963.

who converted Mexico to Christianity between 1523 and 1583 were as brave and remarkably gifted as Cortés and his captains, and their conquest was more significant. Cortés had been the first to remark similarities in the Aztec and Catholic religions. While the Aztecs didn't believe in eternal life or in heavenly rewards for good conduct, they practiced rudimentary baptismal and confessional and communion rites, and their rich polytheism was adaptable to the worship of the saints; their Omeyotl was a supreme deity; Huitzilopochtli was born of a virgin; and the cross (if only as a symbol of the four cardinal points) was already in use. The Spaniards, of all Europeans, were most like them in being cruel, fatalistic, strict with children, and obsessed with death.[4]

Cortés specifically requested of Charles V that the mendicant orders rather than the secular clergy be sent to Mexico. Only the Fathers with their poverty, chastity and ethical rectitude, he realized, would be able to compete with the fanatically chaste Aztec priests. He may also have guessed that compassion would accomplish more than fanaticism, and a learned devotion to the arts have more lasting effect than ecclesiastical pomp and good living. It is true that the missionaries "neglected entirely to use the minute particle of truth which in their eyes the Aztecs might have held." [5] Nor were the Fathers by our standards tolerant men—they boasted of the number of idols they overthrew and the libraries of pre-Columbian texts they burned—yet they preserved the native languages, and to some extent the native arts, and they were concerned to replace the old order with a Mexican culture in which the Indians could participate.

First to arrive and most creative of the three orders were the Franciscans. Pedro de Gante, a lay brother, arrived in 1523. "The Twelve," Friars Minor of the Observance, arrived in 1524. Among them were Martín de Valéncia and Toríbio de Benavente, who called himself Motilinia ("poor man" in Nahuatl—"this being the first word I learned, lest I forget it"). The great scholar Bernadino de Sahagún, soon to write his history of Indian Mexico in Nahuatl, came in 1529 with nineteen more Franciscans. Juan de Zumárraga, himself a Franciscan, governed the diocese of Mexico as its first bishop from 1528 to 1548, being succeeded by a Dominican, who remained in office until 1573, when the Jesuits and the secular clergy took over.

---

[4] Until the twentieth century, the Chamulas in Chiapas melded the traditions by crucifying a young Indian every Easter.

[5] Robert Ricard, *The Spiritual Conquest of Mexico.* Translated by Lesley Byrd Simpson. Berkeley, California, University of California Press, 1966.

Viceroy Mendoza, who characterized the secular clergy as "base, mean and self-seeking," did everything in his power to help the Franciscans, but they were already in command when he arrived. (Nuño de Guzmán's attempt to oust them while Cortés was in Honduras had failed.) Historically, they arrived with one great asset: Religion was the principal preoccupation in every Indian's life, and his own gods had failed utterly to protect him from the invaders; he was ready to try others. Only this can account for the staggering numbers who were converted in the early years. Fray Martín de Valéncia claimed that each of The Twelve converted a hundred thousand in the first five years. Pedro de Gante boasted of baptizing ten thousand in a not untypical day. By 1543 the Franciscans claimed nine million souls. Nowhere in the world had such a conversion been accomplished in so short a time.

How much of it involved true belief? "The Indians need to be attracted to our faith by kindness and love," Zumárraga had said, but he added revealingly: "After they are members of the Church, some pious chastisement is often needed because of their natural temper, which is less neglectful of material than of spiritual matters; and they need a spur, since they do not often want to come to church unless they are compelled."

Defeated, discouraged and confused—especially by the epidemics of disease, which carried off two million of them in a single year, and by the sudden poverty which had reduced many to eating grass and dirt—the Indians, confronted by the fiercely individualistic Spaniards, accepted Christianity in a docile, childlike spirit. They loved the Franciscans because "like us they go about poorly clad, and barefoot, partaking of the same food we eat, abide in our midst and deal meekly with us." They were especially impressed with the zeal with which the Fathers mastered their difficult tongues. And they loved to confess—some, it is related, swimming up to the friars' boats in Tenochtitlán and confessing as they treaded water!

Octavio Paz makes the point that the Fathers "used the key of baptism to open the doors of society, converting it into a universal order *open to everyone*." [6] There were classes, castes and slaves, he says, but no pariahs as in our totalitarian societies. This is true, but the Fathers themselves were well aware that they were treating the Indians, a prey to petty thieving, lying and indolence, as children. They made a point of keeping them in their villages, around the monastery, and they never accepted them into their own ranks.

[6] *The Labyrinth of Solitude, Life and Thought in Mexico.* Translated by Lysander Kemp. New York, Grove Press, 1962.

Whatever qualities of resistance and self-reliance the Indians had shown under Cuauhtémoc were weakened under the parental regimen of the Fathers.

The Dominicans, who arrived in 1536, were more learned than the Franciscans, and less effective in conversion; they put their emphasis on printing and theology, but they were great builders too. They moved quickly into the empty areas the Franciscans had left. Their chain of monasteries extended from Puebla to Tehuantepec, and finally into Chiapas and Guatemala. The Augustinians, who arrived about the same time, were still more learned. They moved north into the "unoccupied" territory of the Otomi and Huastec tribes, and west as far as Guerrero. Their Father Borga built the vast church at Atotonilco and their convents (like the one at Yuriria, which was soon being compared to the Escorial) were famous, almost scandalous, for their magnificence. In their haste to catch up with the other orders, the Augustinians admitted the Indians to Mass before they were baptized. All three orders rejected the collecting of tithes, which Cortés had offered them, as a buying of salvation; they were supported by grants from the Throne and by alms, but of course their vast building projects were made possible entirely by "volunteer" Indian labor. And all three orders were soon warring against each other most un-Christianly for the control of souls—the Augustinians being rebuked by Zumárraga for starting a sumptuous monastery at Ocuituco before the Church was even finished, and the Franciscans for having armed and incited "their" Indians to demolish and burn rival churches.

In view of these rivalries and the missionary zeal of all three orders, it is astonishing that the cult of the Virgin of Guadalupe— the single most effective agency in reconciling Indian Mexico to the Spanish religion and suzerainty—should have been actively opposed by the Dominicans and Augustinians and encouraged by only a few individual Franciscans. One of the latter was Bishop Zumárraga, to whom the illiterate Aztec, Juan Diego, had reported his vision in 1531. The good bishop had been skeptical at first, but when the humble peasant from Tepeyac just north of the capital had brought him a bundle of the most beautiful flowers of Castile from the desert hillside, and he had seen imprinted on Juan Diego's coarse cloak an image of the Virgin, *dark-faced*, in all her splendor, Zumárraga had accepted the miracle and caused the original shrine to be built. (See pp. 217–218.)

The three mendicant orders at the time were not impressed. Cortés and Zumárraga took up a collection for the shrine, and the

Dominican Archbishop, Fray Alonso de Montúfar, Zumárraga's successor, defended it against the opposition of all three orders. The Dominicans and Augustinians, almost to a man, opposed the cult, and their chroniclers do not even mention it. It was violently denounced by the Franciscan Fray Francisco de Bustamente in a famous sermon of September 8, 1556, inveighing against the dangers of false idolatry. The great Franciscan linguist and historian Sahagún was particularly concerned about the Indians' identification of the Virgin of Tepeyac with the Aztec god Tonantzin, "Our Mother," whose worship as the patron of fertility had centered at the same spot. Yet curiously, the Augustinians seem to have had no hesitation in permitting the Indians at Chalma, the second-most-popular pilgrimage place in Mexico, to identify the San Señor with a famous idol at nearby Malinalco. (See p. 212.) They did nothing, however, to encourage the mass pilgrimages. "In this field," Ricard observes, "Fray Alonso de Montúfar, by his perseverance in spreading and propagating the cult of Our Lady of Guadalupe, showed more clear-sightedness and boldness. In a day when the unanimous veneration of the *Virgin Moreña* is perhaps the only tie that persists among the Mexicans, one must admire the perspicacity of the second head of the Mexican Church."

The last great religious figure of the sixteen century was singularly like Cortés in his visionary truculence, his heterodoxy, and his tragic old age. John McAndrew [7] tells the complicated story of Bishop Vasco de Quiroga's utopias and architectural megalomania for the first time in all its ramifications. Pope Paul III had rushed the brilliant Quiroga through Holy Orders in one composite ceremony to receive the bishropric of Michoacán from his old friend Zumárraga in 1536. It was a crash program to try to undo the alienation of the Tarascans whose emperor had just been burned alive by Nuño de Guzmán. Quiroga not only succeeded in this impossible task, but made Michoacán prosperous beyond belief. His program was both idealistic and practical. It was based on the *Utopia* of Saint Thomas More but was more socialistic. The Indians would "avoid the sin of envy" by making things for each other and holding their land in common. Adult males spent two years alternately farming and manufacturing—all on the six-hour day! The products of labor were distributed free—*according to need*. Families were permitted small private gardens for usufruct but not for ownership and sale. Every church and every village ran a large and well-staffed hospital to care

[7] John McAndrew, *The Open Churches of Sixteenth-Century Mexico*. Cambridge, Massachusetts, Harvard University Press, 1965.

for the sick and aged. Modern methods of fishing, glazing, pottery, and manufacturing guitars (in all of which Michoacán still excels) were introduced. Plainsong was taught, and the whole community joined in sing-ins. The whole race would worship—why not?—in a single church!

That was the idea that tripped Don Vasco finally, that gave his numerous enemies the pretext to snarl him in lawsuits for the rest of his ninety-five years. Quiroga's Colegio de San Nicolás, the first in the Americas, survives; but his Cathedral of Pátzcuaro with its five naves never got off the ground.

Colonial Arts

Some of the architectural masterpieces erected by the mendicant orders all over Mexico in the sixteenth century have already been mentioned; others will be described in detail in the last part of this book. "No European nation was ever more kindly disposed to artistic miscegenation than Spain," [8] says Germán Arciniegas. To Cartagena the Moors had brought Damascus. Truly the patio of Santa Monica in Puebla "seems to have been flown directly from Seville," and San Francisco in Acátepec resembles "a china toy blown up to gigantic proportions." But aren't the Colonial churches suffused with Indian influences the memorable ones? They are surely the original ones. Cortés' palace in Cuernavaca and Montejo's in Mérida, the only surviving domestic buildings of the sixteenth century, are curiosities; as architecture they cannot be compared with their Spanish models. And the same applies in lesser degree to such outstanding Mexican examples of the Plateresque as San Augustín in Acolman, or of the Baroque as Tepozotlán's sumptuous pink facade. But in two Spanish styles Spain was surpassed. The extravagant ultra-Baroque gilded decoration, invented by José de Churriguera in Salamanca, was carried far beyond its Spanish models in such exuberantly writhing *retablos* as the one in Tepozotlán's Sanctuary—or in the transepts of the San Augustín Convent in Mexico's own Salamanca. And Francisco Eduardo Tresguerras—sometimes called Mexico's Michelangelo for the genius he displayed in all the arts—made of the Baroque in Celaya and Querétaro a style so personal that it became his own. (See pp. 204–205.)

It may be significant that Tresguerras began his career as a simple mason. The Indians who gave the early monasteries and churches

[8] *A Cultural History of Latin America.* New York, Alfred A. Knopf, Inc., 1967.

their distinctive flavor were masons who occasionally carved wood and stone. Such were native craftsmen at Tlalmanalco, who may have seen the florally wreathed image of the Aztec Xochipilli found there, carrying out their own floral fantasies on the cinnamon-colored columns of the Open Chapel.[9] Later on, Indian craftsmen adapted themselves just as ingeniously to the seventeenth- and eighteenth-century styles. Their masterpiece, and perhaps the masterpiece of Mexican popular art, is the Chapel of Santa María at Tonantzintla, near Puebla. A native adaptation of the wholly Spanish Rosary Chapel in the larger city, it has been felicitously described by the Mexican critic Fernando Gamboa as "a grotto with a pagan interpretation of Christianity." (See pp. 206–207.) In freestanding sculpture—an art that has not flourished in Mexico since pre-Columbian times—the only pieces of any originality that this author has seen are the feathered "angels" playing exotic musical instruments around the dome of San Augustín in Querétaro—Indian work, surely.

Painting in colonial Mexico—except for such primitive frescoes in the churches as the delightful "Martyrdom of San Felipe" in the Cuernavaca Cathedral—was a European import, academic and impersonal.

Literature occasionally got off the ground, but not very far off. Juan Ruiz de Alarcón was born in Taxco in 1581, but since he sailed for Spain at the age of twenty and never returned, this collaborator of Lope de Vega and Calderón in the Spanish theater can hardly be called Mexican. Bernardo de Balbuena, though he was born in Spain and died there, has a better claim to being considered Mexican, since he did spend his youth in Mexico and wrote the first poem glorifying New Spain—and the Indians. This poem, *"La Grandeza Mexicana"* (1604) has been described by Alfonso Reyes as "a mural of Mexico City in graceful tercets, with horses, monuments, theatre, literature, elegance, crafts, and so on, carefully drawn and illuminated by a sunny palette."

The poetry of the intellectual nun Sor Juana Inés de la Cruz (1651–1695) is something else again. Her verses of melancholy alienation and existential moral equilibrium are in tune with the modern temper—perhaps too much in tune for us to estimate her true worth. Octavio Paz, surely a better poet, calls her "one of the key figures in Latin American literature and one of the great Spanish

---

[9] Open Chapels were erected adjoining most of the Franciscan, Dominican and Augustinian fortress churches to accommodate the huge crowds of Indians —a purely Mexican innovation that is described brilliantly and at length in John McAndrew's *The Open Churches of Sixteenth Century Mexico.*

poets of her century." [10] Reyes praises her use of popular speech and her advanced ideas in education and the role of women in society. "It is surprising to find in this woman an originality than transcends the garb she wore." Arciniegas calls her *"Sueños"* (Dreams) "... the most famous Gongoresque poems in America" —dubious praise—and quotes a passage full of clichés and conceits that ends:

> ... Serenely happy in the quiet
> Of her regency of silence,
> She permits no voices
> But those of the birds, who awaken at night
> Murmuring so gravely
> As to leave her silence undisturbed.

But whatever her stature as a poet—and only a poet in the Spanish language can judge of that—Sor Juana was the great revolutionary of seventeenth-century Mexico—no less so for the fact that, like Hidalgo a hundred years later, she "recanted." Though she didn't die before a firing squad, she gave up her precious books and poems and wrote two protestations of faith in her own blood. An illegitimate child and an infant prodigy, Sor Juana had dazzled the literary salons of the capital with her brilliance. She became a nun because her status in society, both as a writer and as a woman, had been humiliating. Challenged in the convent to justify her insatiable intellectual curiosity, she made an epoch-making defense of women's rights. When finally she submitted, the human spirit in Mexico slumbered for a century.

Carlos Fuentes, Mexico's leading contemporary novelist, sees Sor Juana as a victim of the Counter-Reformation that made New Spain a petrified organism. "Our great poet," he says, "felt instinctively that only by leaping into a revitalized humanism could God be made to live again. And in her poetry—which is like Rimbaud's and Baudelaire's in its rebellious making of man into a little god— she took the leap. But of course the Church put a stop to that, and for the last twenty years of her life she was silent. If she'd been permitted to continue, we wouldn't have approached the Inde-

---

[10] Notes to *An Anthology of Mexican Poetry*, edited by Octavio Paz, translated by Samuel Beckett (Indiana University Press, 1958). It is unfortunate that Mexican poetry is known to the American reader mainly through this collection, rendered in a tradition-bound diction, and including none of the living poets, Mexico's best.

pendence tongue-tied, barren of ideas, and terrified of foreign theories.

"Always with us," he concluded, "the vase has tried to shape the substance, or the substance has broken the vase. This dualism is a recurrent theme for Sor Juana's poetry—and of all subsequent Mexican poets, including Paz and Gorostiza." [11]

Colonialism: The Last Phase

Under Charles III (1759–1788), a liberal monarch who adopted many of the ideas of the Enlightenment, Spain's decline was arrested but not reversed. Politically its doom had already been sealed by the last of the Philips when he capitulated to Louis XIV at Rocroi; the silvery glaze of Velásquez and Zurburán, the golden words of Quevedo, Góngora and Cervantes bore no visible relation to Spain's frozen economy and its venal officialdom. Charles III's *visitador* to Mexico, José de Gálvez, did everything in his power to break the stranglehold of the *gachupines*. The *corregidores* were replaced by honest civil servants. Trade regulations were relaxed. A progressive art school, the San Carlos Academy, was established. Able viceroys, notably Antonio de Bucareli and Count Revilla Gigedo, were appointed.

One Carlist reform, the expulsion of the Jesuits, whose political activities had offended the anticlerical despots in Europe, was not appreciated in Mexico. In 1767, the year the Jesuits were expelled, this order had only 2,200 priests in all the Americas, but 700,000 Indians were under their care. The 678 priests in Mexico in many respects had taken up where the mendicant orders left off when the corrupt secular clergy replaced the latter by order of the xenophobic Philip II in 1559. The Jesuits were builders, organizers, patrons of the arts, and the Indians in their care prospered greatly. When word of their expulsion got out, troops had to be brought up to put down local rebellions, and ninety ringleaders were executed.

Mexico by this time was much more open to dissent that it had been. New Spain, in fact, was almost a fluid society. Mexico City had become the largest metropolis in the New World. (Humboldt when he visited it in 1803 gave its population as 183,000, compared to 80,000 in New York, then the largest North American city.) Books had been printed in the capital for two centuries, and now the first daily newspaper, *Diario de Mexico*, made its appearance. There were already several literary periodicals, and archaeological

[11] From a conversation with Fuentes in the author's *Mexican Journal*.

research was beginning. Mateo Alemán wrote the first picaresque novel in Spanish and José Joaquín Fernández de Lizardi was at work on the first antiromantic one, depicting the misery of the poor. Above all, those repressed components of the middle, the Creoles and the mestizos, were beginning to feel their identities and seek ways of expressing their resentment at the Spanish monopoly of political power.

Even before the French Revolution began in 1789, the ideas that activated it were gaining currency everywhere. Subversive thoughts from the "ancients" were quoted. Had not Montaigne said, "The Indians were not the barbarians—the conquistadors were"? Diderot carried this train of thought further. Europeans, he said, had placed a plaque on the New World reading, " 'This country belongs to us.' Why? Is this not as unjust, as senseless, as if some savages were to land by chance on European shores and write on sand or on the bark of trees, 'This country is ours'?" But above all, it was the ideas of Jean-Jacques Rousseau that stirred colonial minds. In 1803 it became necessary for the official *Gazette de Mexico* to publish an edict warning everybody that *Le Contrat Social* was still banned. The time was not far off when the first Mexican constitution would read "Sovereignty springs immediately from the people whose only wish is to deposit it with their representatives."

Independence

The catalytic agent was Napoleon, who invaded Spain in 1807. When Charles IV abdicated in 1808, and along with his son Ferdinand VII fled to France, leaving Joseph Bonaparte on the throne in Madrid, the Spanish colonies refused to recognize the Napoleonic pretender. In Mexico the way to independence had already been prepared by the reaction that followed the death of Charles III. The promising reforms had been abandoned, the good viceroys were replaced by corrupt ones. Resentful Creoles, who had hitherto shown little interest in the libertarian slogans of the American and French revolutions bandied about by intellectuals, began to take notice. Ambitious mestizos, irked by their foreign and clerical "betters," embraced the new philosophy. Since there was no bourgeois middle class as in North America, independence was not thought of in terms of democracy and a free market. The Creole thought of it in his own terms, terms of power for the owners of the haciendas. The mestizo in the village, who had a horse where the Indian had only a donkey, thought of it in terms of moving one step further up, perhaps into the shoes of the minor officials, the lawyers, the parish priests. The Indian, who had nothing to lose and (since he didn't read) knew nothing about the philosophical "rights" of small property owners, thought mainly in terms of looting and revenge. Under the circumstances there wasn't a chance for the kind of orderly constitutionalism that had followed the Declaration of Independence in the North American Colonies thirty years before; but neither was there a chance for the kind of idealistic universalism that, in the persuasive rhetoric of such a romantic authoritarian as Bolívar, smothered any real popular uprisings in South America for more than a century. Most of the Mexican Creoles sided with the Spanish *gachupines* in the ten years of war that was about to break out, and although they would eventually rule independent Mexico, it was not they who had made the revolt against colonial authority, and their triumph over the class war (that the revolt quickly became) would be troubled and temporary.

The leaders of the revolt, then, were neither aristocratic planters like Washington and Jefferson, nor Creole soldiers of fortune like Bolívar and San Martín. They were parish priests from small villages, intellectuals familiar enough with the "subversive" literature of the times to be apostles of freedom, and close enough to their flock (mestizos and Indians) to have no fears of the consequences of activating the underdogs. Miguel Hidalgo y Costilla, the parish priest of Dolores, and Francisco Severo Maldonado, another priest with vaguely socialist ideas who edited Hidalgo's newspaper, *El Despertador*, in nearby Guanajuato, were humanitarians (Creoles in skin color only) who had won the affection of the Indians, much as Bishop Quiroga had two centuries before. José María Morelos, a mestizo with a talent for guerrilla warfare and his lieutenant, Mariano Matamoros, were village priests in Quiroga's old bailiwick, Michoacán.

As far back as 1800, when he had been rector of the University of Valladolid (now Morelia), Hidalgo had been brought before the authorities for "Jansenist" heresies. Jansenism was only a pretext for indicting unorthodoxy, for no one could have been less a puritan than this pleasure-loving padre. The easygoing Church of that time might condone Hidalgo's moral lapses—his dancing, his card playing, his bowling in the streets, even his mistresses and his illegitimate children. After he had received mild censure and taken over the parish of Dolores, they could accept his benevolent camaraderie with the Indians: the symphony orchestra, brick kilns, pottery workshop, beekeeping, wine and silk industry he had developed for them. (It was the civil authorities who tore up his mulberry trees.) What the Church could *not* accept was Hidalgo's liberal-enlightenment philosophy, his surreptitious reading of Voltaire and Rousseau, his calling the Church scholars "a pack of donkeys," his denial of the absolute authority of the Pope, and his questioning the existence of hell.

The year 1810 was marked by Creole conspiracies and uprisings all over Spanish America: conservative, at most "liberal," movements to replace the *gachupín* administrators with governments loyal to the displaced Ferdinand VII. In Mexico, similarly, Creoles had their lodges and clubs ready for such an orderly transition of power, and one such club, headed by the local *corregidor*, was in the city of Querétaro. Ignacio Allende, a young army officer with a reputation for bullfighting, was a member of the club and it was he who recruited the notoriously "enlightened" priest from nearby Dolores to join with them. The club decided to make its move in December. Mexico's independence would be declared and the Creoles would step into the *gachupines'* shoes. But it didn't work out that way. News of the conspiracy leaked out. Allende rode over the mountain to warn Hidalgo that their arrest was imminent, and the impetuous priest decided to act first with the only "weapon" at hand—his loyal Indian followers. Allende, realizing that it was too late to win over the army, agreed to go along with Hidalgo.

Only two decisions since the Conquest had been as fateful to Mexico's future, and this one was taken as haphazardly as the other two. When Cortés decided to break with the Columbus-Velásquez policy of annihilating the native population, and instead to integrate the Indians in the new colony, he had thought mainly in terms of consolidating the power of his fellow conquistadors. When Zumárraga decided to recognize the "miracle" of the dark Virgin of Guadalupe, he had thought in terms of consolidating the power of the Church rather than in terms of providing Indian Mexico with a symbol of its separate identity. Similarly, when Hidalgo rang the church bell at Dolores and gave his famous *grito* (cry)—"Long live the Virgin of Guadalupe! Death to bad government! Death to the *gachupines!*"—he was not acting in behalf of a proletarian insurrection or a war of the races but only (he thought) in terms of Mexico's freedom from Spain, and perhaps, to justify his own defection from the Roman hierarchy by placing Christ once more on the side of the weak and the oppressed.

Hidalgo: A Hero with Doubts

On Sunday morning of September 16, 1810, Miguel Hidalgo y Castilla distributed weapons to his flock, opened the Dolores jail and armed the prisoners, and addressed his motley "army" of mestizos and Indians thus: "Will you make the effort to recover from the hated Spaniards the lands stolen from your forefathers three hundred years ago?" When they had shouted their assent, he led them out and began the march to Guanajuato, the prosperous mining capital thirty-two miles west that was still the Crown's principal source of silver and gold. Guanajuato quickly fell to the invaders, whose members, armed with machetes, scythes, and old muskets, had now become a host of sixty-thousand. The Spanish garrison of five-hundred retreated to the Alhóndiga de Granaditas, then as now a massive pile of stone with a single portal on its longest (210 foot) side. Hidalgo and Allende decided to take it by storm. A fearless Indian named Pipila, protecting himself with a flagstone strapped to his back, set fire to the wooden door. The inflamed mob poured in, giving the garrison no opportunity to surrender, and massacred all five hundred of them. Then they poured out, set fire to the city, and looted it systematically. Before its sack, Guanajuato had been a prosperous city of sixty thousand. After the burning and killing were over, its population dwindled to six thousand, and it never recovered. It was a pattern that was to be repeated, with variations, for 125 years. Hidalgo, though he was and deserves to be the hero of the Independence and the first great leader of the social revolution that ultimately released the Indians from peonage, was personally responsible for the pattern of anarchic uprisings under irresponsible *caudillos* that was to bedevil Mexico until the time of Cárdenas. With the "justification" that the Spaniards had originally dispossessed the Indians, Hidalgo sanctioned pillaging and murder by his followers—over the protest of Allende.

From Guanajuato, Hidalgo's host moved south to Valladolid (Morelia) and then west to Guadalajara by an irregular course. Why they bypassed the capital, which was undefended and indefensible, has never been explained. In Valladolid, the Captain-General of America, as Hidalgo now called himself, issued a utopian proclamation:

Let us establish a Congress composed of representatives of all the cities and villages . . . which will enact mild and beneficent laws appropriate to the circumstances of each community. These representatives governing with the kindness of the fathers, treating us all as brothers, will exile poverty, moderating the devastation of the country.... Crops will be stimulated, industry will come to life; we shall make free use of the intensely rich products of our fertile land and in a few years its inhabitants will enjoy the benefits which the sovereign author of nature has poured over this vast continent.[12]

The insurrection was now spreading. In some towns there were spontaneous uprisings. In others the royalist troops mutinied. San Luis Potosí was seized by a priest, later by a bandit, still later by the royalists. An uneducated peasant fought his way into Guadalajara while the *gachupines* fled to the Pacific. As far north as Texas, the Spanish authorities were routed, but in Oaxaca to the south, Hidalgo's agents were executed. Allende and the other Creole officers associated with Hidalgo did not like the radical turn the rebellion was taking, and in fact the Creole class all over Mexico was beginning to rally to the support of the government in the capital. The news that Hidalgo was restoring the *ejidos* to the Indian villages awakened fears that the haciendas themselves might soon be expropriated. But the news that Hidalgo was thoroughly enjoying power in the west and had accepted the title of Serene Highness may have given his enemies confidence. They had evicted him from Guadalajara, and now they caught up with him at Las Cruces.

Or perhaps one should say that Hidalgo's conscience caught up with him. For once again he stopped just short of the defenseless capital—after winning a decisive battle! Las Cruces lies just sixteen miles from Chapultepec Palace, perhaps no more than ten as the crow flies. And the inscription on the monument there reads that Hidalgo, "the first *caudillo* of the Independence..." here achieved "a glorious victory."

It was indeed. The Spanish federals, led by Col. Torcuato Trujillo, and Lt. Augustín de Iturbide, numbered only eighteen hundred. They were thrown back by the huge *tumulto* of Allende and Aldama. The federals held the pine-wooded slopes of the narrow defile till that point at three in the afternoon when the soldiers of their center came to within hearing distance of the revolutionary

[12] Quoted by Lucas Alamán in *Historia de Méjico* (5 Vols., 1849–52), and by Hubert Herring in *A History of Latin America* (New York, Alfred A. Knopf, Inc., 1955).

speeches. Trujillo at this juncture gave the command to resume firing, and amid shouts of "Treachery!" the freedom fighters gave way sufficiently to permit the surrounded federals to fall back on the capital. Allende begged Hidalgo to resume the march. He knew that the viceroy was preparing to flee and that the revolutionary tide would sweep over the city. But Hidalgo remained stationary until November 6, at which time Félix María Calleja del Rey, the brilliant loyalist generalissimo, swept down from Querétaro and intercepted his rearguard. History was repeating itself. Moctezuma with all his host gave way to Cortés' battalion because the Aztec gods had willed it; could one oppose Quetzalcoatl? Here at Las Cruces Hidalgo heard that the destiny of the colony had been confided by the Viceroy to Our Lady of Remedies. Could one oppose the Virgin? Were not the Church and State indissoluble?

While Hidalgo was debating these questions, his opportunity vanished. He fell back on Guadalajara by way of Querétaro and Valladolid. His followers became disillusioned and divided. In March of 1811, he was captured by trickery and stripped of his priestly robes. On July 31, ten months after the *grito* at Dolores, he was executed by a firing squad in Chihuahua and his head, and the heads of Allende and the other leaders, were displayed in cages that were hung from the cornice of the Alhóndiga.

Inept as a commander, a victim of vanity and dogmatism, Hidalgo's downfall was inevitable. His head full of libertarian doctrine, he believed in the power of the masses, since they believed in *him*. As soon as he began to suffer reverses, the ruthlessness that he had shown at the Alhóndiga and at Valladolid began to prey on his conscience. God was punishing him for his pride! The thin layer of French revolutionary confidence left him. He was a priest again —and a wayward priest who must pay for his sins of rebelliousness and his lack of humility. The tragic denouement of Chihuahua and of his anguished recantation was at hand.

What a man, though, what a hero old Hidalgo was! First with his prohibited silkworms and forbidden books and illegitimate children; dancing and playing cards, defying the Old Order quite openly; and then in the pulpit at Dolores, dressed not in his vestments but in his street clothes, raising aloft the Virgin of Guadalupe as his battle standard; and finally at Las Cruces, wearing his long blue coat with red cuffs bordered with silver galloon, haranguing the poorly armed and clothed Indians. When news reached him at Saltillo that the royalist parliament meeting in Cádiz had decreed pardon for the rebels and invited him to prove his loyalty to Ferdinand, he had replied: "Pardon, your excellency, is for criminals, not for defenders of their country." And when the Holy Office brought charges against him at Valladolid, he answered, "I am accused of denying the existence of Hell, and at the same time of affirming that some Pope is in that place. How can one deny the existence of Hell and yet say that a Pope is in it?"

But greater than Hidalgo the logician or Hidalgo the revolutionist was Hidalgo the humanitarian, with courage and serenity (at the final scene) to match his humanity. He *had* sinned. He *had* shown pride in the righteousness of his position. He *had* carried off two million dollars in silver bars and coin. He *had* given orders for the massacre at Guanajuato and the reprisals (matching Calleja's) at Guadalajara. But—he had been for all that on Christ's side, the side of the poor and the oppressed, of the Indian. It was this certainty that sustained him in the days that followed his recantation. It was this that brought peace to his spirit as he made the last request—candy for the firing squad—and the sublime gesture of placing his hand over his heart, both to make clear the target and to receive there one of the stigmata of his Lord.

Morelos: The Complete Revolutionist

How different a man was Padre Morelos, who now assumed the leadership of the Revolution. José María Morelos y Pavón was neither a crusader nor an intellectual. As a priest he resembled Hidalgo only in two respects; in having his quota of illegitimate children, and in his devotion to the Indian cause. But as a leader Morelos had many advantages. He was a practical man, without vanity or psychological anxieties. And as a tactician he was brilliant enough to have evoked the admiration of such great contemporary commanders as Bolívar, Napoleon, and the Duke of Wellington, the latter having once remarked that "... if I were a Frenchman, I would have made Morelos a Field Marshal." Morelos had no use for the stragglers, bandits and hangers-on who made Hidalgo's army so unmanageable; his own forces were always small, never exceeding twenty thousand men, and they usually struck by night. His lieutenants were chosen strictly on the basis of their ability.

Morelos' motivation was not intellectual either. As a mestizo he had suffered enough discrimination to make him identify with the Indians, and as a practical man he had seen enough of colonial inefficiency to make him ready for any alternative. It was ten months after the *grito* that he joined Hidalgo at Valladolid. Hidalgo may have remembered Morelos as a student there, when he had been rector of the University of San Nicolás Obispo years before; or he may simply have reasoned that a muleteer who knew the roads between that city and Acapulco would be a logical choice to take the Pacific port. On his way to the coast Morelos issued a decree, modestly but firmly phrased; it announced abolition of the caste system, and it urged Indians to regard the income from lands they tilled as their own. But while he was investing Acapulco, the news of Hidalgo's capture reached Morelos. He decided to postpone the siege and instead to lead his army upon the capital.

Morelos had already acquired important allies. There was Hildegardo Galeano, the illiterate grandson of an English buccaneer: imaginative, brave, and unshakably loyal to the Indian cause. There were the wealthy Bravo brothers, who had plotted in secret against Spain, and one of whose sons, Nicolás, had just married the Governor's daughter. There was a young man named Manuel Félix Fernández, later to be known as Guadalupe Victoria. There was Vicente Guerrero, a brave muleteer with a strain of Negro blood, who knew western Mexico as well as any man. But Morelos' greatest acquisition came at the town of Izúcar, where a young priest named Mariano Matamoros joined him. Matamoros was four feet ten inches high and had an ugly pockmarked face; but he had a personal magnetism that was irresistible and an ability in the field almost as outstanding as Morelos'. Matamoros captured Tenancingo on January 23, 1812, and on February 9 rejoined Morelos to take Cuautla. Viceroy Vinegas was now thoroughly alarmed and sent Calleja to Cuautla to besiege that city.

Cuautla lies thirty miles east of Cuernavaca and forty from the capital. Its siege by the royalists' best army lasted seventy-eight days. It was marked by heroics and was ended only by famine. Galeano engaged a captain of grenadiers in a duel. A thirteen-year-old boy with his right arm almost cut off turned back a cavalry company with an abandoned cannon. Calleja cut off the city's water supply and Morelos won it back with a portable tower connected by trenches to Cuautla's defenses. But the food gave out, and soon the besieged were eating rats, insects, and even leather from the doors. When all hope of defeating the superior besieging force or of being relieved had vanished, Morelos took his little band out by night. He was wounded but soon recovered to plan the conquest of southern Mexico, where Calleja would have more trouble getting at him.

On December 25, 1812, Oaxaca surrendered to the revolutionaries. On the way to the southern capital occurred one of those incidents that characterized the Independence wars. Word came to Morelos that Nicolás Bravo's father had been captured. Knowing of the great love between father and son, Morelos offered to free all of his several hundred prisoners if the Viceroy would free Leonardo Bravo, and he also urged the young man to withdraw from the Revolution to save his father's life. The young man refused, and so did the Viceroy. When Nicolás received news of his father's execution, he ordered the three hundred prisoners of Spanish blood to be executed in reprisal. But the following morning, just as the condemned were to face the firing squad, he repented and addressed them with these words:

> Your master, Spain's minion, has murdered my father in cold blood for choosing Mexico and liberty before Spain and her tyranny. Some of you are fathers, and may imagine what my father felt in being thrust from the world without one farewell from his son.... What a master is this you serve! For one life, my poor father's, he might have saved you all and would not.... So I, who am no Viceroy, have three hundred lives for my father's! Go! You are free! Go find your vile master and henceforth serve him—if you can! [13]

That same afternoon the three hundred turned back from their march, and with happy shouts joined Nicolás Bravo.

With the fall of Oaxaca, Morelos was at the height of his powers. Except for the cities of Mexico, Puebla, Valladolid, Guadalajara, and Acapulco, he now controlled all of central and southern Mexico—and he now determined to take Acapulco. With the Pacific port's capture in August, he felt that the time had come to form a legal government. Eight delegates from the captured states met in Chilpancingo and to them the Generalissimo expounded his ideas. The republic (Anáhuac, he called it) would be governed by the people in terms of absolute racial equality. There would be a Catholic state, but without compulsory tithes, and all Church lands would be seized, along with the haciendas of the rich *gachupines* and Creoles, and broken up into small holdings for the peasants. All taxes except excise would be abolished and the Jesuits called back

[13] Quoted from John Anthony Caruso, *The Liberators of Mexico*. New York, Pageant Press, 1954.

to superintend education. The Constitution, providing for universal suffrage, indirect elections, a congress and a supreme court, was never put into effect, for by the time it was completed a year later, Morelos had lost most of his territory.

One reason was that Mexico was much too divided and disorganized to be governed democratically. (Even Morelos himself was obliged upon occasion to act dictatorially, packing the Congress of Chilpancingo to have his way with it and recommending that the Generalissimo—himself—be chosen for life.)

Another was that the long siege of Acapulco during the summer of 1813 was a strategic blunder. While Morelos was engaged in it, the Spaniards appointed the cruel but able Calleja Viceroy, and Calleja wasted no time in defeating the revolutionary armies, now separated from each other by great distances, piecemeal.

Part of his success may be attributed to the news from Spain, which perhaps deterred neutrals from joining the revolutionary cause. Following Napoleon's defeat at Leipzig, Ferdinand had returned to the Spanish throne. The colonies would now be represented in the Cortés, the Indians would no longer pay tribute, the leaders of the revolt would be pardoned—excepting Morelos, who would be exiled. In Mexico City there was a week of fireworks, bullfights and banquets to celebrate. But more important to the loyalist cause than this propaganda windfall was their discovery of a captain with a formula for success. Col. Augustín de Iturbide, who had fought with Trujillo at Las Cruces, was sent to harass Morelos' main army camped on a steep hill above Valladolid. Since the camp was believed to be impregnable, it was poorly guarded. Iturbide's cavalry cut a path through it in the night, and in the resulting confusion the awakened revolutionaries started firing on each other. Now attacked in force, they retreated and were decisively defeated at Puruarán. Matamoros and Galeano, Morelos' ablest commanders, were captured and shot; and soon Morelos himself, with less than a hundred followers, was being hunted in the hills. In October, 1815, Morelos was captured near Tehuacán, and on December 22, he was executed.

Even in his death cell Morelos' consistent integrity and selflessness was winning for him that admiration which the Mexican people have always accorded to his memory. His jailer left the door ajar for him every night, until finally Morelos said to him, "God forbid, dear Martínez, that I should imperil you and your innocent family to prolong my own life."

Iturbide: Tinsel Emperor

The Napoleon of the Mexican Independence was Iturbide; but as Marx was later to say of Napoleon's nephew, history when subjected to imitation tends to repeat itself not as tragedy but as farce. Augustín de Iturbide was a Napoleonic figure, in some ways more admirable and endearing than the Corsican, but he lacked both military genius and the capacity to rule when he had the power. Like Bolívar (a fellow Creole who admired him—and Napoleon—excessively), Iturbide was bemused by his own charisma, which made women swoon and crowds of grown men go beserk, but unlike Bolívar, he mistook the sumptuous appurtenances of high office for the reality. Therefore his death before a firing squad, when he returned from European exile to "liberate" anew the Mexico he had already liberated but which was sliding willfully into ignoble *caudillismo*, was too meaningless to be tragic.

Iturbide's misfortune was to have no principles, no clear idea of what to do or where to lead Mexico; and so when he mumbled idealistic phrases, everybody recognized his true motivation: vanity. Marx would probably have seen his failure as the failure of the Creole class he represented—a class too obsessed with dress, status and making money to govern seriously. But in a real sense Iturbide's success—for he *did* liberate Mexico from Spain—was in activating that class without which liberation could not have been achieved. Hidalgo and Allende were Creoles, but only Indians followed them. Under the mestizo Morelos, mestizo guerrillas proved too weak to take the cities. Where they had failed, Iturbide succeeded; but it was a success that was to deliver Mexico over to a century of betrayals, petty despotisms, and chaos—a chaos that would be unrelieved until the idealism of new Hidalgos and Moreloses would rouse Indian Mexico to march again.

There is as little agreement on what Iturbide was like as there is on what he actually accomplished. His personality was as volatile as his career. That he was tall, handsome, magnetic, conversationally brilliant, effective in battle, and brimming with energy and ambition is a matter of record. That he lacked education, political wisdom, compassion, loyalty and honesty is equally clear. Bolívar, Lucas Alamán and Henry Clay admired him; but most American statesmen of the time—Jefferson, Monroe and Jackson, notably—regarded him as a petty usurper and tyrant.

Iturbide's political career began in 1810, when Hidalgo offered him a lieutenant-generalship if he would join the revolution. Like a typical Creole, he declined on the grounds that property rights and the Church were in jeopardy. His role at Las Cruces, and later on in Morelos' 1813 defeat, has already been described. By 1816, Iturbide had won a reputation as the ablest commander in the royalist army and as Governor of Guanajuato was paying off his private debts by hijacking convoys of precious metals and mining equipment that passed through the state.

The events that would lead to his big opportunity began in 1819. Ferdinand VII, who had planned to crush the revolts in New Spain, discovered that the Spanish Army and the Masons were about to overthrow him, and precipitately switched sides. In fact, he came out for the liberal-revolutionary Constitution of 1812. The news reached New Spain in 1820, and its effect was electrifying. The Church—seeing its very existence threatened by the new laws which abolished the Inquisition, suppressed the resurgent Jesuits, and confiscated the properties of other religious orders—suddenly became the most outspoken force on the side of independence. However, Juan Ruiz de Apodaca, who had succeeded Calleja as Viceroy in 1816, carried out the orders from Madrid obediently; he dispatched Iturbide south with an army to snuff out the dying embers of the revolution still being cherished by Vicente Guerrero, Nicolás Bravo and Guadalupe Victoria. Egged on by Antonio Joaquín Pérez y Martínez, the bishop-elect of Puebla, Iturbide struck out at last for himself. Instead of defeating the revolutionaries, he would enlist their support for Mexican independence! Wasn't that what they wanted? With the powerful Church on their side, how could they lose?

Iturbide began by winning over General Guerrero. His forces now augmented to 3,700 veterans, he obtained a printing press from Bishop Pérez, and at Iguala, by "taking custody" of a sum of 525,000 pesos destined for Acapulco, he was able to print and circulate a manifesto. On February 24, 1821, the famous Plan of Iguala was published. The Plan began like the Declaration of Independence, but the meat of it was in the so-called Three Guarantees. The first declared Mexico a sovereign nation. The second established Roman Catholicism as the state religion. The third proclaimed social and political equality for all Mexicans. (No doubt the third guarantee was included as a concession to Guerrero and his Indian followers.) Nothing was said about the vast inequities in land and the other perquisites of the old ruling classes except that property would be "protected" by the state. But the Plan did suggest that the new nation should be a moderate monarchy; if Ferdinand VII should refuse the throne, then one of his brothers might be tempted. Iturbide himself for the moment contented himself with the designation First Chief—a title that would be rendered equally opprobrious by Venustiano Carranza in the Mexican Revolution a hundred years later. Then Iturbide presented Mexico's new flag to a wildly cheering mob in the capital, explaining its symbolism: green for their independence, white for the purity of their sacred religion, and red for the union of Aztecs(!) and Spaniards. And he then tore the lace that distinguished him as a colonel in the Spanish Army from his shoulders with the words: "Yesterday, I refused the title of lieutenant-general, which you would have conferred upon me, and now I renounce *this* distinction!" [14]

The would-be Caesar now had but minor stumbling blocks to remove before assuming the purple. The cities of Guanajuato, Valladolid and Querétaro had to be secured. Veracruz, and its island fortress of San Juan de Ulúa had to be seized lest the Spanish continue to reinforce their colonial administration. Finally, the capital must be taken, either by winning over the Viceroy, or by assault. Iturbide took Guanajuato, Valladolid, and Querétaro himself. For the investment of Veracruz, he received unexpected assistance from a young officer who had just deserted the royalists: Captain Antonio López de Santa Anna. This impetuous, reckless young man—already establishing a style in chameleon demagoguery that was to bedevil Mexico for half a century—gained partial control of Veracruz and then marched inland to seize Córdoba, center of the lucrative tobacco industry. For the taking of Mexico City, Iturbide received an assist from Spain itself that seemed almost like an act of God. The liberal government in Madrid had sent to Veracruz a new Viceroy to succeed Apodaca, Juan O'Donojú. O'Donojú was a soldier-statesman of Irish extraction who combined in his make-up a passion for anticlerical liberalism and a belief in absolute rule—a perfect instrument for Iturbide's immediate schemes —and finding himself besieged by the royalists still in partial control of the port, he extricated himself by accepting the Plan of Iguala and agreeing to meet Iturbide at Córdoba. The meeting took place August 23, 1821, and a treaty was drawn up declaring New Spain to be a sovereign nation, but a constitutional monarchy, the choice of monarch no longer limited to Ferdinand and his fam-

14 Quoted in *The Liberators of Mexico.*

ily. On September 23, O'Donojú entered Mexico City and took over the government. The *gachupín* troops marched out. And four days later Iturbide arrived with the Army of the Three Guarantees from Puebla and received a triumphal welcome. By the following month the only toehold remaining to the Spanish in all Mexico was the fortress of San Juan de Ulúa.

Two paths now lay open to Iturbide. The deputies had already assembled and appointed him president of a five-man ruling council, which (until his untimely death from pleurisy October 8) included Viceroy O'Donojú. Iturbide could either govern constitutionally, making concessions to the republicans who were already beginning to grumble over the dictatorial powers he was assuming. Or he could dissolve the Congress and attempt to govern with the army, the clergy and the wealthy Creoles as his only support. He started his course down the second path by altering the rules governing the composition of the Congress which had been drawn up at Córdoba. One chamber would be filled with dignitaries of the Church, the Army, and the local governments. The other, in effect cancelling out the first, would be representatives chosen by the (qualified) voters. But even this was too democratic to satisfy Iturbide. He next revised the second chamber to include only members chosen for their importance in the professions. This revision was rejected by most of the deputies, but Iturbide maneuvered it into law notwithstanding. As a result the republicans gave up trying to make their will felt constitutionally and began to plot for Iturbide's overthrow by force.

The initiative for making the Liberator a monarch was taken by a sergeant of the Celaya Battalion—on orders from higher up, of course. On the evening of May 18, 1822, the city mob was joined by soldiers from every part of the city, marching past Iturbide's home with the rhythmic refrain: "Long live Augustín I! Long live the Emperor!" Like Caesar, Iturbide professed reluctance. A friend had said to him, so he related later, "The people are easily made irritable by what they construe as ingratitude. You must make this new sacrifice for the public good; the country is in danger; a moment of indecision may change their acclamations to cries of death." Needless to say, Iturbide was persuaded. The republicans stayed away to a man, but even so the other deputies were so reluctant to make the decision that Bishop Pérez had to bolster their resolve by invading the assembly hall with a claque of monks shouting: "Emperor or death!" The armed guard outside took up the cry and the deputies promptly voted—sixty-seven of the eighty-two present assenting and fifteen dissenting. July 21 was chosen as coronation day.

Iturbide's empire had a short, inglorious history. Hardly were the Emperor and his Empress installed in Chapultepec Palace when the balky Congress renewed its quest for lost authority. The most outspoken and clever of the thwarted legislators was Fray Servando Teresa de Mier, a friar-turned-revolutionary who had fled the country after Morelos' defeat, returned from Havana to participate in the new independence movement, and was imprisoned at San Juan de Ulúa, where he received the news that he had been elected deputy from Monterey. An eccentric with aristocratic pretensions who claimed to be a descendant of Cuauhtémoc, Mier was a great orator and he wielded a wicked pen. "He likened the coronation to a malodorous ointment, and the inauguration of [Iturbide's] Order of Guadulupe, with its knights in their mantles and plumage, to a barbarous dance performed on feast days by ridiculously dressed Indians called for the occasion *huehuenches*, or little old men." [15]

Father Mier led the opposition to Iturbide's attempt to appoint judges, and he had powerful allies in the Masons, whose anticlerical newspapers the Catholic Emperor now suppressed. Two republican conspiracies, meanwhile, were uncovered; but when Iturbide ordered the arrest of the republican deputies (including Mier), the other deputies protested, and some of them joined the republicans. With the Treasury empty again, and a wave of crime sweeping the capital, the harassed Emperor dissolved the Congress.

Iturbide's downfall was initiated by the man whose diabolical skill in undermining governments was soon to become famous. Santa Anna had done as much to help Iturbide to power as any man, but when he sought to increase his influence with the throne by wooing the Emperor's sister, who was nearly sixty, Iturbide made the mistake of canceling the Veracruz officer's courtship with a witticism. Santa Anna's monumental pride was wounded and his admiration for the man so like himself turned to hatred. Taking advantage of the siege of San Juan de Ulúa, in which he had played a typically treacherous part, he marched his regiment into Veracruz one day and proclaimed a republic. Guadalupe Victoria and some of the other republicans came out of hiding to join him. And in the south Vicente Guerrero and Nicolás Bravo raised an army of revolutionists.

At first the rebellion fared badly. The southern revolt was crushed.

[15] Quoted in *The Liberators of Mexico*.

Santa Anna was bottled up almost alone in Veracruz. But at this juncture the Masons, taking advantage of the dissatisfaction of the provincial governments with the autocratic regime in the capital, declared a revolt of their own. The general of the army which Iturbide had sent against Santa Anna, his most trusted commander, was a Mason and joined his anticlerical brethren. The Plan of Casa Mata, drawn up by the Masonic leaders outside Veracruz, was soon embraced by all of the antifederalist states, as well as by Santa Anna and Guadalupe Victoria. Iturbide made a last desperate effort to reconstitute the Congress he had lately mauled, but even the few members who assembled at his bidding lacked the enthusiasm to go it alone with the discredited Emperor. On March 19, 1823, less than eight months after his coronation, Iturbide abdicated.

What was to be done with him? The deputies, who now reconstituted themselves as a Congress, proposed to exile him to Italy with a pension. Father Mier demanded that he be hanged—and quoted Saint Thomas Aquinas in support of it. But the majority had their way, and escorted by Nicolás Bravo, the ex-Emperor with his family and retainers set out for Veracruz. The magnanimous Guadalupe Victoria came to say good-bye, was presented with a gold watch, and gave in return a silk handkerchief which Iturbide carried with him to the end.

The end came not in Italy, however, but in Mexico, and reflected more honor on the flamboyant Augustín I than on his enemies. Whatever one may think of Iturbide, he was no coward, and he had more concern for his destiny as a Mexican savior than for his comfort as a pensioner among the exiled aristocrats in Leghorn. On his fortieth birthday he dictated a manifesto offering his services to the Mexican people and replying indignantly to charges that he had enriched himself while in office. From Leghorn he proceeded to London, arriving there January 1, 1824. Receiving an invitation (possibly spurious) from Ferdinand VII to lead an expeditionary force against Mexico for which he would receive in return the viceroyalty for life, he tore it up. He resolved instead to return to Mexico on his own and addressed a letter to the Congress, warning it of the danger from Spain and stating that he was coming, with arms and ammunition, to offer his services and then retire. But the triumvirate of Bravo, Victoria and Pedro Celestino Negrete, attempting to govern the country already rife with conspiracy, feared that his presence would inspire widespread revolt. They declared him a traitor. Landing on the coast of Tamaulipas July 13,

Iturbide fell into the hands of a local commandant whom he had once befriended. The commandant delivered him over to a firing squad. Less than ten years later Santa Anna, of all people, declared Iturbide a national hero and ordered that his portrait be hung in every public office in the country.

3

THE WAR WITH THE UNITED STATES, THE REFORM, THE DICTATORSHIP (1824–1909)

THE eighty-six years that stretch between the fall of Iturbide and the Mexican Revolution are by all odds the darkest, least creative, in Mexico's history. This is not to say that before the curtain fell in 1910 the cluttered stage had not been illumined by occasional flashes of high drama, or that among the few actors disputing its center with the villainous principals there were none worthy of emulation. The confrontation of the Zapotec Indian Benito Júarez and the Hapsburg Pretender Maximilian, which enlivened the second of the three Acts, was a study in characters diametrically opposed and each in his fashion admirable. But perhaps only a theater critic from abroad, with no personal stake in the national destiny, could admit as much. *Any* honest reviewer, however would be obliged to say that Act One was a shambles, and Act Three a fall from grace that quickly degenerated into a descent to the abyss. By Shakespearean analogy, Santa Anna was an Iago all the way; Juárez an Othello type, incorruptible but grim; Maximilian an ineffectual Hamlet stranded in a world he never made; and Porfirio Díaz, Macbeth.

Act I, that was to end with the most disastrous event in Mexico's history, the war with the United States, opened auspiciously enough in the fall of 1824 with those two old heroes of the Independence, Guadalupe Victoria and Nicolás Bravo, assuming office as the first President and Vice President of the Mexican Republic.

To show why both men failed dismally, and why the third old hero of the Independence, Vicente Guerrero, who succeeded them, fared no better, it is necessary to explain why Mexico was a republic in name only, and why it had become ungovernable. In the first place the Indians, who made up the bulk of the population, came out of the Independence with no gains at all. The Creoles had assumed power and the mestizos constituted the "liberal" opposition; the disfranchised Indians had no stake in the private property or in the game of elective musical chairs which the other two classes played. Some of the Indians who had fought with Hidalgo and Morelos for a social revolution continued to fight—either through inertia or because impressed into service. They constituted the cannon fodder in the "armies" of the embattled factions. But most withdrew into their mountain villages, and remained there until 1910. The army, when it wasn't raiding the villages for conscripts, was putting its services at the command of the highest bidder among the politicians.

Shooting suspects and confiscating property at will, the army was accountable only to its own courts of law. And this was the case also with the clergy, by now "the propagandists and the paymasters of reaction," as Parkes calls them, who had reacquired vast land holdings and mortgages, had virtually abandoned their missions among the Indians, lived tax free on their estates, and carried on an unremitting war against secular education and freedom of opinion.

As for government, the various regimes that shuttled in and out of power during this sorry period were trapped by the state's insolvency. The mines, which had supplied the viceroyalty with most of its revenues, never recovered from the lootings of the revolutionary peasants. Until the dictatorship of Porfirio Díaz late in the century, there was never a balanced budget in Mexico, and, according to the Mexican historian Francisco Bulnes, whenever the deficit was more than 25 percent, a revolution took place. Foreign investors soon became the only source of capital, with the result that bankers and industrialists from abroad held a mortgage over what was left of the Mexican economy. The governments of the Creole landowners were at the mercy of the bankers, for if they couldn't pay the generals and bureaucrats, these drones would promptly make a deal with the opposition party. The mestizos, with a much greater sense of nationalism than the Creoles, didn't really come to power until Benito Juárez led them in the War of the Reform in the sixties, but their constant demands for an end to special privileges for the clergy, the military and the landowners kept the Creoles in too much of a state of imbalance to ever effectively consolidate power. The result was that Creole conservatism entrenched itself in the capital under army *caudillos*, while mestizo liberalism, under provincial caciques, fought for an end to arbitrary federal control. While power between these classes remained divided, governments seized power and were ousted with bewildering frequency.

The Rise of Santa Anna

The present seems like a dream, a pale reflection of the past. All is decaying and growing fainter, and men seem trusting to some unknown future. One revolution follows another, yet the remedy is not found. Let them beware lest half a century later, they be awakened from their delusion, and find the cathedral turned into a meeting house, and all painted white; the *railing* melted down; the silver transformed into dollars; the Virgin's jewels sold to the highest bidder; the floor washed (which would do it no harm), and round the whole, a nice wooden paling freshly done in green—and all this performed by some of the artists from the *wide-awake* republic farther north! [1]

For all her presentiment that the state of affairs in Mexico was ephemeral, the observant Scottish girl who had married the first Spanish Ambassador to independent Mexico would have been astonished to know how soon the Americans, whose intervention she prophesied, would be cleaning up the debris in the Mexican capital. In her pleasant memoirs of the years of prologue, Fanny Calderón describes the oft-"retired" Santa Anna at his country seat, Manga de Clavo, near Veracruz. When she and her husband breakfasted with him, he had a "philosophic, melancholy expression" and spoke "frequently" of his famous leg, shot off in the defense of the port, when the French had seized its fortress in 1838 in a futile attempt to collect their Mexican debts. "It is strange," she noted, "how frequently this expression of philosophic resignation is to be remarked on the countenances of the deepest, most ambitious, and most designing men." She also tells the story of Santa Anna, during one of his eight presidencies, being called out of an audience with

[1] Mme. Calderón de la Barca, *Life in Mexico*, 1843.

a bishop and not bothering to come back: The President's favorite fighting cock had taken sick, it seems.

Antonio López de Santa Anna was born in Jalapa, in the province of Veracruz, in 1795. We have already seem him support and then betray Iturbide. During the do-nothing regime of Guadalupe Victoria, he lay low. His three estates in Veracruz province, covering 483,000 acres, made him one of the richest landholders in Mexico. No doubt he watched with interest the virtual domination of the nation's economy by British capital, and the clumsier efforts of French, German and American businessmen and diplomats to keep up with British imperial enterprise. But it was not until the rival factions who called themselves conservatives and liberals were prepared to overthrow the tottering government that he reentered politics. In 1827 a conservative rebellion under Vice President Nicolás Bravo had been suppressed by Vicente Guerrero. But in 1828 Santa Anna, who had supported Guerrero, suddenly switched to the side of the liberal *puros* who were opposing the candidacy of Gómez Pedraza for the presidency. The liberal leaders were Valentín Gómez Farías, an honest but naïve physician from Zacatecas, and Lucas Alamán, a mining engineer and historian with a subtle mind and authoritarian views. Santa Anna "pronounced" for them and was driven south to Oaxaca. But the liberals in the capital quietly removed old Guadalupe Victoria from the national palace, installing old Guerrero in his place, and Santa Anna was saved.

His opportunity to assume the center of the stage came when the Spaniards, who had finally abandoned San Juan de Ulúa, seized Tampico. It was thought that chaotic Mexico would welcome them back, but the Spaniards proved just as disorganized. On the way from Cuba the navy quarreled with the army, with the result that the landing force was abandoned on the beach, contracted yellow fever, and willingly surrendered to the first Mexican to reach the port—Santa Anna! This bloodless victory was parlayed by the cunning publicist-general into such a feat of arms that when Guerrero was ousted and executed, what could be more natural than that the Hero of Tampico should be invited to overthrow the reactionary dictatorship that had succeeded the "martyred" *independentista?* Especially since he had seized Veracruz (pocketing its rich customs duties) and would have as his running mate the popular anticlerical liberal Gómez Farías? But then, either because Santa Anna respected the power of the Church or because he recognized that liberalism had no real base in the Mexico of 1832, he suddenly withdrew to Manga de Clavo, feigning sickness. For a while Farías carried on alone, whittling away at the abusive privileges of the clergy and the army, trying to establish a system of secular education, even holding out promises of relief to the beleaguered Indians. But it was not to be. The Creoles, under cover of Santa Anna's "disinterested patriotism," struck back. The Church, aided by a plague of cholera which turned the superstitious *léperos* (rabble) in the capital away from their liberal deliverers, hailed Santa Anna's coup as "the holiest revolution our republic has ever seen." In April of 1834, with Congress dismissed, the anticlerical legislation declared null and void, Gómez Farías and his colleagues driven into exile, and the rebellious provinces turned over to the tender mercies of the army, the self-styled Napoleon of the West assumed the dictatorship.

The Loss of Texas

With Santa Anna maintaining his despotic rule by slipping in and out of the presidency, the focus of meaningful events shifted far to the north.

The northernmost provinces of New Spain had never been securely held or effectively colonized. Florida had been ceded to the United States by treaty in 1819. Louisiana had fallen to the French much earlier, and the French in turn had sold it to the United States. Texas, New Mexico and California (the latter two containing most of what are now the west-central American states from Missouri to Oregon, including Arizona) were tenuously held wildernesses, populated mainly by the most savage Indian tribes. Most of this wilderness, including California, was unmapped, and parts of it were claimed by the British and the French as well as by the parties of American explorers, settlers, trappers, freebooters, and fugitives from justice who crossed it from time to time.

Until the Independence, Mexican penetration of Texas consisted of a scattering of missions, camps and adobe villages. The population in 1823 is estimated to have been no more than three thousand—not all Mexicans, by any means. There had already been three Anglo-American attempts to move into this vacuum, all of them abortive. But the first genuine Anglo-American settlement was made on the Brazos River by Stephen F. Austin, in 1822, and for a while it looked as though peace would obtain. An upright New Englander, Austin confirmed his grant legally in Mexico City in 1833. The Mexicans thought the Americans could be converted into good Mexicans—at least into colonists who would resist annexation—but they guessed wrong. More and more Americans poured into the tax-free land of promise, and by 1833 the population had increased tenfold. Some of the settlers from the South brought their slaves with them; and none of them (except perhaps Austin) were disposed to accept Hispanic law or the inefficiency of the bureaucrats. The Mexicans retaliated by trying to force Catholicism on the settlers and by barring further immigration. Nevertheless Austin's peace party, with its faith in Mexican liberalism, imposed restraint—until Santa Anna overthrew the federal constitution and sent an army north in December of 1835 to disarm all who sympathized with his political foes. When this army was driven back across the Rio Grande, Santa Anna, momentarily out of the presidency, accepted command of the defeated northern army himself. Riding back to power on its victorious coattails would be in the Santa Anna style.

Still looking for effective leadership, the Texas settlers were in disarray when the energetic Mexican crossed the Rio Grande. He had marched his three thousand soldiers almost as many miles, and they were well equipped. He caught up with the American advance guard in San Antonio. About 140 men, commanded by Lt. Col. W. B. Travis, and including such frontier heroes as Davy Crockett and James Bowie, were surrounded in the old mission building, the Alamo. How Travis drew a line in the dirt, giving those who did not choose to cross it the opportunity to escape, and how the stricken Bowie demanded to be carried across the line in his bed, has often been told. The little band held out for two weeks, refusing to surrender, and accounting for several hundred Mexicans. Then the trumpets sounded the *deguello,* the Mexicans scaled the walls, and the survivors were slaughtered to a man. The bodies of Travis, Bowie and Crockett were tossed from bayonet to bayonet.

Only a few days before, a Texan declaration of independence had been drafted. "Remember the Alamo!" provided the settlers with a battle cry. Sam Houston, a giant of a man whom the Indians called "Big Drunk" and who was fearless, became their commander. At the San Jacinto River he called upon the fleeing population to turn and face Santa Anna. The sack of the Alamo, and his unopposed butchery of 371 American prisoners two weeks later at Goliad, seems to have gone to Santa Anna's head. When Houston turned on him from the cover of an oak forest, the Napoleon of the West was enjoying a siesta and his men were cooking their dinner. With a loss of only two men and twenty-three wounded, Houston killed, wounded or captured the entire Mexican army. Santa Anna's second-in-command, Col. Juan Almonte, helped Houston round up the fugitives. The General himself was captured the following day, and although he was quite ready to recognize Texas' independence in return for his liberty, the Mexican Government wasn't. Houston, nonetheless, was elected president of Texas in September of 1836, and the following year the republic's independence was recognized by the United States, Great Britain, France, and Belgium. But charges that it was being used as a pawn by the slave states plagued Texas, and it was not until March 1, 1845, that the new state, claiming that its boundary with Mexico was now the Rio Grande, was admitted to the Union.

The detachment of Texas from Mexico was illegal all the way, but it was an action carried out against a nation at that time without republican institutions and in fact without responsible government. "The occupation of Texas," Bernard De Voto says, "neither usurped nor absorbed a community, a culture, or an economy. Instead, it created all three ... Texas, New Mexico and California were precisely the portions of Mexico where Spain's imperial energy had faltered and run down. To this frontier Great Spain had come and here it could go no farther, here it began to ebb back. It had succeeded most in the genial California lands, but not much and long ago, much less in New Mexico, least of all in Texas. Stephen W. Kearny and Alexander Doniphan brought more safety, stability, and hope to the New Mexicans in two months than Spain had given them in two centuries, or Mexico after Spain. It was the last episode in the erosion of an empire." [2]

The War with the United States

James K. Polk of Tennessee was nominated by the Democratic Party in 1844 as a "dark horse," to oppose Martin Van Buren. Van Buren had warned that the annexation of Texas might provoke Mexico to war. The eleventh President of the United States was long regarded as a Southern politician who favored expansion as a means of advancing the interests of slavery. But the publication of Polk's diaries in 1910 put an end to that notion. Polk's consuming ambition was to expand the United States westward to its "natural" territorial limits, and his major objectives were always Oregon, California, and New Mexico, in that order—territories that had no chance of becoming "slave." Moreover, following the defeat of Mexico, Polk successfully opposed the clamor to take over the whole of

[2] Bernard De Voto, *The Year of Decision: 1846*. Boston, Houghton Mifflin Company, 1942.

Mexico—territory in which slavery might then have thrived for a decade or two, since there were few to oppose it. But before the war began, Polk was convinced that New Mexico and California could be secured without resort to arms, and who could facilitate their purchase better than the prisoner who had just fallen into American hands? Had not Santa Anna already offered to trade Texas for his personal freedom? And had he not demonstrated time and again that he could fool the Mexican people into believing that he spoke for their best interests?

The proposition, seemingly so logical, failed. Polk did not recognize that a man as unprincipled as Santa Anna would be just as capable of reneging on his promises to the United States as he had been of betraying his political allies in Mexico—more capable since, after all, Santa Anna *was* a Mexican and would have to explain to his fellow countrymen the acquisition of the bribe money he had been promised (rumors concerning it were already in the air). Polk also underestimated Santa Anna's capacity to make Mexico forget his duplicity and to raise armies capable of offering resistance to invasion; and he underestimated the Mexicans' disposition to fight for their own soil south of the Rio Grande—even under Santa Anna's disreputable banner.

Between 1836 and 1840 the political situation in Mexico had struck bottom. The so-called Pastry War found the debt-provoked French bombarding Veracruz, and the street mob in the capital, confused as ever, first shouting "Down with the Jews!" and then "Down with the Saxons!" Yucatán, under a liberal government, had virtually seceded. Indian tribes in the north, with the fairly efficient Spanish gendarmerie gone, were raiding the Creole haciendas at will. Only the news that Santa Anna was on his way home frightened the liberals into calling back from exile their one honest leader, Gómez Farías. But in 1841 Santa Anna was back. First he overthrew the government. Then, when the new Congress threatened reforms, he retired to Manga de Clavo. And finally, in 1843, Nicolás Bravo, almost senile by now, produced a new Constitution under which the President was to have the powers of a dictator—and of course Santa Anna assumed the presidency. Parkes describes with restraint his *ambiance* at this time:

> As dictator Santa Anna had ample opportunity to appear in his Napoleonic role and to display the various facets of his richly disharmonious character. He proved to be remarkably energetic in collecting money. By exacting forced

loans from the Church, by increasing import duties twenty per cent, and by selling mining concessions to the English, he raised a revenue twice as large as his predecessors'. These new resources were then distributed where they would prove most useful; thousands of new officers were added to the army payroll, and the government contractors found it easy to make fortunes. Santa Anna's amputated leg was disinterred from its grave at Manga de Clavo and solemnly buried in the cathedral. His statue was erected in the plaza, with one hand pointing toward Texas, which he was still promising to reconquer—though it was remarked that it also appeared to be pointing towards the mint. A new theatre, *El Gran Teatro de Santa Anna*, was built, and was proclaimed to be, with one exception, the largest in the world. When the wife of the dictator was seized with a mortal sickness, a parade of twenty thousand persons, headed by the archbishop, carried the host to her deathbed. [A month later, however, the dictator was remarried—to a girl of fifteen.] Santa Anna himself, like Napoleon, wore simple clothes, as though disdainful of personal display, and endeavored to add to their effect by clothing his staff in scarlet uniforms; when he dined in state six colonels stood behind his chair, and when he sat in his box in the theatre, a glittering array of generals sat beside him. Those admitted to his intimacy found the same courteous manners as before, the same melancholy expression, the same professions of zeal for the greatness of Mexico, and the same capacity for occasional acts of generosity.[3]

Unfortunately for Santa Anna, and for Mexico, the officers about to lead the armies of the United States across the border were a different breed. In one category were Indian fighters of the frontier, hard-bitten cavalrymen like Doniphan and Kearny and Zachary Taylor. Doniphan and Kearny not only understood guerrilla warfare, but they were masters in the pacification of hostile peoples, firm but not cruel, conscientious, farsighted. Taylor knew only how to inspire his troops by sitting bolt upright on his horse through the hottest of engagements; after the battle it was his custom to issue streams of purple prose for the benefit of the battalion of newspaper correspondents dragged along to promote his candidacy for the presi-

[3] Henry Bamford Parkes, *A History of Mexico*. Boston, Houghton Mifflin Co., 1938, 1950.

dency to succeed his commander-in-chief, Mr. Polk. As a general, Taylor was incompetent. The indecisive victories he won over the Mexicans in the north were achieved only through superior deployment of artillery and the brilliance of such subordinates as William Jenkins Worth, John Anthony Quitman, Jefferson Davis, and Ethan Allen Hitchcock.

The second category consisted of young subalterns from the corps of cadets, organized effectively at West Point following the War of 1812. These subalterns played a minor part in the first phase of the war under Taylor, who despised "scientific" soldiers. But their role was decisive in the final phase that brought about Mexico's capitulation. If they had not lived on to achieve fame twenty years later in the biggest and bloodiest war the world had seen up to that time, their names might have been forgotten. They included Braxton Bragg and Pierre Beauregard, George McClellan and George Gordon Meade, George Thomas and Thomas Jonathan (Stonewall) Jackson, Ulysses S. Grant and Robert E. Lee. The military genius later to be displayed by the last two took root and flourished, it is safe to say, by proximity to and with the encouragement of a military genius as phenomenal as theirs was to become: that of the Commander-in-Chief of the American Army, Winfield Scott.

President Polk, who thought of war entirely in political terms, had no intention of giving the command to Scott, who referred to him not too privately as "Little Jimmy Polk of Duck River," [4] and who was a Whig. But when the bumbling Taylor became the darling of the opposition party—and proved incapable of advancing beyond Mexico's northern provinces, the pressure became too great for Polk to resist. Even so he failed to reinforce or even supply Scott's expeditionary force advancing from Veracruz up Cortés' old trail to the capital; and when the little army of six thousand men, without reinforcements or effective communications, defeated Mexico decisively, Polk's gratitude expressed itself in recalling Scott in disgrace. But that is getting ahead of the story. Polk's immediate problems were two: (1) how to make the war palatable to the American public, and (2) how to govern the vast wilderness territories—comprising half of the entire area of Mexico—which he proposed to take.

Both problems solved themselves—without any help from Polk. Thoughtful Americans, almost without exception, opposed the war. They regarded it as immoral in principle—and they were not concerned that the actual fighting was precipitated by Mexican politi-

[4] Glenn W. Price, *Origins of the War with Mexico: The Polk Stockton Intrigue.* Austin, Texas, University of Texas Press, 1968.

cians so sure of victory that they refused Polk's many offers to reach a peaceful solution of the Texas boundary dispute.[5] Emerson and Thoreau and James Russell opposed the war; in fact, among the poets, only the young Whitman could be called a hawk. Abolitionist statesmen like William H. Seward and Charles Sumner spoke out against it. Horace Greeley called it "unjust and rapacious." Even Lieutenant Grant regarded it as a conspiracy of slaveholders and wrote, "I felt sorry that I had enlisted." Abraham Lincoln made a speech against it that cost him his seat in the House of Representatives. Theodore Parker made a greater speech in Boston which concluded:

> I maintain that aggressive war is a sin; that it is a national infidelity, a denial of Christianity and of God. . . . The political authors of the war on this continent, and at this day, are incapable of a statesman's work, or else guilty of that sin. . . . Yet the Government and its Congress would throw the blame on the innocent and say war exists "by the act of Mexico!" If a lie was ever told, I think it is this one. Then the "dear people" must be called on for money and men, for "the soil of this free republic is invaded," and the Governor of Massachusetts, one of the men who declared the annexation of Texas unconstitutional, recommends the war he just now told us to pray against, and appeals to our "patriotism" and "humanity" as arguments for butchering the Mexicans, when they are in the right and we are in the wrong! . . . I am not at all astonished that northern representatives voted for all this work of crime. They are no better than southern representatives, scarcely less in favor of slavery and not half so open. They say "Let the North make money and you may do what you please with the nation" . . . for though we are descended from the Puritans we have but one article in our creed we never flinch from following, and that is—to make money, honestly if we can, if not, as we can! [6]

It was no use. The issue may have been (in part) making money, but it certainly wasn't slavery, and though the moral argument was irrefutable, the mood of the young country was exuberantly expan-

[5] The evidence is summarized on p. 155 of Vol. 1 of *The War with Mexico* by Justin H. Smith, reprint edition. Gloucester, Massachusetts, Peter Smith, 1963.
[6] Quoted in *The Year of Decision.*

sive and not to be denied. The frontier oratory of Senator Thomas Hart Benton prevailed. The phrase "manifest destiny" was coined. The adolescent jingoism of Walt Whitman perfectly expressed the American mood of 1846:

> It is from such materials—from the Democracy, with its manly heart and its lion strength spurning the ligatures wherewith drivellers would bind it—that we are to expect the great FUTURE of this Western World! a scope involving such unparalleled human happiness and rational freedom, to such unnumbered myriads, that the heart of a true man *leaps* with a mighty joy only to think of it!

Late in 1844 Santa Anna's dictatorship had been brought to an end by his former ally, Mariano Paredes y Arrillaga. With the country this time hopefully decreeing his "permanent exile," Santa Anna had taken ship to Cuba. But in Havana he managed to convince Polk's agents that should American forces in Texas make a token advance from the Nueces to the Rio Grande, he, Santa Anna, would use this as a trump in persuading President Paredes to cede peacefully the territories President Polk desired and over which Mexico no longer exercised effective control. Accordingly, on May 13, 1846, Polk sent secret instructions to the naval task force patrolling Mexico's Gulf Coast to allow any ship carrying Santa Anna to pass through to Veracruz. And on the same day the United States declared war on Mexico.

Polk, mesmerized by Santa Anna, envisioned a brief occupation of the northern provinces, an investiture of the seaports, a march overland through New Mexico to California, and a peace treaty confirming the new acquisitions. It didn't work out quite that way. Mexico's northern states were supposed to "rebel," but they didn't. An expedition into Chihuahua by Gen. John Ellis Wool became cut off from its supplies and forced to return to Texas. Mexico's second-largest port, Tampico, was indeed occupied by a naval party. But Gen. Zachary Taylor's disorganized army of volunteers stalled at the frontier city of Matamoros. Taylor's repulse of the Mexican "invasion" of Texas at Palo Alto (May 8) and Resaca de la Palma (May 9)—the precipitants of Polk's declaration of war May 13—had been too much for Taylor. So far, only the New Mexican expedition was going according to plan.

The leaders of that long march, Kearny and Doniphan, had received a thousand Missouri volunteers May 13 and were prepared to use them effectively. Marching sometimes as much as thirty miles a day, they proceeded to clear the historic Santa Fe Trail. The savage Comanches were driven back and the friendly Indian tribes skillfully won over. On August 12, an advance party rode into Santa Fe and began to negotiate with the surprised Mexican authorities. The latter had tried to get the padres and landholders to convince the people that Kearny's army was coming to debauch them, but the people had been debauched and exploited by Spain for so many centuries that any change looked like a change for the better. The American expedition arrived at Santa Fe on August 18, and ran up the Stars and Stripes. Kearny had taken New Mexico without firing a shot.

The conquest of California was almost as bloodless, but more complicated. To oppose John Charles Fremont marching down from Oregon and Kearny marching north from Santa Fe, the Mexicans had generals but no troops. The territory had been virtually empty when Andrew Jackson tried to buy it, and it was still empty. But the handful of Americans who had come to settle near Sutter's "Kingdom" or trapped the Yosemite had sent home stories of the two crops a year and sixty bushels of corn per acre the great valleys would yield; and Fremont, the grandiloquent pupil of Kit Carson, who had married Senator Benton's beautiful daughter Jessie, had blown this propaganda up into a best seller. The idea that "Americans must occupy their continent" inevitably climaxed with the California dream. Besides there were those Pacific ports that Russia had vacated but Britain might seize, unless . . .

Fremont and Robert Field Stockton, not waiting for the war, marched in, and a California Republic was proclaimed. San Diego was "liberated" on July 29, and Los Angeles on August 14. But by the fall, the "natives" of these and other coastal settlements had become thoroughly disillusioned with the rascals who were their new masters and had taken back everything they had lost. So it remained to Kearny, who arrived in December, to reconquer and pacify California; which he did. Los Angeles fell for the second time January 10, 1847. When Kearny left California in June, the territory was almost as reconciled to its change of nationality as New Mexico had been.

Meanwhile on the border, Taylor was fending off attacks and moving forward with the greatest difficulty. Much to his surprise (and Polk's) the Mexicans were defending their country with great bravery. If they had had determined, resourceful leadership, Taylor would have been no match for them. Lieutenant Grant had taken a toll of eight to one at Palo Alto only because he concentrated the fire of his artillery batteries so that the Mexicans could not get near them. The Battle of Resaca de la Palma had been won because the Americans were better marksmen, and in the virtually leaderless engagement had acted effectively *as individuals:*

> Few of [the Mexicans] here or later could shoot straight. Government policy, taking account of revolutions, had forbidden the citizenry to bear arms. Mostly, too, they were pressed men—gathered up by gangs from among the peons, to eke out the standing army, which was at least disciplined if poorly supplied and preposterously over-officered. There was little reason why they should fight at all. Did it matter which Mexican faction or which invader was quartered on them, raped their women, drove off their cattle, and levied on their crops? But they did fight, at Palo Alto and most other battles, with heroic doggedness. If one day of battle was frequently enough for them, so that on the second day they broke and ran, part of that routine flight may be ascribed to the usual failure of the commissary to bring up supper and breakfast, and the rest to their general officers who, by the second morning, were either panic-stricken or betraying one another.[7]

On August 16, Santa Anna, having been permitted to pass through the American blockade, reached Mexico. Nicolás Bravo had already overthrown the Paredes government in his behalf. With his characteristic energy, Santa Anna wasted no time in raising a new army. There wasn't time to finance it by the usual method—goading Gómez Farías into threatening expropriation of the Church and then extracting several millions from the frightened clergy with the promise to act as their savior. So Santa Anna seized the mint at San Luis Potosí and melted down its ninety-eight silver bars. He neglected, however, to train his army. The twenty thousand men bribed or impressed into service "had not by this date held a general maneuver, not even on division level, and the artillery had never fired so much as a blank shot." [8] Accompanied by its multitude of *soldaderas,* and trying desperately to prevent deserters from melting into the trackless mountains along the way, this army struggled ponderously toward Saltillo to oppose Taylor.

[7] De Voto, *op. cit.*
[8] Oakah L. Jones, *Santa Anna.* New York, Twayne Publishers, Inc., 1968.

September 19–24 the American army of 6,600 had taken the city of Monterrey from a slightly larger force of 10,000 Mexicans under Gen. Pedro de Ampudia. Taylor got the credit as usual, but the real heroes were his generals of brigade, Quitman and Worth, and the soldiers knew it. Worth could have annihilated Ampudia's army, but was not permitted to by Taylor, who instead granted an eight weeks' armistice, leaving the retreating Mexicans to join forces with Santa Anna.

The big battle took place at Buena Vista, near Saltillo, on February 22, 1847. And this time it was Santa Anna who let victory slip from his grasp. He had the greater numbers, and by the end of the second day he had the Americans outflanked and reeling. But on the morning of the third day, instead of pressing his advantage, he ordered a retreat, which turned into a panic. Taylor, by doggedness alone and the initiative of his subordinates, had won; but his army was so badly mauled that Polk was finally forced to give the command to Winfield Scott.

Scott's plan all along had been to ignore northern Mexico, capture Veracruz, and reach Mexico City by the shortest overland route. Once he had his orders, he moved swiftly. Veracruz surrendered March 29, 1847, after Capt. Robert E. Lee's engineers dismounted the big guns from Comdr. Matthew Perry's fleet and zeroed in on the fortress of San Juan de Ulúa. After a four-day barrage that lobbed 6,700 projectiles into the fort and city, the Mexican commander surrendered. Scott permitted none of the lawlessness that had disfigured Taylor's campaign. When an American raped a Mexican woman, Scott had the soldier court-martialed and hanged.[9]

[9] Russell Potter Reeder, *The Story of the Mexican War.* New York, Meredith Press, 1967.

The agonizing decision of whether to penetrate the harbor by naval action, take the city by storm at night, or lay siege to it by land in order to bring about its surrender by bombardment and starvation, was reached by Scott in consultation with his Little Cabinet, which included Captain Lee and Lt. Col. Ethan Allen Hitchcock. Naval action, favored by Farragut, the future naval hero of the Civil War, was rejected as too slow; the army could not risk what Scott called the *vomito* (malaria, dysentery) by lingering in the tropic lowlands. The second solution, Scott estimated, might cost two- to three thousand American lives and an "immense slaughter" of noncombatants. "For these reasons," Scott said, "although I know our countrymen will hardly acknowledge a victory unaccompanied by a long butcher's bill (report of killed and wounded) I am strongly inclined—policy concurring with humanity—to 'forego their loud applause and aves vehement' and take the city with the least possible loss of life. In this determination I know, as Dogberry says truly of himself, I 'write me down an ass.' " American losses totaled nine, all told, but this was nine too many for Hitchcock, a New Englander of the Peace Party, who commented mordantly: "Our approach and our active proceedings have been con-

A well-equipped new army which Santa Anna raised in another spectacular burst of energy was cut to pieces in the Cerro Gordo Pass, twenty miles east of Jalapa, April 17–18. Again it was the brilliant Captain Lee, this time taking advantage of Santa Anna's failure to fortify a hill overlooking the gorge,who ensured the elimination of half of the Mexican army's effectives. Scott released all of his prisoners, buried their weapons, and pressed on. With the six thousand men he had left, he took Puebla on May 15. For three months he rested there, trying to negotiate an armistice, with Polk plaguing him all the way. Failing in this, he marched reluctantly past the volcanoes to the capital.

On August 19 and 20, Scott won the two battles of Contreras and Churubusco, in what are now outlying districts of Mexico City. For a second time he tried to negotiate an armistice and failed. At the Molina del Rey, where Scott made his only miscalculation, Santa Anna had victory in his grasp, but gave way and called for a retreat just as he had at Buena Vista. September 12–13 the Americans took the fortress of Chapultepec by storm. The castle which housed the Military College was penetrated by assault parties with scaling ladders after a furious artillery barrage in which Grant and Jackson played outstanding roles. The American losses were heavy. Santa Anna ordered relief for the young cadets who were defending the citadel, but they refused to leave; some were slain at their cannon, and one wrapped himself in the flag and leaped from the cliff rather than surrender.

The way to the city now lay open as Generals Quitman (in one shoe) and Worth led their bloodstained brigades down the causeways that still remained from Aztec Tenochtitlán. Santa Anna retired to Villa Guadalupe, and the *léperos* sacked the National Palace. On September 14, Scott entered the Zócalo and the American flag was raised. For five months, until Polk recalled him in disgrace, Scott governed Mexico firmly and well. The last word about his feat was spoken by Napoleon's conqueror, the Duke of Wellington: "Scott's campaign was unsurpassed in military annals. He is the greatest living soldier." Scott himself gave credit to the future commanders of the Civil War:

---

ducted under the direction of scientific Engineers & everything has proceeded according to known rules of the Art of War. Hence the loss has been very slight—of course I mean comparatively—no loss in this infamous war is slight. We have not acted neighborly towards our weak brother." (Quoted in *Chronicles of the Gringos: The U.S. Army in the Mexican War, 1846–1848. Accounts of Eyewitnesses and Combatants*, edited by George Winston Smith & Charles Judah. Albuquerque, New Mexico, University of New Mexico Press, 1968.)

I give it as my fixed opinion that but for our graduated cadets the war between the United States and Mexico might, and probably would, have lasted some four or five years, with, in its first half, more defeats than victories falling to our share, whereas in less than two campaigns we conquered a great country and a peace without the loss of a single battle or skirmish.[10]

By the Treaty of Guadalupe Hidalgo, signed February 2, 1848, Texas, New Mexico and Upper California were ceded to the United States for a payment of $15 million and the cancellation of all unpaid American claims. Considering the military positions of the two countries at the termination of hostilities, the terms were considered in Europe to be unprecedentedly mild. Independent Texas had long before opted for American statehood. It was hardly to be expected, observed Alexander von Humboldt, Mexico's benefactor and friend, that California and New Mexico "could be indefinitely withheld from the uses of civilization and improvement."

As for the war itself, it had been conducted, wrote the knightly Lee, "in a manner no man might be ashamed of." "The elevated and kindly character of Taylor and Scott," wrote the Mexican historian Roa Bárcena, "lessened as far as was possible the evils of war," and the Americans treated the Mexicans, he added, with "the most noble courtesy." Even Theodore Parker, the most intransigent American opponent of the war, acknowledged that it had "been conducted with as much gentleness as a war of invasion can be." How, then, had the embattled Mexicans failed so signally to rout an enemy uninspired by aggressiveness and poorly supported at home? The answer was that the Mexicans were the victims of their political immaturity:

> The want of public virtue had filled the army with miserable officers, the legislative halls with dishonest, scheming, clashing politicians, and the whole nation with wrathful, disheartened people, secretly thankful to find their oppressors, whom they could not punish themselves, punished by the Americans. . . . Primarily Mexico was defeated because she did not fight; and she did not fight because she had nothing to fight for.[11]

[10] Quoted in *The Story of the Mexican War*.
[11] *The War with Mexico*. All quotations in this paragraph are from Volume 2 of Justin Smith's exhaustive study.

Santa Anna had tried to raise new armies to cut the Americans off from their base in Veracruz, but the Creole landowners preferred peace to guerrilla warfare. José Fernández Ramírez, a Congressional delegate of more than usual discernment, noted that at this point the Mexican generals, with the exception of Gabriel Valencia

> have given proof of what they have been, are, and will continue to be: cowards, ignoramuses, and men wholly devoid of even one spark of personal honor. Judged by their ability, they scarcely would make good sergeants. Judged by their character, they are what one of our hapless poets has said of them:
>
> > Tortoises in the country,
> > Vultures in the city.
>
> Select just one percent of them to make an exception. And if you could see these men today still walking along the avenue in droves with their wretched stars and medals gleaming on their breasts—and not one evidence of shame about them! [12]

Deposed from the presidency, the flamboyant Santa Anna was given a banquet by the grateful American officers, and shipped off to Jamaica. Mexico, deprived of half of her territory, faced with secessionist movements in the north and south, and bankrupt as usual, prepared for a long uphill struggle.

Juárez and the Reform

There is a theory, sometimes borne out, that when the clock of history is about to run down, a great man appears and starts the wheels turning again in an upward cycle. Except perhaps in the case of the United States at this precise time—where Abraham Lincoln ended the procession of political schemers who had brought on the ugly little war with Mexico and then escalated it into the fratricidal holocaust of 1861–65—no country was ever blessed with a more timely deliverer than Mexico when Benito Juárez appeared out of nowhere to save the country from itself.

If a dramatist of genius had been looking for Santa Anna's exact opposite, he would have invented Benito Juárez. Born March 21, 1806, in a small mountain village in the state of Oaxaca, Juárez was

[12] Quoted in *Santa Anna.*

a full-blooded Zapotec Indian. Five feet in height, homely, totally lacking in vanity and selfish ambition, and with a slow-working intellect that never deviated from the concept of *what is good for the people of Mexico*, Juárez was a latter-day Puritan, a self-made man who never thought of self, a kind of secular saint. He was a family man. He drank only wine, and that sparingly. He wore dark clothes, usually black, and rode (even to war) in a black carriage. He believed in the integrity of the law above all things. His honesty was proverbial and extended from his personal affairs to those of the state. His reserve was so great that his enemies took it for arrogance, and his friends (of whom he had few) sometimes for stupidity. Like all true democrats he was pragmatic and optimistic, and believed that education was the key to social and economic equality. He was a great builder, and he had a will that never faltered. If he had faults, they stemmed from his lack of a sense of humor, his insensitivity to the arts, his political paternalism. He was, and still is, hated by most of the religious for his anticlericalism; but the truth is that Juárez was a deeply religious man who never lost his belief in God and tried only to curb those abuses of Christianity which had multiplied with the Church's most un-Christian economic and political privileges.

Oddly enough, Juárez' career began under the aegis of Santa Anna. In 1844 the young Indian, who had been brought up and trained as a lawyer by a kindly middle-class family in Oaxaca following his parents' early death, was appointed secretary to the cabinet of the state governor. The Governor was a Santa Anna conservative. Juárez, already a liberal, no doubt shared the general belief at that time that Santa Anna could save the country; but he resigned from his post in protest when the Governor drafted into the army a student who had criticized his policies.

Juárez' break with Santa Anna and the conservatives came later. He had been appointed to the governorship in 1847. In 1852, incredible as it seems, Santa Anna was brought back from his exile. The conservatives were about to oust the second of two *moderados*, José Joaquín Herrera and Mariano Arista, who had been ruling Mexico honestly and intelligently since the war. When the coup succeeded, Santa Anna was made dictator. The young generation of liberals, like Melchor Ocampo, the Governor of Michoacán, and Juárez in Oaxaca, were doomed—especially after Lucas Alamán, Santa Anna's sponsor, and the one moderate reactionary he would listen to, died in 1853. Once more the central government ruled with a mailed fist, and federal troops took over the state capitals. The town councils were disbanded, Congress was dissolved, and all taxes formerly received by the states were turned over to the central government.

This time, however, the liberals knew what they wanted. The Plan of Ayutla, published in 1854, called for a temporary dictatorship by the military chiefs of the rebellion, to be followed by the calling of a convention to draft a new constitution. The guerrillas in the state of Guerrero were led by Juan Álvarez, an old Morelos lieutenant, and Ignacio Comonfort, a Creole whom Santa Anna had dismissed as customs collector in Acapulco. Juárez and Ocampo bided their time in exile, across the American border in New Orleans.

Santa Anna marched west, but Comonfort, besieged in Acapulco, was not to be taken. The dictator gave up the pursuit, stomped back to the capital and began putting his money in banks abroad. When the money gave out, he sold southern Arizona (the Gadsden Purchase) to the United States for $10 million. Then he sold Mayan Indians from rebellious Yucatán to the Cuban sugar plantations for twenty-five pesos a head. It was no use. Comonfort was acquiring munitions from the United States, and soon all the northern and western provinces were in rebellion. In August 1855, Santa Anna fled to the coast and took ship for his hacienda in Venezuela once more. Ironically the name of the vessel that bore him away was *Iturbide*. Santa Anna made several attempts to regain power before his death in Mexico City twenty years later, but the Mexican people had had enough of him at last. When the government commemorated the Battle of Churubusco, at which he had commanded the troops opposing General Scott, Santa Anna was not even invited to attend. He died a few months later, forgotten.[13]

When the new government of liberals was organized in November of 1855, a junta headed by Santa Anna's perennial antagonist, Gómez Farías, declared Juan Álvarez President. Almost immediately the new Minister of Justice and Public Instruction, Benito Juárez, inaugurated the Reform by decreeing the abolition of the separate courts through which the clergy and the military had maintained their power. A second law, passed in June of 1856, decreed the sale of all Church estates, either to the existing tenants or to any person who might choose to "denounce" the landlord. This was the *Ley Lerdo*, devised by Comonfort's treasury minister, Miguel Lerdo de Tejada, and its effects were disastrous; instead of dividing

---

[13] But not before he had made one last dubious contribution to civilization. Resting briefly in Elizabeth, New Jersey, where he was trying to contact William H. Seward in 1864, Santa Anna was observed by James Adams chewing chicle from his Veracruz estate. The invention of chewing gum followed shortly.

up the vast haciendas among those in need and capable of farming them, it concentrated their ownership in a still smaller class, mostly foreigners, and it broke up the communal lands *(ejidos)* belonging to the Indian villages, turning them over to the land-hungry mestizos who had been unable to afford haciendas themselves.

Nor was Comonfort the man to enforce these laws for the benefit of those who had fought his battles. His heart was in the right place, but he was weak. He feared to alienate the Church and the army; even more he feared his aging and extremely devout mother. "He was afraid," Juárez wrote later, "of the privileged and reactionary classes. He expressed extreme disgust because to the council formed in Iguala there had not been named one ecclesiastic, once venturing to say that it would be good if the council were composed half of ecclesiastics and half of the other classes of society. He wishes also that there should be left employed in the army the generals and other officers that up to the last hour had served the tyranny that had just fallen." [14]

Comonfort remained in power just long enough to see enacted the Constitution of 1857, which incorporated both the *Ley Juárez* and the *Ley Lerdo,* and over which Juárez as president of the Supreme Court presided. It was a weak document on the Anglo-Saxon model, wholly unsuited to Mexican realities, giving the legislature greater powers than the executive; but it did include, in addition to the two controversial laws, the famous Article 123 giving the government control of the Church—theoretically. That was enough for the Church, which promptly excommunicated everyone who had sworn allegiance to the Constitution. The Church also fomented rebellions led by the resourceful militant priest Francisco J. Miranda, an illiterate Indian who was a fanatical Catholic, and Miguel Miramón, an aristocrat of French origin who had risen rapidly in the army. Comonfort went into exile. Juárez became President but was forced to move the government to Veracruz, where it carried on shakily during the three years of civil war that ensued.

When Juárez arrived in Veracruz May 4, 1858, he had fewer than 350 soldiers and almost no money, but forces more or less loyal to him controlled parts of the north, south and west. In Oaxaca he had such able commanders as Marcos Pérez, Díaz Ordas and Porfirio Díaz. That ancient follower of Morelos, Juan Álvarez, still

[14] Quoted in Charles Allen Smart, *Viva Juárez: A Biography*. Philadelphia, J. B. Lippincott Company, 1963.

held Guerrero. Santos Degollado and Melchor Ocampo were active in the north. But all central Mexico was in the hands of the Indian general Mejía, Miramón, and a new paladin of the Church, Leonardo Márquez, soon to be known for his atrocities as "The Tiger of Tacubaya." It was a religious war that was being fought, fanned by Juárez' new decree separating Church and State and guaranteeing religious freedom, and finally (1859) confiscating all Church property except the actual buildings without compensation. But it was also a class war: Indians from Guerrero and Oaxaca and *rancheros* from the north were on Juárez' side. Creoles from the capital and principal cities, assisted by the clergy, constituted the opposition; with armies of professional soldiers and Indian religious fanatics, they won most of the battles.

The intervention of the European powers into this chaotic situation was facilitated by the embroilment of the United States in the Civil War. But before the war began, a treaty had been drawn up anticipating that conflict. This was the McLane-Ocampo agreement which, in return for a paltry four million dollars, would have written off the isthmus of Tehuantepec and permitted American troops to enter northern Mexico "to keep order." Fortunately it was defeated in the United States Senate before Ocampo's reputation (and indirectly Juárez') could be permanently damaged. During Abraham Lincoln's administration the American Government was consistently friendly to Juárez, but just as consistently evasive when it came to doing anything practical to aid the beleaguered liberals; Lincoln was much too close to losing the Civil War to tip the balance by alienating France, England, or Spain. But munitions were generally available along the border to which Juárez' forces had retreated; and once the Confederacy was defeated they began to flow south in a rush. An imperial European outpost across the Rio Grande was the last thing the United States wanted to see.

Juárez, meanwhile, was face to face with just that. The liberal government had returned to the capital briefly in 1861. There were a handful of able, loyal men assisting Juárez—Ignácio Zaragoza, Leandro Valle, Santos Degollado, Jesús González Ortega, and of course the Lerdo de Tejada brothers and Ocampo—but these were not nearly enough. To govern, deals had to be made with the conservative bureaucrats, and soon the liberal officials were outnumbered. Tottering on the edge of bankruptcy, the government desperately sought new sources of revenue, while the British and Spanish paymasters tightened the screws. Closer and closer to the capital's outskirts came the clerical armies of Miramón and Mejía. The stage was set for Napoleon III to make his own bid for the prize.

Napoleon's wife was Spanish and rabidly Catholic. The distraught, unscrupulous Emperor himself was looking for any adventure abroad that might distract the French from his failures at home. He had already fumbled in Italy, and in the Crimea. In 1859, Miramón had obtained a quick loan of $750,000 from a Swiss bank by putting up as collateral $15 million in Mexican bonds. The Emperor's brother had acquired title to many of these bonds, and in March of 1860 the French Government demanded that the Mexican Government (now Juárez', not Miramón's) pay up, or else. Juárez stalled through 1861, was reelected President by a narrow vote of 61 to 55 electors, and lost by assassination or ambush three of his closest associates, Ocampo, Santos Degollado and Valle. In January of 1862, the French landed 2,500 troops at Veracruz; Spanish and British forces, already there "to ensure the collection of revenues," made a deal with France and withdrew.

The first engagement was won by Mexico. The French, reinforced to 6,000 men, moved up onto the plateau and invested Puebla. On May 5, 1862, General Zaragoza attacked them with a smaller force and drove them back to Orizaba. This was the famous battle of *Cinco de Mayo*. "If the French had taken Puebla," Smart says, "they would also, in the light of later events, have taken Mexico City. Napoleon's plans certainly would have been much more quickly and completely realized, and France would probably have openly recognized and supported the Confederacy, and England might well have done the same. In short, the battle of *Cinco de Mayo* was an important victory not only for the Republic of Mexico, but also for the United States." [15]

Unfortunately, Juárez underestimated French strength and intentions. The French army was permitted to retire in good order, and the five hundred prisoners taken were courteously returned. On March 16, 1863, the French army came back to Puebla. This time Ortega and Comonfort were in command, and they lost. The way to the capital was now open, and Juárez, without enough men left to defend it, moved the government north to San Luis Potosí. The French marched in and this time the fickle *léperos* greeted them with flowers paid for by the French. Napoleon's problem now was how to govern Mexico.

[15] Smart, *op. cit.*

The Short Unhappy Reign of Maximilian

Santa Anna, from his latest exile in the Virgin Islands, had written Louis Napoleon: "The overwhelming majority of the nation is longing for the restoration of the empire of Moctezuma." Santa Anna was no friend of the Indians, of course; when he said Moctezuma he was employing poetic license: he meant Iturbide. And when he talked of the "overwhelming majority of the Mexican people," he spoke only for himself. Some of the Emperor's better-informed friends warned him that a new pretender to the nonexistent Mexican throne might be received a bit roughly. But Louis Napoleon was still ready to try; after all, it wouldn't be *his* neck.

The prospective puppet on whom the Emperor's vacillating gaze fell was Archduke Maximilian, younger brother of the Emperor Francis Joseph of Austria. Maximilian, aged thirty, was tall, blond, brave, benevolent and humane. He was also vain, a bit of a snob, a do-gooder who had never moved outside of court circles, grand tours, and honorific employment. His experience of politics, and of the lowly he sincerely desired to elevate, was derived entirely from books. He was lately married to Carlota of the Belgians, a china-doll type whose ambition to save the world exceeded his own but was less pure, being motivated mainly by a sulky passion to cure her own sick psyche.

Into the Mexican maelstrom moved this unlikely, hapless pair, following a plebiscite which Maximilian had demanded, to test their "popularity"; the plebiscite, of course, was rigged. They arrived at Veracruz, that funnel and vent for all the conquerors and clowns, on May 28, 1864. Juárez was not there to greet them. In fact, he had by now been pushed by the home-grown imperialists to the northernmost extremities of Mexico. Comonfort had been assassinated. His military chiefs, Ortega and Doblado, had been defeated. His American friends still had their hands tied. A Confederate force had moved in to help "colonize" Mexico. French armies were moving up to the border almost unopposed. Juárez' family, from its refuge at the Mexican Consulate, 210 East Thirteenth Street, in New York, had just sent the harassed President the terrible news that his eldest and favorite son had died. The one bright spot—Porfirio Díaz' brilliant campaign in defense of the south—was glimmering: Díaz had been forced at last to surrender Oaxaca, though he refused to pledge allegiance to the invaders and eventually escaped to fight again.

Juárez' optimism and steady determination saved Mexico. The well-intentioned Maximilian, who had spent the voyage preparing an elaborate manual of court etiquette, gravitated between his palaces at Cuernavaca and Chapultepec, wringing his hands over the plight of the Indians and discovering for himself that the clergy were "lacking," as he put it, "in Christian charity and morality." When he confirmed the laws of the Reform by a decree of December 27, 1864, the Emperor lost the support of the clergy, the royalists, and Empress Eugenie without gaining any adherents among the Juaristas, who didn't recognize his right to issue decrees at all. Lee's surrender to Grant in April was another blow to the royalist cause. Secretary of State Seward warned Austria that if Maximilian should receive any further support, the American Minister to that country would ask for his passports.[16] Anticipating enforcement of the Monroe Doctrine, Napoleon began to withdraw the forces which alone sustained Maximilian. Gen. Mariano Escobedo recaptured Monterrey and Laredo.

Even so, the pressure was not removed from Juárez, who was squeezed by another French thrust from Chihuahua into El Paso del Norte (now called Ciudad Juárez). So strapped for money was he at this point that the Mexican President was forced to borrow a thousand dollars from one Jesús Carranza of Chihuahua, whose son, Venustiano (see pp. 109–110) was then seven.[17] But Juárez' powerful American friends—who included the assassinated Lincoln's successor, Andrew Johnson, as well as Generals Grant, Sherman, and Sheridan —were now prepared to support him even should he be forced out of Mexico. The Italian patriot Mazzini, and other friends abroad, were laying plans to organize a Republican Legion of volunteers to come to Mexico's assistance. And following the decisive Prussian victory at Königgrätz on July 3, 1866, Napoleon was forced to recall Bazaine's French army to protect France itself. Maximilian's Empress drove away from an embassy of desperation to the Empress of the French with the news that Louis Napoleon was the Devil and that he had tried to poison her with orange juice.

As the republican forces now began to move south in pursuit of the retreating Miramón, the war became increasingly savage. Each side accused the other of atrocities, reprisals, mass executions; and there is enough evidence to sustain the charges of both parties. The

---

16 H. Montgomery Hyde, *Mexican Empire*. London, Macmillan and Co., Ltd., 1946.
17 Smart, *op. cit.*

end came when Maximilian and his generals, their force now reduced to eight thousand men, were besieged in Querétaro.

Maximilian was popular in the royalist city. With characteristic courage he exposed himself to danger in the streets. When Juárez' army, led by Escobedo and Riva Palacio, had swelled to forty thousand, and they were serving cat pie at the best tables (including the Emperor's), the townspeople still loved him, taxed themselves to pay his army's wages, gladly melted down the church bells for cannon and shot. But it was at the inevitable end, when Col. Miguel López had betrayed the citadel to the Juaristas for a handful of silver, that Maximilian looked best. At the Hill of Bells, on the seventy-first day of the siege, he surrendered with his staff, which included such romantic adventurers as Prince Felix zu Salm-Salm (Agnes Salm was later to offer her body to the prison commander, when she thought that the genuineness of a bribe to permit Maximilian's escape was being questioned). The Emperor's last two messages to Juárez—one a request that Miramón and Mejía be spared, the other a letter urging the liberal leader to reconcile all Mexicans without bloodshed—make one forget the Black Decree he was duped into signing the year before. As the Emperor passed to the firing squad, the people of Querétaro again appeared on their balconies—in mourning, weeping openly. He gave the place of honor in the center to the brave Miramón; comforted Mejía, who was hardly well enough to stand, handing him his smelling salts; gave what little gold remained to the execution party, with the injunction reminiscent of Hidalgo's fifty years before: "*Muchachos*, aim well; aim right here." Then a few words to the onlookers: "I forgive everybody, I pray that everybody may also forgive me. And I wish that my blood, about to be shed, be for the good of the country. *Viva Méjico! Viva la Independéncia!*"

Juárez' decision to have Maximilian shot has been debated for a century. At the time, liberals from all over the world, including such friends of Mexico as Garibaldi and Victor Hugo, wired impassioned pleas for mercy. There is a legend—and a celebrated wax work at San Luis Potosí to illustrate it—that Princess Salm embraced the inflexible President's knees in a final plea for Maximilian's life. "I am grieved, madame," Juárez is reported to have answered, "to see you on your knees before me; but if all the kings and queens of Europe were at your side, I could not spare his life. It is not I who take it away; it is my people and the law, and if I did not do their will, the people should take his life as well as my own."

There has been less debate over the more fateful decision of August 14, 1867, amending the Constitution to increase the President's powers *unconstitutionally*—that is, without the concurrence of the state governments. In the long run, Juárez was only doing what had to be done, what would be done more drastically by the Revolution of 1910–20, to ensure effective government in a country with an illiterate peasantry and no democratic traditions. But in the short run he was opening himself to charges of authoritarianism and preparing the way for a dictator who might not have his personal integrity or scruples about applying the *Ley Lerdo* to the Indians' *ejidos*. In the presidential election of 1871, Juárez won by a narrow margin over the two other candidates, Sebastián Lerdo de Tejada and Porfirio Díaz, but a rebellion broke out almost immediately in Oaxaca led by Porfirio Díaz' brother Felix.

The rebellion was snuffed out ruthlessly. Felix Díaz was killed. Porfirio Díaz escaped in a priest's disguise to the mountains of Nayarit. But on July 18, 1872, Juárez died of a heart attack—triggered, symbolically, by one of the lowly beneficiaries of his reforms who had gripped his knees in gratitude too lovingly.

What had Juárez accomplished in these last five years of comparative peace? He had succeeded in identifying the Reform with Independence. He had destroyed the special privileges of the military and the clergy. He had laid the groundwork for a system of secular education. He had begun the industrialization of the country by completing the railroad from Veracruz to the capital. Above all, he had given a personal example of honesty, selflessness, and dedication to the common weal that could be transgressed but never forgotten.

Sebastián Lerdo de Tejada, who succeeded Juárez as President, had greater intellectual gifts but none of the old Indian's will and appeal to the masses. He was arrogant and indolent. And faced with another Díaz rebellion, he made the tactical mistake of giving the American railroads the right to extend their lines into Mexico. "The attitude of the United States," Parkes notes, "was henceforth to be a decisive factor in every Mexican revolution. Since [Díaz' successful bid] . . . no Mexican revolutionary bid for power has failed if it has been allowed to use United States territory as its base of operations; none has succeeded if the United States government has been unsympathetic." [18]

[18] Parkes, *op. cit.*

The Dictatorship of Porfirio Díaz

The story of how Porfirio Díaz came to power, how he maintained himself through eight presidencies, and how the world marveled at the glittering palace of peace and prosperity he had wrought, only to discover when the facade collapsed that it contained nothing but the corpses of his victims, the groans of the starving, and the piles of worthless paper he had taken for the nation's movable wealth, is a classic in the annals of dictatorship. Except for the fact that Díaz' early career was honorable and that he took flight to die in bed, the story exactly parallels that of the Dominican "benefactor," Rafael Leonidas Trujillo, in our time. Díaz was part-Mixtec Indian, and Trujillo was part-Haitian Negro, and both spent their long lives trying to live down those antecedents and crush the "inferior" race from which they sprang. Both came to power by subverting a defective constitutional system. Both consolidated their power for three decades with the help of the Church and the armed forces, compromising both in the process. Both stifled opposition by corrupting the press and the courts, playing off one local administration against another, and terrorizing the majority with a secret police apparatus and a vicious rural constabulary. Both carried on a love-hate relationship with the United States, which had lately occupied their countries. Washington, which first smiled upon the two *caudillos* beneficently for the "protection" they gave big business, covertly aided their enemies when they began to flounder in senility. Both despots were virtually illiterate, glorified "progress" through "science," built roads, spacious esplanades, factories and arsenals on a lordly scale, and patronized the worst imported vulgarity in the arts. Both were too afraid of competition to groom capable successors, so that when they fell, a period of nationwide lawlessness followed inevitably.

We have seen Díaz as an effective guerrilla leader in his native Oaxaca during the wars of the Reform, and as one of the ablest commanders in the struggle to eject the French. What happened to change his course? Unfortunately, when Maximilian was defeated at Querétaro and the victorious republican government returned to Mexico City, Juárez' suspicion of his ambitious young general's loyalty was aroused. He greeted him coldly and gave a less successful commander preferential treatment. If indeed Juárez made the prescient remark that "Díaz is a man who kills while weeping," it may have gotten back to Díaz. The Oaxacan was not a man to forget a slight. "Properly handled," Parkes observes, "Díaz might have remained loyal.... By treating Díaz as though he were dangerous, Juárez encouraged him to become so." The result was that after the election of 1871 Díaz accused the government of having rigged the election, demanded less government and more liberty, and—ironically, in the light of his later career—came out for curbing the power of the executive and of the President's right to succeed himself in office.

When Lerdo sought reelection in 1876, after saying No to American railroad tycoons who had asked permission to extend their lines south from Texas, Díaz knew that his moment had come. He now had no trouble recruiting men and supplies in the United States. One of his lieutenants seized Matamoros across the border. He himself slipped into Oaxaca in disguise by way of Havana and Veracruz, and organized a striking force in his native state. When the Lerdistas in the capital split over the succession problem, Díaz marched in and had himself declared provisional President. From then on until 1911 he was the master of Mexico.

How did Díaz manage to perpetuate his rule for those thirty-five terrible years? What created the almost universally held illusion in the rest of the world that Mexico was enjoying a golden age of peace, prosperity and progress? [19] Who, beside the dictator himself, was responsible for the ugly reality?

When the third of his three armed rebellions against the constitutional government of the Reform succeeded in 1876, Díaz took the leaders of his motley force—bandits, criminals, and soldiers disgruntled with Juárez' anticlerical, antimilitarist policies—and put them in charge of the state governments. There, so long as they remained loyal to him (and all but a very few did), they were permitted to plunder their provinces and execute their enemies. Their rewards came in the form of charters with cash subsidies permitting them to organize companies and build railroads. (The amount of $40 million was appropriated for these railroad subsidies alone during Díaz' first four years in office.) With this money in

[19] One perceptive reporter of the time saw through it. *Barbarous Mexico,* by John Kenneth Turner, published in Chicago in 1911 by Charles H. Kerr & Co., is the frightening record of two trips through Díaz-land in 1908 and 1909 by a newspaperman who posed as an investor. Since he exposed just as mercilessly the role of American business and government in supporting the Díaz regime, few of Turner's articles ever appeared in the newspapers which shared the illusion of the despot's benevolence. The title of his book, he states at the outset, "is intended to apply to Mexico's form of government rather than to its people."

their pockets the governors were free to carry out their assignments with a labor force either enslaved or paid starvation wages. When the Indians refused to move off their lands or be impressed into service, the lands were seized and the Indians were either hunted down and killed or deported in chains to other parts of Mexico.

When, for example, the Yaquis of Sonora—long known as the strongest, soberest, most industrious of Indians—took to the mountains to escape peonage, an army was sent north to subjugate them. Soldiers received $100 for every pair of ears that proved a Yaqui killed. Those who surrendered with their families on promises of amnesty were marched overland by the thousands to Veracruz, and from there transported in the holds of ships to Yucatán. Those who survived were bought for $65 a head by the two dozen or so henequen planters,[20] who had acquired the penninsula by this time, thanks to Díaz. There the Yaquis remained, sharing their slavery under the lash with the subjugated native Maya population, working under the tropical sun twelve hours a day on a diet of one meal of beans and rotten fish, locked up at night with their women in noisome, overcrowded prisons.

In other parts of Mexico, conditions were worse. In the notorious Valle Nacional in the state of Oaxaca, tobacco was cultivated by fifteen thousand slaves, 95 percent of whom died of disease, malnutrition or beatings every year. The dead (and the rebellious) were thrown to the alligators. Replacements were supplied by the *jefes políticos* and *enganchadores* (snarers) from all over Mexico.[21] The hated *jefe político*, who often paid as much as ten thousand dollars annually in rental fees for his lucrative job, sold his recalcitrant Indians into slavery. The *enganchador*, with the connivance of the government, kidnapped men, women and children of the lower classes off the streets of the villages and cities, and sold them to labor contractors. Raiding the pulque saloons of the capital for

[20] Every year, 250,000 pounds of henequen (sisal) were being exported from the port of Mérida to the American cordage trust by these henequen kings, at eight centavos a pound, the cost of production being less than a centavo. One of these "kings," Olegario Molina, had holdings of fifteen million acres in Yucatán and the neighboring Territory of Quintana Roo, where the slaves worked under conditions even more terrible. Some of the plantation owners lived in palaces in Mérida, but many lived abroad, and few ever troubled to visit their estates in person.

[21] "The Valle Nacional slave holder has discovered that it is cheaper to buy a slave for $45 and work and starve him to death in seven *months*, and then spend $45 for a fresh slave, than it is to give the first slave better food, work him less sorely and stretch out his life and toiling hours over a longer period." (*Barbarous Mexico*)

workers too drunk to resist was one means frequently employed.

State governors, federal henchmen, foreign favorites, and members of Díaz' own family were rewarded with more than slave labor, however. They were rewarded with land. The most desirable lands in the country, and not merely the Indians' *ejidos*, were registered, and when their owners could not prove ownership to the government's sly lawyers, they were evicted. Hundreds of thousands of small farmers thus lost their property.

Wealthy Americans, as well as the dictator's friends and henchmen, were able to acquire vast acreage for almost nothing. William Randolph Hearst, and Harrison Gray Otis, owner of the *Los Angeles Times*, each acquired cattle ranches of over a million acres in Chihuahua; their papers would probably have beatified Díaz anyway. Had the dictator not already given Mexico's mines and smelters to the Guggenheims? ... Mexico's best rubber lands to the Inter-Continental Rubber Company? ... the monopoly of beet sugar to the American Sugar Trust? ... control over the much-vaunted National Railways to E. H. Harriman? ... and 90 percent of the nation's wholesale and retail trade in oil to Rockefeller's Standard Oil of New Jersey?

Imperialism and Downfall

But the billion-dollar American investment in Mexico, which by 1910 exceeded the total capital owned by the Mexicans themselves, began to be threatened in the last Díaz decade by that 10 percent which the dictator withheld. Just as he played off the state governors against one another, so he began to favor the Spanish, the French and especially the British capitalists at the expense of the Americans. The Spanish controlled the tobacco in Valle Nacional and elsewhere. The French were granted a monopoly of the textile industry. The British, headed by Lord Cowdray, whose firm had been invited in to drain Lake Texcoco, began to receive preferential treatment in the oil fields of Tampico over the Doheny and Rockefeller interests already there. Díaz was taking the chance that Uncle Sam might no longer smile, that instead of singing the tyrants' praises and persecuting his political enemies who escaped across the Rio Grande, he might provide a haven for the refugees and even arm them.

But as long as the dictator had no opposition on Mexican soil, why should he worry about that? It was his boast that a mule train laden with gold could be driven across the country in broad daylight without a nugget being stolen. His *rurales* controlled the countryside, and his secret police and elaborate spying apparatus watched over the cities and ports. Besides, weren't such courageous critics of his regime as Tomás Sarábia, Antonio Villarreal, and the brothers Flores Magón languishing in American prisons on trumped-up charges? And weren't American statesmen from Theodore Roosevelt and President William Howard Taft to William Jennings Bryan and Elihu Root on record in his behalf? [22]

If Díaz, like the Medicis, had used even a part of his power to make Mexico a leader in the arts and sciences, history might excuse his despotism—at least in part. But this was not the case. Not a single inventive work in any of the arts was produced under the dictatorship. Díaz himself was a man without culture, almost an illiterate; he read only his press clippings; and he surrounded himself with sycophants. In the beginning these were mestizos like himself; later on they were Creole intellectuals who professed to follow the positivist philosophies of Comte and Spencer and called themselves *científicos*. Among their number were Rafael Reyes Spindola, owner and editor of *El Imparciál;* Francisco Bulnes, a historian-apologist for reaction and belittler of Juárez, who led the spurious "opposition" in Congress; and Romero Rubio, who controlled the gambling houses and the police in the capital and gave his teen-age daughter to the 51-year-old dictator in marriage.

Científico doctrine had it that Mexico should be governed by white men, that the Indian was a beast of burden, and that the country could progress only by importing foreign capital and Anglo-Saxon institutions. Many were, or became, millionaires, and as intellectuals they rationalized their wealth as well as their dependence upon Díaz. Only two had real stature. Justo Sierra, Minister of Education and reviver of the moribund National University, sang the joys of liberty—under the aegis of what he called "spontaneous Caesarism"—but he rejected the dogmas of both positivism and Catholicism and sheltered such inquiring young minds as Antonio Caso, José Vasconcelos, and Alfonso Reyes under his wing. José Yves Limantour, the son of a French plunger from San Francisco, who had made a fortune when the Church holdings were broken up under Juárez, was, like Sierra, personally honest, but he felt none

[22] He was "to be held up to the hero worship of mankind," according to Root. "The Moses and Joshua of his people," Andrew Carnegie called Díaz. Even Leo Tolstoi, who should have known better, called him admiringly a "prodigy of nature." The American Peace Society made Díaz an honorary vice-president for having brought peace to Mexico!

of the latter's need to decry the pyramiding of monopolistic wealth. As a banker, he believed that, given a balanced budget, all other problems in Mexico would solve themselves. As the Treasury Minister, who had nationalized the railways, Limantour did not think it improper that the banking firm in which his brother was a partner should buy up the stock and then sell it back to the government at a profit; nor that the *científicos* should award contracts for public works to companies they controlled, collecting legal fees for their services in the bargain; nor that in the state of Mexico where he lived 84 percent of the people were engaged in farming, while 99.5 percent owned no land at all.

Still less did it concern Porfirio Díaz that in his own state of Oaxaca, where 99.8 percent of the people had no land, the acreage of the principal haciendas ranged from 2,500 acres to 193,000. This ghastly imbalance had become the norm. And only a man who was cruel, hypocritical, stupid or cowardly could have presided over it with equanimity. Díaz was all four. As a child he had revenged himself on a favored brother by filling his nostrils with gunpowder while he slept and touching a match to it; and years later, when he had installed that same brother, by then a drunkard, in the governorship of Oaxaca and an uprising in Juchitán had killed him, Porfirio Díaz revenged his death by having his troops surround that city during a band concert and massacre everyone listening to the music in the central square.

His hypocrisy was illustrated by his treatment of Juárez, the schoolteacher of his boyhood who had given him his opportunity to rise through the military service. First Díaz encouraged Bulnes to blacken Juárez' reputation; but later, when he needed a symbol of virtue to hide behind, he had an extravagant monument erected in honor of the great man on the capital's Alameda Park and at its dedication he wept crocodile tears while eulogizing his "great teacher."

Díaz' essential stupidity and cowardice did not become a matter of public knowledge until the weeks before he fell. Up to then he could not believe that the people of Mexico did not love him, much less that he could be ousted by the little man with a squeaky voice and no arms or resources whom he referred to scornfully as an "imbecile." In a panic, Díaz told Limantour to give the people what they wanted. Everything that Francisco Madero asked for they could have—no reelection, effective suffrage, sale of the public lands to small buyers on reasonable terms, even an auction of the unproductive parts of the vast privately owned tracts. So why did the people continue to march and mill about in the streets? What did they want? When he heard that his resignation was what they wanted, he cowered in his shuttered library on Calle Cadena and gave one last desperate order. Machine guns were mounted on the roof of the National Palace in the Zócalo, where an unarmed crowd had assembled, and at a signal they fired blindly into the packed square, killing and wounding hundreds. When only a downpour of rain dispersed the enraged survivors, Porfirio Díaz knew that he was done for. Nursing a toothache, the old man signed his resignation, crept into a waiting carriage, donned an appropriate disguise, and slunk out of the city to a railroad siding where General Victoriana Huerta was waiting with an armored train to conduct him to Veracruz. The slow boat to Paris had been waiting a long time.

4

THE REVOLUTION
(1910-1924)

In countries plagued by autocracy, and therefore partial to the violent remedies which alone appear to affect this dread disease— France, Russia, Mexico, for example—there have been revolts, rebellions, *coups d'état,* and changes of the palace guard, but only one real Revolution. The catacylsmic events of 1789–92 in France were a watershed not only for that country but for Europe; none of the countless overturns since have changed the expression of either France or its neighbors. The equally cataclysmic events of 1914–17 in Russia unsettled neighboring China as drastically, and the rest of the world is still reacting one way or another to the shock waves. The similarly melodramatic events of 1910–20 in Mexico are certainly *the* Revolution as far as Mexico is concerned, but—so far at least—the doctrines spawned by it have not proved exportable. Which may, in part, be a reflection of a milieu too primitive to have nurtured ideologies, though it could also be regarded as a tribute to a people by instinct too civilized to tolerate fanatical ideologues.

In terms of our century, the Mexican Revolution of 1910–24 enjoys a special primacy. It was the first successful peasant uprising against a landed oligarchy. It was the first nationwide proletarian revolt against industrial capitalism. And it was the first revolt against Big Power imperialism on the part of an underdeveloped country. As such, it influenced the later Russian Revolution to a considerable extent. And its "positive" consequences—social security, joint capital-labor management, agriculture under partial control of farm-producers' cooperatives, and in embryo all the features of the welfare state—have been a generic part of the evolution of most Western societies ever since.

Phase One: Madero, Apostle and Martyr

It is still not recognized, and perhaps least of all in Mexico itself, that Francisco I. Madero was the real hero of the Mexican Revolution. The other leaders in the great drama, with their sanctionings of various forms of social extermination, did the obvious in terms of self-interest. Madero alone acted *against* his personal and class interests, believing in the rights of all men, and in principle. As the son of a millionaire *hacendado*, he had every reason to support Díaz and the status quo. As the first leader of the Revolution, he had every interest in executing his enemies—which he consistently refused to do. As a politician, he could have remained in power indefinitely had he brushed aside constitutional government and given the Zapatistas what they demanded without legal procedures. But as a genuine democrat, Madero felt he had to oppose the extremism of both the Victoriano Huertas and the Zapatas. His rise, triumph and downfall have all the elements of Greek tragedy. Fate (the times, Mexico's immaturity, an American ambassador's perfidy) overcame him. Morelos and Juárez had as much integrity, but the one was cruel and the other righteous. Madero is of the order of Lincoln and Gandhi.

Which is not to say that Díaz' little "imbecile" from Coahuila with the squeaky voice was without weaknesses; he had many. Yet, somehow, these were weaknesses that made the strength of others look ugly. He was unaware, in the beginning, that Mexico needed a thorough social revolution, or wanted one. He refused to believe that even in the Mexico emerging out of Díaz' police state, compromise would necessarily favor evil men or moderation be equated with cowardice. He underestimated the ambitions and cupidity of most men, including those of his own ubiquitous family.

When Evaristo Madero, Francisco's grandfather, died in 1911, he had fourteen children, thirty-four grandchildren and fifty-six great-grandchildren, and was reputed to be one of the ten richest men in Mexico. His fortune, founded on the cutoff of cotton exports during the American Civil War, was diversified by 1900 into rolling mills and refineries, cattle and guayule haciendas, wine distilleries and banking. Evaristo Madero served one term as Governor of

Coahuila (1880–84), but the stimulus he gave to education and culture aroused the suspicions of the dictator, who replaced him with a forceful young loyalist, Gen. Bernardo Reyes. Thereafter the Madero family remained out of politics, confining its liberal and humanitarian inclinations to the administration of its vast northern estates, and by the time Francisco Indalecio, the first of fifteen children born to Francisco Madero, Sr., was old enough to go to school, it was natural that he would be sent away to the United States and Europe to acquire a progressive education rather than to the backward and reactionary capital of Porfirio Díaz.

Young Francisco had been a sickly child, introspective and inclined to enter the priesthood; he never grew to more than five feet two, but by the time he returned from his six years abroad, he was strong, an excellent horseman and swimmer, and with a physical courage to match the extreme sensitivity and idealism that were already his outstanding characteristics. His religious inclinations had shifted to spiritism and the study of oriental philosophies. He was particularly impressed with the Hindu *Bhagavad-Gita*, which denies material values and counsels the achievement of peace and spiritual salvation without hatred for one's enemies—but through unremitting action. Returning to a share in the administration of the family estates, young Francisco at once put these ideas into action by pioneering in the latest agricultural and industrial methods, raising the salaries and improving the working conditions of his labor, providing schools for the young and dispensaries for the sick, and (with his wife, Sara, who shared his missionary spirit and was equally loved by their dependents) personally caring in his own home for those who needed special therapy or guidance.

Inevitably, Madero began to realize that charity, paternalism, and enlightened business-labor relations were not enough. Especially in a nation where their practice met with total resistance; and where 97 percent of the rural population now owned no land, and the other 833 *hacendados* were doing nothing for the nine million landless peasants who worked their estates and kept them in a state of ignorant, enforced peonage. So in 1905 Francisco Madero entered politics, much to the dismay of his family at first. He founded a newspaper in Coahuila, *El Democrata*, and he helped organize a state party dedicated to the principle of "No Reelection" for Díaz' lackeys.

By 1908 Madero had disassociated his movement from the extremist Liberal Party, directed from abroad by the Flores Magón brothers, who favored anarcho-syndicalism; from the Pure Liberal Party, whose emphasis was mainly anticlerical; and from the followers of General Bernardo Reyes, the exiled rightist who was concerned only to replace Díaz in power. An imprudent interview, given to James Creelman by the aged dictator, indicated that Díaz would not seek reelection and would welcome the appearance of an opposition party. This aroused nationwide expectations of change and stimulated Madero to begin work on a book that would quickly become a best seller, *The Presidential Succession in 1910.* To his father's objections he had written prophetically, "One ought not to consider personal losses . . . when he is treating . . . of the Fatherland for which it is necessary to be resolved to sacrifice even one's life." To his grandfather, Don Evaristo, who had written his "beloved grandson" that "you ought to know that redeemers end up crucified," he replied: "I have seen so clearly the hand of Providence protecting our family that I firmly believe that the protection has been given us not only to enjoy it, but to extend its benefits." [1] Madero's book contrasted Juárez' enlightenment and respect for the law with the corruption of absolute power as exercised by Santa Anna and Díaz; but for tactical reasons it concentrated its fire on Reyes and on Ramón Corrál, the enslaver of the Yaquis, who as vice-presidential candidate was being groomed to succeed the dictator. Madero criticized inequities in land, the neglect of education, and concessions to foreign exploiters, but his emphasis was on the conquest of democratic power by peaceful means. So obvious were the disinterestedness, humanity and nobility of the author, which came through on every page, that Madero became a national figure overnight, the recognized leader of the opposition to Díaz.

In June of 1909, Madero began to stump the country. He was not a great orator, but his sincerity, lucidity, and valor in the face of many attempts to prevent him from being heard, won over his audiences. By 1910 he was the popular choice to head the Anti-Reelectionist ticket and in April of that year he won the party's nomination.

An interview with President Díaz was now arranged, and Madero came away from it convinced that nothing short of revolution would force the dictator to step down. By this time Madero's family had rallied to his support, and with their financial assistance he visited twenty-two of the twenty-seven states. Díaz, thoroughly alarmed at last, had him arrested in Monterrey. By election day Madero was transferred to the jail in San Luis Potosí. Five thousand other Maderistas were seized, and rebellions broke out in Yucatán and elsewhere.

[1] Quoted in Stanley R. Ross, *Francisco I. Madero: Apostle of Mexican Democracy*. New York, Columbia University Press, 1955.

The expected news that Díaz and Corrál had "won" prompted Limantour to intercede for Madero's conditional release, but plans for a national uprising had already been laid. On October 7, friends spirited Madero across the border at Laredo, where he issued the statement, "I am here because citizens of the United States are free and their liberties are guaranteed by the Constitution and maintained unmolested. In Mexico it is different." He announced that he was assuming the provisional presidency of Mexico "until the public shall choose their government according to law," and he published the Plan of San Luis Potosí as the manifesto of the Revolution.

The situation on both sides of the border, preceding Madero's reentry into Mexico and the abortive attack on Casas Grandes March 5, was confusing. Who was supporting the revolt, and in whose behalf would it be won?

To Madero's father in San Antonio, the Revolution was being supported by people of "quality." "The monied interests of Mexico are taking an active part," he wrote, but added significantly, "my son is fighting the battle of the exile and the forgotten man." Characteristically Venustiano Carranza, the Maderist Senator from Coahuila, was waiting to see whether Madero would succeed before committing his resources. To Pascual Orozco, the leader of the Maderist guerrillas in Chihuahua, it was a personal matter; he would fight ably for Madero if it would enable him to seize the state governorship. Orozco's lieutenant in charge of the "bandits," Francisco Villa, was temperamentally on the side of the underdog, having taken to the hills years before after shooting the owner of a hacienda who had raped his sister; he admired Madero and distrusted Orozco. Far to the south, in the state of Morelos, Emiliano Zapata was organizing peons who had escaped from the sugar plantations; his mounted bands of "brigands" were already burning some of the haciendas around Cuernavaca, slaying the landowners and the *rurales*, and demanding land as their share in the revolution. In Yucatán and Puebla small groups of Maderists were making desperate and uncoordinated attacks on the local governments.

Porfirio Díaz, meanwhile, had ordered the seizure of the Madero estates, and was deploying his peace-corrupted armies in ten different directions to take care of the outbreaks. But he was beginning to discover that his soldiers were unreliable and his commanders too old and inured to city life to respond effectively.

The attitude of the United States was ambiguous. On the one hand, it was felt that the dictator and his pro-British *científicos* had outlived their usefulness and that any replacement might prove less sympathetic to Lord Cowdray. On the other hand, it was recognized that Madero was "unreliable" and that some of his supporters were actually "dangerous." The result was neutrality in the conflict, which in the long run aided the rebel cause; in the short run, however, it was the threat of Madero's arrest by American authorities on Díaz' demand that forced Madero out of Texas prematurely, and almost to his death.

The Battle of Casas Grandes was not a total loss. The valor of the wounded Madero endeared him even more to Mexico. Armed rebellions continued to spread in the south; and the federal troops failed to pursue Pascual Orozco, with the result that he and Villa were permitted to envelop the frontier city of Ciudad Juárez on April 18 and take it by storm May 10.

The fall of Ciudad Juárez was the beginning of the end for Díaz. By the gas headlamps of a car in the border customshouse a treaty was signed with the Federal Government on May 21, 1911. Under its provisions Díaz and Corrál agreed to resign by month's end; Francisco de la Barra, the Ambassador to Washington, would serve as interim President until general elections could be held; hostilities would cease, the revolutionary forces would disband, and the interim government would satisfy popular demands and indemnify damages caused by the Revolution. Díaz had no alternative; by May 21, Zapata had taken Cuernavaca, Cuautla and all the territory west to Chilpancingo. Two thirds of Mexico was in rebel hands. Why, then, did Madero settle for so little? He was concerned over the growing violence. In Ciudad Juárez he had saved the captured general from execution at the risk of his own life. Orozco had tricked Villa into arresting him, and that time Madero had saved himself only by rushing out of the tent and appealing to the troops. He sympathized with the Zapatistas' clamor for bread and land, but he wanted their claims to be satisfied legally. He wanted constitutional government to emerge out of an orderly transition of power. He believed that following elections the federal forces would serve his own government loyally. He trusted De la Barra. He was sure that the Mexican people were ready for democracy.

Madero took the train for the capital on June 1. Everywhere along the way he was received with the wildest enthusiasm. A severe earthquake in the capital the morning of June 7 didn't interfere in the least with the wild welcome he received. A hundred thousand people cheered deliriously as he passed along the Paseo de la Reforma on his way to the Palace. The Revolution had triumphed.

But had it? Its leader, the man the people were cheering, did not occupy the presidential chair. "The interim period," Ross comments, "proved to be a grave political error. What was so necessary for the reestablishment of peace was a strong government animated by a desire to satisfy the aspirations of the people. Instead, the interim period was one of ambiguity and confusion, with the government simply drifting.... During those few months, deep and dangerous divisions developed among the revolutionary chiefs." [2] In a sense victory had come too quickly. There was no cohesive party with a consistent revolutionary philosophy. A few Maderists were included in De la Barra's cabinet, but they were in a minority. Madero himself was robbed of his authority by the demands flooding in upon him from all sides—demands which he still had no power to satisfy. Perhaps the biggest error of all had been to leave the federal army intact while disbanding the revolutionary forces. The *rurales* and *jefes políticos* had fled. In some provinces the disbanded revolutionaries seized power. In others they became outlaw gangs, preying on the countryside. Should the federal army be deployed against them? Madero was caught in an angry cross fire. His friends on the left attacked him for not supporting popular demands for land, higher wages, local political control. His enemies on the right demanded federal intervention to restore "law and order."

Under the circumstances Madero acted with admirable energy and characteristic optimism. While still in Ciudad Juárez, he had promised the Yaquis of Sonora to repatriate them and restore their stolen *ejido* lands. Representing the government, he carried through these promises by signing a treaty with the tribes on September 1, providing interim relief and tax exemption for thirty years. Other disaffected peoples, faring less well, felt themselves betrayed. The problem of what to do with Zapata was the most serious.

Zapata and his staff came to the capital to confer with Madero early in June, and on June 12, Madero was received by the revolutionary leader at Cortés' Palace in Cuernavaca. Madero agreed to restore the communal lands as soon as it could be done within the law, and Zapata agreed to disband his irregulars. But the guerrilla leader, however much he may have trusted Madero, was aware that the interim government, whose newspapers were calling him the "Modern Attila" and charging that he planned a new insurrection, might take advantage of him if he disarmed altogether. The negotiations were prolonged and acrimonious, and Zapata's suspicions were not mollified when De la Barra sent an army under General Huerta

[2] Ross, *op. cit.*

to Cuernavaca. The Zapatistas responded by seizing several nearby towns. Madero denounced this move and went to Cuautla, where he assured Zapata that "our enemies do not resign themselves to the defeat they have suffered." He appealed once more to the insurgent leader to discharge his soldiers. Zapata complied—or seemed to. But no sooner had Madero returned to the capital when Huerta broke the truce and advanced on Cuautla. Infuriated, Madero broke with De la Barra, charging that the Zapatistas would now have good reason to believe that he had visited them in Morelos at the risk of his life in order "to betray them." Zapata resumed the offensive, the federal forces were thrown back, and Huerta accused Madero of hampering his efforts to restore order.

The elections took place on schedule the first week of October, 1911, and even Henry Lane Wilson, the American Ambassador who shared De la Barra's aversion to Madero, reported that "order prevailed everywhere." They were, in fact, the cleanest, most democratic elections in Mexico's history, and Madero received 19,997 votes in the electoral college to 148 for all other candidates. General Reyes, whom Madero had permitted to return to Mexico with the agreement that he would not run but would accept the Ministry of War if Madero won, had broken his promise; after being stoned in Mexico City by an angry crowd, he retired into exile again. José María Piño Suarez of Yucatán was elected Vice President by a narrow margin over De la Barra and several other candidates.

The interim government of De la Barra, the so-called "White President," had lasted five months and ten days. The presidency of Francisco Madero lasted a year and three months. The same problems that had plagued Madero during De la Barra's incumbency continued to plague him in the National Palace. Never has a democratic ruler exercised more conscientious devotion to his task, greater consistency, more fairness, more respect for the law; but it seemed as though Madero's very virtues were his undoing. The press was given complete freedom, and abused it by vilifying Madero; he was accused of practicing nepotism, his sanity was questioned, his wife was insulted. "Prostituting their sacred trust, they (the press) exaggerated, distorted, and engaged in sheer fantasy. Revolts were enthusiastically reported, and disorders were magnified. The old rumors of foreign influence in the revolution were revived. The government was attacked both for not solving the agrarian problem and for intending to solve it!" [3]

[3] Ross, *op. cit.*

Madero's generosity and forgiveness were poorly repaid. The conservatives retained in the cabinet from the De la Barra regime fought the liberals constantly. General Reyes came back into the country through Texas, tried to foment an armed rebellion, and when few joined it, surrendered and was imprisoned in the capital. Felix Díaz, the deposed dictator's nephew, seized Veracruz and then surrendered it; Madero was advised to execute him for treason, but Díaz too was imprisoned in the capital.

Many efforts were made to deal with the agrarian question. Madero admitted that "one of the greatest national necessities is ... to divide the great properties and to encourage small agriculture," and he moved in this direction, but too slowly. A start was made in restoring the *ejidos* to those from whom they had been seized. Millions of acres of illegally alienated national lands were recovered by the government and a plan was made to parcel them out in small lots. The gadfly of the Revolution, Luis Cabrera, attacked this policy of peace-first-economic-reforms-later in a speech in the Chamber of Deputies; he demanded that the Executive be given power to expropriate *private* lands to satisfy the land-hungry peasants. The reactionary press screamed as though this had already been done.

Labor was similarly encouraged to make its presence felt. Workers were permitted to organize and strike for the first time. A radical trade-union leadership began to develop.

Appropriations for education were almost doubled. The government established rural schools where none had existed. Food was provided for poor students in the capital. Indian education was suggested for the first time by Alberto J. Pani, Sub-Secretary of Public Instruction.

During 1912 there were rebellions in both the south and the north. With the President's permission but not his concurrence, Zapata had published his Plan of Ayala within a month of Madero's assuming the presidency. It demanded that peasants occupy at once the lands of which they had been despoiled, and that a third of the estates remaining in private hands be expropriated with indemnification—those refusing to comply forfeiting everything. By January 19, the Zapatistas had pillaged and torn up so much railroad track that martial law had to be declared in Morelos, Guerrero, Tlaxcala and parts of the states of Puebla and Mexico. Goaded by the Right, Madero sent a federal army under Gen. Juvencio Robles into the area and Robles on his own initiative embarked upon a campaign of extermination. Madero recalled him and sent in his place Gen. Felipe Angeles, Director of the Military College and a revolutionary at heart; Angeles failed to win over Zapata but he held him in check. Meanwhile, in Chihuahua, Pascual Orozco seized Ciudad Juárez again, hinting that the object this time was to replace Madero with a more uncompromising reformer; actually Orozco had the backing of the big landowners, cattle barons and mining interests. Villa, who recognized this, opposed him. Madero dispatched a federal army north to assist Villa, reluctantly giving its command to General Huerta. Villa and Huerta quarreled, and Villa was sent to the capital under arrest. Huerta pursued Orozco relentlessly, retaking Ciudad Juárez in mid-August. Madero had lost prestige with the northern radicals and was becoming dangerously beholden to the old Díaz military clique.

At this juncture Governor Venustiano Carranza of Coahuila called an emergency meeting of the four northern governors—was he too preparing to rebel? No one was sure.

The Ten Tragic Days

As the wolves began to close in on Madero in January of 1913, his position was further embarrassed by the conduct of his brother Gustavo, and by that of the American Ambassador, Henry Lane Wilson. The President's aggressive younger brother had been the chief money raiser on the road to power; now he manipulated the government's forces in Congress and tried to counter the influence of the Right. It had been Gustavo's "terrorist mob," Madero's enemies said, who had stoned General Reyes' supporters in the streets. The Porra ("Stick"), as the gang was called, was repudiated by the government party, but the overzealous Gustavo Madero had become such a political liability to the President by this time that Madero agreed to send him on an honorary mission to Japan.

Madero would have liked to send Henry Lane Wilson at least as far away, but he contented himself with the thought that by March 4 the newly elected liberal Woodrow Wilson would be in the White House and would withdraw President Taft's hated appointee. Ambassador Wilson was meanwhile directing all his efforts to securing the overthrow of Madero before that time should come. Whether or not it was true that the Ambassador was associated with the Guggenheim mining interests, traditionally rivals of the Madero family in Coahuila, it was true that his background as a banker and real estate speculator perfectly ill-fitted him for his post as ambassador to a revolutionary government. Thin-lipped, wearing a toupee, he looked disapprovingly at the idealistic President, regarding him as a crackpot, at best a naïve amateur in the realm of "realistic" politics. Wilson hated the President as soon as it became clear to him that Madero would not give favors to American capital. He wrote inaccurate and inflammatory reports to the State Department in Washington. He harassed the Mexican Government with constant protests and claims for indemnity. He pressed the claims of all other nationals—except the rival British—though they were none of his business. He denounced the "discriminatory and confiscatory" oil tax—a tax of three centavos a barrel! When Orozco was making his bid for power, Wilson cabled the State Department on behalf of the American Colony Committee for a "self-defense" requisition of 1,000 Krag-Jorgenson rifles and 250,000 cartridges, two days later doubling the number of guns requested and asking for 1,000,000 rounds of ammunition—requests which were not granted. When he discovered that Madero was preparing to tell Woodrow Wilson that the U.S. ambassador was *persona non grata*, the officious envoy stepped up his efforts to force Madero out.

When the conspiracy was hatched, it was typical that everybody knew about it except Madero. Gustavo, hearing about it in Veracruz, canceled his trip to Japan and rushed back to the capital to warn his brother that Generals Díaz and Reyes would be released as the first step in the *golpe*. President Madero, though handed a list of every officer involved, handed it back with his customary benign smile and the jocular comment that only the question mark after Huerta's name was a mistake. ("Pancho doesn't believe it!" said the despairing Gustavo to his friends next day.)

The conspirators, hearing that word had leaked out, struck without further delay.

Before dawn on February 9, the two mutinous generals were released from their cells, and columns of soldiers under their orders converged on the National Palace and arrested Gustavo Madero. The situation seemed to be saved, however, when Gen. Lauro Villár, the military commander there, alertly recaptured the Palace and released the President's brother. General Reyes was killed in the Zócalo during this skirmish, as were some five hundred civilian bystanders. General Díaz retreated to the Ciudadella, the capital's low-lying arsenal, a few blocks to the southwest.

It was typical again of Madero that, having been informed of these events in Chapultepec, and advised to remove the government to a safe place in the loyal countryside, he instead mounted his horse and rode down the Paseo to the Palace, smiling and waving to the onlookers and ignoring the sound of gunfire in the distance. It was also typical of him that once in the Palace he replaced the wounded loyalist Villár with Victoriano Huerta, about whose treachery he had already been warned.

Ten nightmarish days of sham battle now ensued between Díaz and his rebel soldiery, bottled up in the Ciudadella, and the "loyal" federal forces under Huerta in the Palace. The federals could easily have routed the rebels but were deliberately withheld by Huerta as he maneuvered for the opportunity to bring about Madero's downfall without appearing to have had a hand in it.[4]

Madero went to Cuernavaca and returned with General Angeles, whom he was advised to put in command, but didn't. Gustavo was now receiving so many reports of Huerta's secret negotiations with emissaries from Díaz in the Ciudadella that at one point he arrested the disloyal commander personally, covering him with his pistol for several hours, only to have the President return and insist on giving Huerta another chance to take the arsenal. Huerta, instead, was permitting food and arms to get through to the beleaguered rebels.

The embattled city, meanwhile, presented an appalling spectacle. Day and night it was raked by desultory cannon and machine-gun bursts in which thousands, mostly spectators, were killed. Decomposing bodies and piles of uncollected garbage filled the streets. Epidemics of disease broke out. Gas and electric lines were severed. And in the eerie light of uncontrolled fires by night, escaped criminals from Belém prison, breached by artillery fire, looted and murdered at will.

The aimless confrontation could have had comic-opera aspects but for two factors. The nobility of the President's character, his bravery, and his naïveté, were now transparent. The infamy of the American Ambassador, who was now working night and day to trap him for the drunken Huerta in a spider's web of false claims and hypocritical appeals, was not revealed until later. What Henry Lane Wilson managed to bring about in those ten days of intrigue was far more reprehensible than what the American armies had done to Mexico in 1847, when the struggle for power had been quite open and Mexico's leaders had been corrupt and treacherous; and the consequences of Ambassador Wilson's malign activities were in the long run far more poisoning to the United States' reputation south of the Rio Grande. The Ambassador accurately reported the substance of

---

[4] Edward Bell, an American eyewitness, toted up the immense superiority in men and arms at Huerta's disposal and stated categorically that Madero's commander could have taken the Ciudadella "in any designated half hour." (Edward I. Bell, *The Political Shame of Mexico*. McBride, Nast & Co., 1914.)

Huerta's intrigues to Washington—*but not to Madero*. Wilson visited the Ciudadella, encouraging the rebels to hold out, and did nothing to secure the release of John Kenneth Turner, the American writer who admired Madero and had exposed Porfirio Díaz. He transmitted to the State Department fabricated reports of popular sympathy for the rebels and uprisings all over the country, demanding American intervention to protect American nationals and their property, and mobilized as many of the envoys of other nations as he could to talk Madero into surrendering to Huerta. Then he spread so many rumors to the effect that the American fleet and army were on the point of intervening that Madero's foes in the Congress, and even some of his weaker supporters, joined in begging the President to resign to save Mexico from invasion. By the time Madero had become suspicious enough to wire President Taft for confirmation of this—and received in reply a telegram disavowing any such intention —it was too late. Finally, when Huerta had seized Madero and Piño Suarez in the Palace and tricked them into signing their resignations with the promise that they would be conducted to a waiting warship in Veracruz, Henry Lane Wilson could have saved their lives; instead he encouraged Huerta to murder them lest they return at some future time to save the Revolution.

The end came the afternoon of Tuesday, February 18, when Madero was seized at the Palace by a battalion of disloyal troops from Oaxaca under orders from Huerta. The President and Vice President were hustled to a nearby building, where they were soon joined by the loyal General Angeles, arrested while his batteries continued to shell the Ciudadella in defiance of Huerta's cease-fire. Gustavo Madero was taken to the Ciudadella, where at the foot of Morelos' statue he was lynched by a mob which first beat him, picked out his eyes and shot away his lower jaw.[5] The conspirators assembled in the American Embassy, where Wilson greeted Felix Díaz with the triumphant cry, "Long Live General Díaz, savior of Mexico!" When the diplomats asked the Ambassador what the fate of "poor Madero" would be, he is reported to have answered, "They will put him in a madhouse where he should always kept. As for the other [Piño Suarez], he is nothing but a scoundrel. So if they kill him it will be no great loss." And when the Chilean envoy protested, "We must not allow it," Wilson replied with supreme irony:

[5] The particular animus against Gustavo among the military, according to Bell, was that he alone "had stood in the way of men who had been making money through graft in army supplies and in other dealings with the government." (*The Political Shame of Mexico*.)

"We must not meddle in the internal affairs of Mexico!" [6] Later he brushed aside impassioned pleas for mercy from Señora Madero and from Vasconcelos. By the time the new American President, Woodrow Wilson, took office a few days later, and recalled the Ambassador in disgust after rejecting his frantic pleas to recognize Huerta, it was too late. On February 22, under the walls of the Federal Penitentiary, the Mexican President and Vice President were forced out of a car and shot.

News of the double assassination was received with disbelief and horror in the United States and everywhere else in the world. In the capital only Lord Cowdray, and the other British magnates who had supported Huerta from the start, rallied to the new despot's support. Already the Mexican nation was in arms to avenge the martyrs' deaths and reestablish the Revolution in blood and iron.

Phase Two: Villa, Zapata, and Carranza

The three military adventurers in whose hands the fate of Mexico rested for the next two years were quite incapable of ruling their country. Francisco Villa was a romantic primitive, a bandit-turned-revolutionary; he had the heart and generous inclinations of a Robin Hood, but when his temper got the best of him he disposed of his enemies with the summary methods of an Al Capone, suffering agonies of genuine outrage over those colleagues who mistook his sense of justice for cruelty or bad faith. Emiliano Zapata was another kind of primitive, a peasant realist with one unshakable idea: to see the Indians of southern Mexico take back by any means what history and the landlords had despoiled them of. Venustiano Carranza was a cynic, a bourgeois revolutionist with a colossal ego, resolved to use the Revolution to transfer the land, the resources and the power of the Díaz gang to a more modern band of overlords. Villa and Zapata were trusted only by their own followers: Carranza, who overcame them by playing them off against each other, was trusted by no one.

It was Carranza, the elderly governor of Coahuila, who struck first against the criminals entrenched in the capital. Huerta was not only looting the Treasury and employing thugs to murder anyone who spoke out against him, but he had become such an incurable drunkard that the affairs of state were now being conducted in saloons all over the capital. Carranza had a small army at his disposal

[6] Quoted in Ross, *op. cit.*

in the northern state, perhaps recruited to overthrow Madero on his own. When news of Madero's murder reached him, he placed his army under the command of Pablo González, a general soon to became famous for never winning a battle. Taking the clever title of First Chief of the Constitutionalist Army for himself, Carranza published the Plan of Guadalupe, calling for a national uprising to oust the usurper. Then he left Coahuila to the ravages of the federal troops and slipped over the mountains to Sonora on the Pacific, where a much more promising rebellion was under way, offering it his "leadership."

Sonora's rebels were enjoying the political guidance of Adolfo de la Huerta (no relation to Victoriano) and the military command of Álvaro Obregón, a general whose approach to war resembled that of Winfield Scott, and whose efficient lieutenants included Plutarco Elías Calles and Benjamín Hill. Under their auspices a Yaqui army was preparing to drive the federals south into Sinaloa.

In Chihuahua, the henchmen of the drunken Huerta had seized the Governor, Abrahám González, an old friend of Madero, and thrown him under the wheels of a train. Command of the Maderistas fell naturally to Francisco Villa, who had escaped from the jail in the capital to which Huerta had consigned him after the campaign against Orozco. Getting to the United States by boat, Villa began his conquest of Mexico with eight companions. They swam their horses across the Rio Grande, and Villa wasted no time recruiting an army among the *vaqueros* and cattle rustlers of Chihuahua he knew so well.

In the south, Zapata's wide-ranging insurgents were getting intellectual guidance from Antonio Díaz Soto y Gama, a socialist orator who overplayed his role of being a *pelado* in white cotton pants and sombrero by sporting the tight pants and supersombrero of a *charro*,[7] thereby depriving Zapatismo of some of its primitive authenticity.

But the spotlight for the time being was on Pancho Villa, whose *división del norte* was beginning to win a series of pitched battles, prepared by skillful guerrilla raids and climaxed by furious cavalry charges. Its progress south to the capital took place, when the tracks were not torn up, on the tops of boxcars, the soldiers potting jackrabbits and cooking on sheets of tin as they jolted along, sometimes accompanied by their women. Villa was both fortunate and unfor-

---

[7] The Mexican "cowboy," then as now an affectation of upper-class playboys. There was no affectation in Zapata himself. For an interesting account of his early life and the injustices he had the courage to oppose, see "Zapata," Lola E. Boyd, in *Americas*, September, 1968. Washington, D.C., Pan American Union.

tunate in having attached to his staff a young officer, Martín Luis Guzmán, who later become a great novelist and historian of the Revolution—fortunate in that none of the details of his flamboyant personality were lost, unfortunate in that his paranoia and terroristic lapses were preserved for posterity with as much precision.[8]

The portrait of Villa that unfolds is fascinating. We see Doroteo Arango, aged 16, avenging the rape of his 12-year-old sister by the *hacendado*. "Mama dear, it is my fate to suffer. I'll be the Number-One bandit in the country before I'll see my family dishonored. Give me your blessing, commend me to God, and He will know what to do." We see him returning a few months later as Robin Hood: "I gave my mother five thousand pesos and among my close relatives distributed four thousand more. I bought a tailor shop for a man named Antonio Retana who had very poor eyesight and a large and needy family.... In eight or ten months I had given away all that was left of the fifty thousand pesos." In 1910 "distrusting everyone and everything," we see him having first talks with Don Abrahám González, before that old revolutionary became a martyr to democracy. "He asked me to join the Revolution and fight for the oppressed people.... I felt the anxiety and hate built up in my soul during years of struggle and suffering change into the belief that the evil could be ended.... I understood without explanation—for nobody explains anything to the poor—how our country ... could become the inspiration for our best actions and the object of our finest sentiments. I heard the name of Francisco I. Madero for the first time. I learned to love and revere him, because he, a rich man, was devoted to the struggle for the poor and the oppressed."

We see Francisco next at Ciudad Juárez, learning his first lessons in war and politics. Here, on the eve of 1914's anonymous holocaust in the trenches, we find him enjoying hugely the last romantic battles. "The flashes of gunfire overpowered the mind. Señor! It took brave men to assault those positions. It was an honor to be in that battle, and a greater honor to have assembled that army of free men.... Señor, how sweet the cannons sound when they are firing on the enemy." Politics was an enigma to Francisco, but in the field where the only problems were how to divide the loot, how to "audit fairly" the captured gambling houses, to whom to give the craps and

---

[8] The novel, *The Eagle and the Serpent* (translated by Harriet de Onis, Dolphin-Doubleday paperback, 1965) was first published in 1928, and is auto-biographical-reportorial in character. *The Memoirs of Pancho Villa* (translated by Virginia H. Taylor, University of Texas Press, 1965) was published three decades later; it is based in part on five manuscript notebooks left by Villa and in part on Guzmán's memory of the campaigns in which he participated.

roulette concessions (Brother Hipolito got them), and how many prisoners to shoot, his conscience did not trouble him.

With Madero murdered and the action shifted to the civil war against the Huertistas, Villa was now in command of the Northern Division. In the great pitched battles at Torreón and Zacatecas and Paredón he was well served by his lieutenants. These included Tomás Urbino and Juan Medina; the dashing Maclovio Herrera, who hated Villa but bided his time; the noble ex-Federalist Felipe Angeles, who had served Madero to the end and who deployed Villa's artillery brilliantly; and the chief of Villa's *Dorados* (Golden Boys), Rodolfo Fierro. It was Fierro who had galloped after an escaping train at Tierra Blanca, leaping aboard to brake and capture it; it was Fierro who had disposed of such irritating critics as William Benton and Ambrose Bierce; and it was Fierro who nursed a swollen trigger finger after personally shooting three hundred Orozcista prisoners who were forced into the open from their pen and given a chance to escape over a wall fifty feet away:

Not for one minute did Fierro lose his precision of aim or his poise. He was firing at moving human targets, targets that jumped and slipped in pools of blood and amidst corpses stretched out in unbelievable postures, but he fired without other emotion than that of hitting or missing. He calculated the deflection caused by the wind, and corrected it with each shot. Some of the prisoners, crazed with terror, fell to their knees as they came through the gate. There the bullet laid them low. Others danced about grotesquely behind the shelter of the well-curb until the bullet cured them of their frenzy or they dropped wounded into the well. But nearly all rushed toward the adobe wall and tried to climb it over the warm, damp, steaming heaps of piled-up bodies. Some managed to dig their nails into the earth coping, but their hands, so avid of life, soon fell lifeless.... And to the shouts of one group and the other were added the voices of the soldiers stationed along the fences. The noise of the shooting, the marksmanship of Fierro, and the cries and frantic gestures of the condemned men had worked them up to a pitch of great excitement. The somersaults of the bodies as they fell in the death agony elicited loud exclamations of amusement from them, and they shouted, gesticulated, and gave peals of laughter as they fired into the mounds of bodies in which they saw the slightest evidence of life....

"Unsaddle my horse and make my bed," ordered Fierro. "I'm so tired I can't stand up,"... He knelt down and crossed himself... stretched out his feet until he touched his orderly. "Hey you. Don't you hear? One of these dead men is asking for water." "Yes, chief." "You get up and put a bullet through the snivelling son of a bitch. Let's see if he'll let me get some sleep then."... Under the shelter of the shed Fierro slept.[9]

The Convention of Aguascalientes

At Aguascalientes, where a convention was held in October of 1914, Villa met with Zapata's representatives and made a fateful decision. The success of both Constitutionalist armies—Villa's Northern Division driving down central Mexico, and Obregón's winning all its battles along the Pacific as it approached Guadalajara—had been made possible by the lifting of the American arms embargo. Woodrow Wilson, after recalling Henry Lane Wilson, had decided to support the Carranzistas in their civil war against Huerta, though there was a moment of incredible stupidity on the new American President's part when he tried to hasten Huerta's fall by seizing Veracruz. (This blunder, almost forcing Carranza to join hands with Madero's assassin, accomplished nothing except to rid Veracruz of malaria and intensify suspicion of American motives anew.) Now, at Aguascalientes, when Villa and Zapata decided to make a complete break with Carranza, the Revolution was split down the middle. For it was inevitable that Obregón, rather than take orders from the two unpredictable guerrilla chieftains, would throw his support to Carranza—for the time being, at least.

Villa had already threatened to shoot Obregón when the latter had visited his headquarters shortly before the Convention assembled. He had also become incensed with Carranza's advisers, who counseled the First Chief to keep the violent commander of the Northern Division in check lest the Revolution be discredited at home and abroad. "The chocolate drinkers and sweet-scented friends of the First Chief were a greater danger to the Revolution," Villa confided, "than Huerta's armies. Carranza still seemed to be a sincere Revolutionary, but his choice of advisers was a weakness." [10] Now he decided that Carranza was *not* a sincere revolutionary, and the fol-

[9] *The Eagle and the Serpent.*
[10] *Memoirs of Pancho Villa.*

lowing progression of Guzmán's descriptions of Carranza seem to
parallel Villa's thinking:

> His habit of combing his beard with his left hand, which
> he would put under the snowy cascade, palm outward and
> fingers curved, throwing back his head a little with each
> movement, seemed to indicate tranquil habits of thought
> which made unthinkable—so I thought at the time—all the
> violence and cruelty. . . . Within Don Venustiano's orbit
> intrigue and the lowest kind of sycophancy grew rank; the
> trimmers, the tale-bearers, the bootlickers, the panderers
> had the inside tracks. . . . By this time I had learned a lot
> and knew that Carranza, old and stubborn, would never
> change. He would go on responding to flattery, rather than
> acts, to servility rather than ability. . . . He took care to
> promote one of his own generals—even a defeated one—five
> or six days earlier to keep Villa a little lower on the roster.
> . . . Now [he] yielded to the temptation of becoming a
> despot, which is irresistible to the redeemers and liberators
> of Mexico.[11]

Guzmán saw the Convention of Aguascalientes as a turning point.
"The idealistic motive, which still persisted in a few, had practically
disappeared. It was not the Revolution that they were fighting for,
but its spoils." Only General Angeles in Villa's camp and Gen. Lucio
Blanco in Obregón's seemed disturbed; they and a handful of intellectuals like Guzmán, Alberto J. Pani, Luis Cabrera and José Vasconcelos, who gyrated in agonized indecision between the two camps.
Only they appeared to be aware of the tragedy of the Revolution—
"the moral impossibility of not supporting it, and the material and
psychological impossibility of achieving through it the regeneration
that would justify it." What had happened was that the Revolution,
"a movement essentially idealistic and generous had fallen into the
hands of the most selfish and the most unprincipled." Guzmán was
balanced enough, as a man and as a novelist, to appreciate the good
with the bad: He recognized the conflicting humanity and bestiality
in such a man as Francisco Villa, the statesmanship inherent in Carranza's position if not in his character, the power to reconcile Mexico
that lay behind Obregón's calm self-confidence and genial ruthlessness. The novelist Manuel Azuela and the painter José Clemente
Orozco, however, were too emotionally involved in the betrayals

11 *The Eagle and the Serpent.*

they witnessed in this period ever to present the leaders of the Revolution in any guise but as swindlers, hypocrites and cynical destroyers of humanity.[12]

The Convention of Aguascalientes was enlivened by several characteristic speeches on the part of the principals. Zapata's spokesman, Soto y Gama, called his chief the heir of Karl Marx, St. Francis of Assisi, and Jesus Christ. Villa, weeping copiously, proposed that he and Carranza simultaneously commit suicide as proof of their sincere desire to see the Revolution reunited. In the end, however, it was decided to nominate Eulálio Gutiérrez, a general from San Luis Potosí, provisional President of Mexico, and to seize the capital before Obregón and Carranza could reach it. Troop train after troop train rolled southward.

By the time the insolent officers of the Villista army had entered the capital and seized the finest houses, the Zapatistas were already there, peacefully quartered in Xochimilco, wandering about curiously along the abandoned boulevards, knocking at the doors and asking for something to eat—much to the surprise of the fearful city folk who had heard only lurid stories of their raids on the haciendas of Morelos. A historic meeting took place between Zapata and Villa in the National Palace, but their conversation, unfortunately, was not recorded; only a photograph memorialized the fantastic occasion. Nothing, except their respective spheres of influence, was decided. Zapata withdrew from the city, and Gutiérrez, surrounded by a band of ineffectual intellectuals wringing their hands over the mounting excesses of the Villistas, became in effect Villa's prisoner.

Villa's paranoia was becoming uncontrollable. He read an editorial that Obregón had written about him in one of Carranza's papers: "Pancho Villa is a traitor, an assassin, and a robber. He betrayed Sr. Madero in Ciudad Juárez and tried to assassinate him. . . . He tried to betray Huerta when this traitor was still faithful to Madero. He assassinated the Englishman William Benton. . . . He tried to

---

[12] Both master creators were from the state of Jalisco. Mariano Azuela's *The Underdogs* (Signet Books, 1963) which Orozco illustrated, presents an episode in one of Villa's campaigns entirely in terms of the corruption and brutality overtaking its protagonists:

"We've got to go on fighting."

"Good. But on what side?"

Demetrios, nonplussed, scratched his head.

"Villa? Obregón? Carranza? What's the difference. I love the revolution like a volcano in erruption; I love the revolution because it's the revolution!"

(For a discussion of Orozco's mural indictment, based on the months when he witnessed atrocities on both sides while attached as a cartoonist to Carranza's forces in Orizaba, see pp. 194–195.)

assassinate me.... He seized millions of pesos and dollars.... He
exploits gambling in his territory for the purpose of living a sinful
life and squandering money on himself and his family, etc., etc."
But Villa could think of no other way to protect himself from such
slanders than to assassinate those who were begging Gutiérrez to
get rid of him. He even went so far as to imprison a woman who
laughed at his advances in a restaurant. Gutiérrez charged him with
having ordered Fierro to shoot Guillermo García Aragón and David
Berlanga, and with threatening the life of Vasconcelos. Villa, hurt
to the quick, replied: "Señor, I can tell you nothing about the death
of General García Aragón, who was alive when my escort delivered
him to Zapata's men. As for David Berlanga, it was necessary to
shoot him so no one would think for a minute that you and I are
at odds." Finally, when Villa placed his political chief under "protective" house arrest, Gutiérrez said to him, "I want to be a long
way from you and Emiliano Zapata, Sr. General; I want to free
my conscience of the crimes the Villistas and Zapatistas are committing under my government. If I have no trains at my disposal,
I will even ride a burro to get away from you." It was hardly surprising that when Villa was called out of the city to confront a
military threat from Obregón, Gutiérrez seized the opportunity to
escape with his own troops and join the Carranzistas.

The end for Villa's bid to control Mexico was not short in com-
ing, but it was bloody. Fierro was defeated at Guadalajara and at
Tuxpan by Manuel Diéguez, one of Obregón's officers, early in 1915.
Villa was forced to abandon the capital and face Obregón at Celaya.
Felipe Angeles' good advice, to dispose of Carranza in Veracruz
first, went unheeded. General Angeles then advised him to harass
Obregón with guerrilla raids rather than to meet him head on:
"Obregón is cautious, Sr. General. He never attacks unless he is sure
of superiority in men and materials." But again Villa disregarded
Angeles' advice. Too late he wished he hadn't. "But I could not
curb my men. They crossed embankments and fields from which
came the fire of Yaqui infantrymen and machine guns; and they
kept on going when they saw that the enemy cavalry had sought
shelter in the city. Señor! What an error it was for my troops to
rush ahead, without artillery protection or the aid of infantry,
against an enemy who, if they were suffering great losses, were
inflicting still greater ones."

Obregón had already learned the first lesson of World War I:
His hundred machine guns were dug in behind barbed wire where
they couldn't be reached, and they stitched holes in the army of

Francisco Villa that April 7. (Villa himself tried to modernize, using an airplane as an artillery spotter, but it was shot down by rifle fire). With the loss of his artillery in the second battle of León, which lasted forty days, Villa was finished. He made an attempt to hold Sonora but was defeated in that northwest corner of Mexico by Obregón's lieutenant, Plutarco Elías Calles. Finally he retreated to the mountains of his native Chihuahua, where he could never be defeated [13] but where he became again the bandit chief he had been before the Revolution gave him the chance to become something for which nature had not intended him.

Emiliano Zapata's defeat in the south was left to Pablo González, who didn't tarnish his reputation for never winning a battle, but who did complete the ruin of the haciendas of Morelos, and in so doing deprived the Zapatistas of any nourishment in the fertile valleys they knew so well. In his native hills Zapata was as invincible as Villa in his, but González (on orders from Carranza) finally brought about his death by treachery, inviting the legendary peon chief to a parley and shooting him down from ambush. Even the hardheaded Zapata couldn't believe that his enemies would go so far to prove their "friendship" for him as to massacre their own soldiers before his eyes in cold blood.

Carranza was accounted for by assassination, too, but not until 1920. The four years during which he retained power uneasily were not without their political gains—at least on paper. Economically, the country was looted by Carranza's five hundred "revolutionary generals." (The real ones, Obregón and Calles, had retired into Sonora to await Carranza's expected demise.) Not since the days of Porfirio Díaz had the ordinary Mexican been exploited so shamelessly. Under the combined impact of the civil war and an epidemic of influenza, the population had been reduced by a million and a half. A new verb, *carrancear* (to steal), became popular. But back

---

[13] Even John J. ("Black Jack") Pershing, who later became commander of the American Expeditionary Force in France, failed. When President Wilson dispatched him across the border in 1916 to "bring back Villa, dead or alive," Pershing came back empty-handed. Villa's man had slain sixteen engineers on a train and burned the town of Columbus, New Mexico. Later, in 1920, the gift of a 25,000-acre hacienda in Durango came to him as a reward for his submission to provisional President De la Huerta. Villa farmed this ranch efficiently with tractors and threshing machines, but he was assassinated there in 1923, probably on orders from Calles, whose succession to the presidency he opposed. Felipe Angeles was executed by a firing squad in Chihuahua in 1918, on Carranza's orders. Fierro, after executing Villa's old comrade, Tomás Urbino (on Villa's orders) died in a quicksand—reputedly with his pockets too loaded with gold to struggle out.

in the fall of 1916, a constitutional convention had been held; the idea had been to de-fuse the ever-present Zapata menace, still the clamor of labor in the capital, and defy the United States, which was then turning hopefully toward Villa as a more viable protector of northern mining interests. At the convention Luis Cabrera proposed some radical laws, and because they were backed *in absentia* by General Obregón to embarrass Carranza, they were passed.

Under Article 123 the working class was given a more advanced bill of rights than any then obtaining in the world. The right to organize and strike was affirmed. An eight-hour day was promised. Advanced social benefits such as profit sharing and a minimum wage were all proclaimed in black and white. Article 27 implemented Juárez' Reform Laws by placing the rights of the Indians in their *ejidos* ahead of the usual liberal concept of absolute rights in private property; it also established the nation's inalienable ownership of water, minerals and oil—though concessions to develop these *temporarily* were conceded to foreigners. Under Article 120, Juárez' anticlerical legislation, prohibiting the Church to own property—which had been abrogated under Díaz—was reaffirmed. Marriage was made a civil contract. The odious foreign-born priests were outlawed. And any criticism of the state by the clergy was prohibited.

Little or nothing was done by Carranza to enforce these laws. But expectations were aroused among the Indians and the peasants. A powerful labor federation, the *Confederación Regional Obrera Mexicana* (CROM) was organized by Luis Morones in 1918, and the following year it spawned a Mexican Labor Party to sponsor Obregón's candidacy for the presidency.

Obregón came out of retirement only when it became clear that Carranza, who had been inaugurated President in March, 1917, had no intention of enforcing this Constitution for which the civil war had been fought—or of retiring. Effective suffrage still didn't exist, and without it there was nothing to prevent Carranza from placing his puppet, Ignácio Bonillas, the Ambassador to Washington, who was contemptuously referred to in Mexico as "Meester Bonillas," in line to succeed him. Nothing, that is, except Obregón, who mounted his rebellion upon Carranza's attempt to break a strike in Sonora. The Governor of Sonora was Adolfo de la Huerta, Obregón's young friend, who promptly declared the state's independence and dispatched an army south under Plutarco Elías Calles. Before it even reached the capital, Carranza was in flight to Veracruz with five million pesos from the national treasury. He never made it. First he was betrayed by his commander in Veracruz, and finally

he was murdered as he slept in a small Indian village whose cacique
had promised to guide him to safety.

Phase Three: Obregón

Álvaro Obregón's character is very well established by Villa, who
hated him before he was defeated by him. Villa describes him at the
moment when he had the Sonora general in his power:

> I ordered the captain at the door to go and bring an escort
> of twenty men to shoot Obregón if he did not reconsider
> his treacherous acts. To this, Obregón replied, "I don't
> know whether you really intend to shoot me, Señor Gen-
> erál. But I say only this: by shooting me you do me a
> favor and yourself great harm. I am in the Revolution to
> lose my life for glory while you are not in it to lose your
> honor. And have no doubt that if you shoot me, your honor
> will be lost."
> He said this calmly and without the slightest arro-
> gance....[14]

Vasconcelos told me once that Obregón had green eyes. According to Guzmán, there were golden glints in them "reminiscent of
a cat's; a continual smile spread over the rest of his face. He had
a way peculiarly his own of looking sidewise, as though the smile
of his eyes and that of the corners of his mouth were going to con-
verge in a lateral point situated in the same plane as his face. There
was nothing military about his appearance.... He affected untidiness
as though it were one of his campaign virtues." [15]

On the authority of the one-eyed Eduardo Hay, who served with
him, Obregón was of a serene temperament, untiring energy and
prodigious memory; tactically he drew the enemy out, made him
commit himself, like a good poker player. Guzmán says that he
lacked the audacity and gift for those sallies that made Villa famous,
nor could he maneuver with such art as Felipe Angeles: "He always
took the offensive but with defensive methods." That is another way
of saying that he never accepted battle until he was sure of winning.
But Guzmán didn't like Obregón, and he called him "a person who
was convinced of his own immense importance, but who pretended
not to take himself seriously.... He was not a man of action, but

[14] *Memoirs of Pancho Villa.*
[15] *The Eagle and the Serpent.*

an actor. His ideas, his beliefs, his feelings were intended, like those of the theater, for the public. They lacked all roots and inner conviction. In the literal meaning of the word, he was a comedian." But the painter Siqueiros, who was on Diéguez' staff and saw Obregón just after he had lost his arm at Celaya, admired both his military genius and his sense of humor; he thought that the casualness was put on deliberately to cover an inflexible determination, and he told me that when Obregón asked the surgeon where his arm was and was told he'd never see it again, the general replied: "You just throw a few pieces of gold on that table, Colonel, and my arm wherever it is will come crawling here on all five fingers!" [16] Perhaps, however, only an outsider like Parkes could understand what it was in Obregón's peculiar make-up that provided so opportunely what the Revolution needed at this moment:

> Few men could have been, by temperament, less revolutionary. A native of the half-Americanized state of Sonora, he had the mentality of a practical businessman. His strength lay in his singularly lucid grasp of realities, his insight into the possibilities of a situation. He had none of that romantic devotion to impossible ideals which constitutes both the charm and the ineffectualness of the Mexican temperament. He thought in prose and not in poetry. He initiated processes by which the grievances of the Mexican people might be remedied, but he had no intention of pursuing reform too rapidly. Economic efficiency and political peace meant more to him than democracy and freedom.[17]

Obregón's ascent to the presidency had not been without risks. There must have been some kind of deal with Carranza in 1916, the General agreeing to retire to his chick-pea plantations in Sonora, the First Chief agreeing to be succeeded by him in 1920. But the sight of Carranza in power must have infuriated the general. Had he won a hundred battles with Huerta and Villa, almost destroying Mexico in the process, for this? Were these little civilian flatterers and corruptionists, now bleeding Mexico white, the end product of those efforts? Even more revolting must have been the sight of Car-

---

[16] Obregón himself says in his memoirs that he was momentarily so crazed by pain following the loss of his arm, that he attempted suicide—with a pistol that turned out to be unloaded.

[17] Henry Bamford Parkes, *A History of Mexico.* Boston, Houghton Mifflin Co., 1938, 1950.

ranza in the famous Zimmermann Telegram affair, promising U-boat bases to the Germans in return for Texas, New Mexico and Arizona, thus almost embroiling Mexico in another disastrous war with the United States. The spectacle of Bonillas being groomed as a puppet —"The world has lost a first-class bookkeeper," said Obregón of his fellow-Sonoran scornfully—was the last straw. Obregón came to the capital, and when it was clear that he was being pursued by assassins in the pay of Carranza, he escaped in disguise to Michoacán and took charge of the growing revolt.

Three days after Carranza's death, Adolfo de la Huerta assumed the provisional presidency and set the wheels in motion for Obregón's election September 5. For those six months there was peace in Mexico. "De la Huerta was an honest, forthright man, noted for his sincerity, good humor, and excellent singing voice. (He had had operatic ambitions.) His manner was frankly conciliatory...." [18] Even Obregón's old enemy, Villa, was conciliated. Zapata was gone, and Zapata's apostle, Soto y Gama, was friendly. When Obregón took office on November 4, with De la Huerta as his Treasury Minister and Calles as his Minister of Government, a long peace seemed assured.

It is impossible to understand Obregón's achievements and limitations without bearing in mind that democracy still did not exist in Mexico, and that the foundations of capitalism, the modern industrial state, which had begun to appear under Porfirio Díaz, were in ruins. President Obregón did nothing to encourage democracy—in fact, the genial largesse with which he rewarded his henchmen went farther than under Carranza—but he put capitalism on its feet again. He paid lip service to the Revolution, as every Mexican President since his time has done. Politically speaking, Mexico remained a dictatorship, though a more benevolent one than Díaz'. There was freedom of the press and a multiplicity of political parties, none of which had any real authority. Labor, united under Luis Morones' leadership, became strong and aggressive. This was in part because labor had backed Obregón against Carranza, and in part because a flourishing capitalism functions best with a strong nonrevolutionary labor movement. But industry also required capital, and capital was only available in the United States. Recognition was essential for this; but first Washington had to be assured that the new Mexican rulers were not Bolsheviks, as many in the reactionary Harding administration insisted they were. De la Huerta went to Washing-

[18] William Weber Johnson, *Heroic Mexico: The Violent Emergence of a Modern Nation.* Garden City, New York, Doubleday & Company, Inc., 1968.

ton and made a pact with Thomas W. Lamont, settling the question of Mexico's revolutionary debts in a way that was acceptable to Lamont's partners in the House of Morgan. Obregón then made it plain that Article 27 of the 1917 Constitution would not be applied retroactively to put the nation's oil and ores out of reach. When these things were done, recognition followed. Ambassadors were exchanged on August 30, 1923.

In agrarian policy, Obregón was even more conservative. Peonage persisted, and the *hacendados* were given full license to rule their plantations as princes, with private police forces, as in the past. Three million acres of government land were distributed among 624 villages to discourage incipient Zapatism, but since the peasants were not given seed, or farm implements, or credit, this extension of the traditional *ejido* system did not fare well. According to the 1930 census, 320 million acres still remained in the hands of a few thousand *hacendados*.

Only in the field of education was there spectacular change. José Vasconcelos, who had been close to both Madero and Villa, served in the short-lived government of Eulálio Gutiérrez after the Convention of Aguascalientes and been director of the National Preparatory School for two weeks—until Carranza arrested him—was made Minister of Education by Obregón. Vasconcelos was an inspired man, but his inspirations were amazingly contradictory. On the one hand, he hated dictatorship and every form of praetorianism, believing that the salvation of the world lay in a broad dissemination of the classics and the diffusion of a purely Spanish culture throughout the Americas (he later became a devout Catholic). On the other hand, he was obsessively anti-American and anti-Indian, carrying his phobias in these respects so far as to advocate a kind of Hispanic racism. "We decided for Obregón," he says in his autobiography,[19] "in spite of the unsavory character of his candidacy, because of his pure Spanish blood." He compared the racial "purity" of Guadalajara with Puebla, "a typical mestizo city," and Oaxaca "absorbed by the Indians." And as for the Revolution in its Indian aspects:

> The hidden doctrine of the school of Zapata was the return
> of Mexico to the primitivism of Montezuma. This return
> was preached by European creoles like Diaz Soto and by

[19] *A Mexican Ulysses: The Autobiography of José Vasconcelos.* Translated and abridged by W. Rex Crawford. Indiana University Press, 1963. For all its quirkiness this is *the* great Mexican autobiography.

Yankee newspapermen; the aristocrats of the capital, taking part in the movement in a kind of defensive mimicry, practised the doctrine in the form of the dress they wore... the *teocalli* of human sacrifices is the only Aztec institution that survives. The followers of Zapata perfected it with machine-guns and automatics.

Vasconcelos admitted that his nature was "better fitted for hymns and praises than for reflecting." He was also frank to say that "facts do not interest me." But in the Mexico of 1920, his integrity and devotion to learning were almost unique.

Obregón was amused by him, and loved to tell the story of the peasant on the railway platform at Guanajuato who didn't know the name of his own village, because he had never had occasion to refer to it: "Give the old man five pesos," the President said to his secretary, "and tell Vasconcelos to send him a collection of the classics." But Obregón backed his eccentric Minister. The organization of the ministry was borrowed from Lenin's first education chief, Anatole Lunacharsky. Translations of the *Iliad* and the *Odyssey*, Goethe's *Faust*, Dante's *Divine Comedy*, Cervantes' *Don Quixote*, even the philosophy of Vasconcelos' favorite Plotinus, were distributed in editions of hundreds of thousands. More practically, thousands of young teachers, imbued with Vasconcelos' dedication, went into the back country and opened schools where none had ever been. "The rural schoolteacher," Parkes says, "became the successor of the priest, carrying forward that task of civilizing the Indians which the sixteenth-century friars had initiated but which, for more than three hundred years, had been totally neglected."

But Vasconcelos' most lasting contribution was not to philosophy, which he loved, nor to literature, which he cherished, nor to the dance (he staged operatic ballets), but to painting, for which he had (at best) an antiquarian's taste. He was color-blind, admittedly. He preferred the work of the derivative classicists among the younger generation of artists breaking out of Porfirio Díaz' hothouse academy—Roberto Montenegro, Fernando Revueltas, Fernando Leal. Diego Rivera, who had sat out the Revolution in Paris and Madrid, painting post-Impressionist and Cubist canvases, he despised for succumbing to "the vogue of folk-art" and glorifying the Noble Indian. He found Orozco's apocalyptic frescoes, he told me once, "grotesque." Siqueiros was a Carranzista and on his way to becoming a Communist. But the fact of the matter was that Vasconcelos gave all these painters their first walls, when it was not good politics to do so, and he stuck by them when philistines demanded that their frescoes be destroyed. He gave the prolific Diego the arcades of the two courtyards at the Ministry of Education to decorate as he chose, and he gave Orozco the better part of the National Preparatory School.

The results were electrifying. Mexico, which hadn't produced a painter of real stature since the anonymous Maya who painted Bonampak in the ninth century, was suddenly becoming world renowned for its revolutionary muralists. Rivera left an imperishable record of Indian Mexico—its markets and fiestas, its work patterns and guerrilla raids—on the Ministry walls; and at Chapingo a masterpiece. Orozco, with his greatest murals still ahead of him in Guadalajara, painted in the Preparatory School with a tragic grandeur and monumentality that hadn't been approached in fresco since the Italian Renaissance.

The De la Huerta Caper

General Obregón's administration, meanwhile, was running into trouble. As usual under dictatorships, the problem of succession was proving explosive. General Calles was known to be Obregón's candidate, but Calles had many enemies. Some hated him because he supported tough leftist policies favoring labor and the peons. The clergy hated him with good reason because he was outspokenly anticlerical. Others hated him simply because he was ruthless and, unlike Obregón, never smiled. Many of the state governors had their private grudges against Obregón and Calles, but when the Carranzista general, Francisco Murguia, "pronounced" from Texas, published a well-documented list of 121 enemies of the regime who had been murdered, and marched into Coahuila, they waited to see what would happen. When Murguia's army was defeated and the general died before a firing squad shouting, "*Viva Carranza!*" they had their answer.

The liberals in the capital who wanted to see constitutional freedoms honored found a more popular candidate to head the opposition in the person of Adolfo de la Huerta. De la Huerta resigned from the cabinet in September of 1923, but he didn't announce his candidacy until December. What prompted him to turn against his old Sonora comrade was that his successor in the Treasury, Alberto J. Pani, announced that he had found the Treasury empty—looted, was the implication. De la Huerta was a notably honest man, and that was too much. Unfortunately for him, the state governors who promptly joined him in rebellion had nothing in common with this gentle liberal and his friends; they included, among others, the man who had betrayed Carranza, and none of them were trusted by labor or the peons who remained staunchly on Obregón's side. Nor did the fact that 60 percent of the federal army had defected mean much, for Obregón was liberally supplied with weapons, including bombing planes, from the United States. The old axiom that no rebellion unsupported from across the Rio Grande could prosper still held. The rebels almost captured the capital, but in three months they were crushed, and most of their leaders were shot. De la Huerta escaped into exile, resuming his singing career in Los Angeles. Obregón, who might have disposed of praetorianism, instead in his triumph created fifty-four more generals to replace the disloyal ones. Calles in the summer of 1924 moved painlessly into the presidency.

The ten-year reign of Calles as *jefe máximo* of Mexico, which finally established the machinery for an orderly transition of power in the postrevolutionary state, was the opening phase of the peaceful modern period and so belongs in the next chapter. But Obregón's death, though it didn't occur until 1928, when he was preparing to assume the presidency for another four years, with Calles' concurrence, belongs here. As with all the other principals of the Revolution—Madero, Villa, Zapata and Carranza—it came violently. On his Sonora estate, the general had been relatively contented. He went about unshaven and in his work clothes, and to a Japanese diplomat who had come to decorate him and apologized for finding him in disguise, he had answered, "This is my natural state. It was when I was in the National Palace that I wore a disguise." Back in the capital, however, Obregón was recognized by everyone and immediately became the focus of a series of bomb plots. The instigators were Catholic, driven underground by Calles' persecutions. Obregón's two opponents for the presidency had been removed by assassination. Obregón himself was killed at a restaurant, La Bombilla, on Avenida Insurgentes, by a young artist who didn't know how to handle a pistol but who approached so close to show the President-elect his sketch that he couldn't miss.

5

MEXICO TODAY (1925–1968)

IN one of Orozco's frescoes at the National Preparatory School a starving beggar is dropping a coin into a church collection box; unseen to the beggar, his coin is being received beneath the padlocked box by a fat hand covered with jewels in a cuff of clerical lace. A hero in the frescoes of both Orozco and Rivera was Felipe Carillo Puerto, the martyred Governor of Yucatán who had been gunned down with his five brothers against a wall during the De la Huerta rebellion; the insurrectionaries were incensed by this "Red Christ's" promise to take the land away from the clerical-landlord clique and give it back to the Mayas.[1] Far from having made peace with the Revolution, the Catholic Church, granted amnesty against Juárez' anticlerical Reform Laws of 1857 by Porfirio Díaz, had increased its vast land holdings and pervasive influence among the superstitious peasants under Carranza, and by 1926 was prepared to reenter politics. The Catholic Vasconcelos severely criticized the Church for not having supported Madero, whose only "crime" was to have asked for equality for Protestants. The tolerant Obregón had charged that the clergy had backed Victoriano Huerta with a gift of forty million pesos, but Obregón hadn't enforced the anticlerical provisions of the 1917 Constitution until the building of a monument to "Christ the King" in Guanajuato threatened to mobilize the peasants there and in the western states against his govern-

[1] The Yucatecan's celebrated romance, which inspired the mariachi song "La Peregrina," is explored in interviews with his fiancée, Alma Reed (who later became Orozco's friend) in the author's *Mexican Journal: The Conquerors Conquered*. New York, The Devin-Adair Co., 1958.

126

ment. The Church had retaliated by backing the De la Huerta rebellion and in the aftermath it had been the *cristeros*—as the militant Catholics were called—who had terrorized the capital with bombs and finally assassinated Obregón. Calles had no compunction about taking the offensive against the Church and ending its landed power once and for all.

Calles and the One-Party State

"The Turk," as the dark-faced,[2] slouching, glowering dictator was called, would have been regarded as a typical fascist a decade later. His only consistencies were his anticlericalism and the brutality with which he disposed of his enemies. Like all fascists, he made much of the labor movement. Membership in CROM jumped from 100,000 to 2,000,000 under Calles' patronage, but the dictator turned it into an auxiliary of his power apparatus by corrupting its easily corruptible boss, Luis Morones, with kickbacks, limousines and diamond rings; and when it suited Calles to break a strike, as in Sonora, he broke it by shooting the Yaqui miners.

Calles posed as the peons' Great Friend too. Declaring himself the heir of Zapata, he distributed eight million acres to the *ejidos*, but the banks established to supply the new proprietors with credit loaned most of the money to big landowners with political pull. Calles hated the rich, yet the Callistas, who stepped into the shoes of the *científicos* without any of the intellectual pretensions of the Díaz gang, became the wealthiest men in Mexico; the location of their weekend palaces in Cuernavaca, clustering around Calles' own, became known as "The Street of the Forty Thieves." When the National Palace was encased in scaffolding for the addition of a third story, capital wags said it was being crated for shipment to Sonora.

The near-civil war with the Church broke out in 1926, when the state governments began limiting the number of priests authorized to practice. In Tabasco, the most extreme case, one priest per thirty thousand inhabitants was permitted—provided he be over forty and *married*. The Church retaliated by disavowing the Constitution of 1917. The government then struck back by *enforcing* the Constitution—no foreign priests, no criticism of the government, no more convents or monasteries. In reply the Church suspended all religious services and boycotted everything purchasable except food. A Callista general published his "liberal doctrine":

[2] Calles was reputedly of Lebanese or Syrian extraction. He had been schoolmaster and a saloonkeeper before the Revolution claimed him.

My religion is the fatherland, reason my deity, truth my dogma, and Morelos, Juárez and Madero my trinity. My saints are Cuauhtémoc and Hidalgo...the Pope is my Lucifer, the priests my demons, the nuns my temptation. My temple is the universe, majestic on a serene night. Viva México! Viva the Reform! Viva the ragged ones! Death to the traitors! Viva Juárez! Viva Calles, who carries on the work of Juárez! [3]

Soon it was all-out war. One side fought with bombs and assassinations; the other, with firing squads and hangings. "The North American ruling class," Vasconcelos wrote, "wanted to see Catholicism disappear from Mexico, for it represented Latinity, the type of civilization which makes us what we are, and which stands in the way of their moral conquest which would consolidate their interference in the fields of economics and politics. Everything could be forgiven Calles, because he served them as an arm with which to strike at the Church." [4] This was an extreme view of both the Mexican and American positions. The struggle to reclaim the Church's vast holdings and end its stranglehold over education had been going on for a century. No doubt Protestant America smiled to see the Church losing out, but only Business influenced policy in Harding's Republican Washington, and the anti-Catholic Calles was esteemed as a friend of Business just as the pro-Catholic Díaz had been. As a matter of fact, it was Dwight Morrow, the Morgan partner whom Calvin Coolidge sent to Mexico as Ambassador in 1927, who talked Calles into easing the tension with the Church—the Church had already lost the "war"—and permitting Church services to be held again.

Morrow was a cultured gentleman who commissioned Diego Rivera to fresco the gallery of Cortés' Palace in Cuernavaca. The new Ambassador got along well with Calles and no doubt was instrumental in getting the dictator to reassure the oil companies and to cut back on his redistribution of land. Seeing Morelos and Zapata glorified in paint was a small price to pay for getting Mexico back on a course of stability with "sound" fiscal arrangements. Morrow

[3] Quoted in William Weber Johnson's *Heroic Mexico: The Violent Emergence of a Modern Nation*. Garden City, New York, Doubleday & Company, Inc., 1968.

[4] *A Mexican Ulysses: The Autobiography of José Vasconcelos*. Translated and abridged by W. Rex Crawford. Bloomington, Indiana, Indiana University Press, 1963. Vasconcelos ignored the fact that the Vatican was opposed to the civil-war tactics of the Mexican Church. (See *The Meaning of the Mexican Revolution*, D. C. Heath and Co., 1967, pp. 33ff.)

applauded the roads, dams and irrigation systems that Calles was building; and he won additional popularity by sponsoring goodwill tours by Charles Lindbergh (who became his son-in-law) and Will Rogers. When the dummy Mexican Supreme Court declared that foreigners who had acquired subsoil rights to Mexico's oil before 1917 were in fact the owners, few were surprised.

Calles' most lasting contribution to Mexico, for better or worse, was his sponsorship of the single monolithic political party that has governed Mexico ever since. The creation of this party, which has changed its names three times but never its pervasive domination, has precluded the emergence of democracy in Mexico, at least democracy in the Anglo-Saxon sense of voting for viable alternatives on the local and national levels. But the problem of succession, which had always plagued Mexico, was solved; democratic gains could now be registered in the economic sphere under conditions of assured stability.

The transition to this system began shakily. Following Obregón's assassination in 1928, Calles, with Morrow applauding, read a statement to the assembled governors of the states announcing the end of *caudillismo*. Then he stepped out of the presidency. But the next three presidents, who held the office until 1934, were puppets, with Calles pulling the strings. The first, elected by Congress for an interim term, was Emilio Portes Gil, a former Governor of Tamaulipas. Calles announced the formation of the Partido Nacional Revolucionario (PNR) on the day the new President took office.

Although Portes Gil carried agrarian reforms forward with more speed than Calles had, his principal contribution was in bringing all the political parties in the country into the new holding company, skillfully isolating such controversial figures as Morones and Soto y Gama.

Calles' candidate to succeed Portes Gil, Pascual Ortiz Rubio of Michoacán, was duly nominated by the PNR in 1929, but an unexpected opposition candidate suddenly appeared on the scene in the person of José Vasconcelos. Vasconcelos stumped the country vigorously denouncing dictatorship, militarism and corruption. But when the votes were counted and he was awarded 20,000 to Ortiz Rubio's million-plus, he fled to Texas like Madero (to whom he compared himself), confidently waiting for a rebellion—which never materialized. Under Ortiz Rubio the program of land distribution came to a halt, with the excuse that the *ejidos* had failed. In a sense they had, getting no help or credit from the government on which to operate efficiently. CROM, Morones' big labor federation, had already been smashed under Portes Gil; Communist unions were first encouraged to function in its place, then outlawed in turn. The anticlerical campaign was first soft-pedaled and then renewed with virulence, especially in the state of Tabasco, where Governor Tomés Garrido Canábal, a fanatic who had named his sons Lucifer and Lenin, deployed bands of "Red Shirts" to hunt down the terrified priests who had refused to obey the law by marrying.

Calles dumped Ortiz Rubio in 1932 and replaced him with Abelardo L. Rodríguez, described unkindly but not inaccurately by Vasconcelos thus: "A man who had never dared to be a candidate, not even for the office of deputy, who would not have stood up to the heckling of a single public meeting, Abelardo Rodríguez became President by unanimous vote. He spoke English badly, but Spanish even worse, and had become a millionaire as an administrator or governor of Baja California, where there is no business other than sentry boxes, houses of prostitution, and an International Casino. Sharing his take with two or three Presidents, he moved up the ladder." [5]

Under Rodríguez' presidency there were disquieting street fights in the capital between Communists and "Gold Shirts," fascist bands dedicated to fighting "Bolsheviks and Jews" with Callista backing; but there was also the promise of real progress and a degree of democracy within the PNR itself when a left wing dedicated to achieving the ideals of the Revolution was organized. It was assumed that the party's official candidate for 1934, Gen. Lázaro Cárdenas, would pay lip service to these ideals and take orders from Calles, his chief, as he always had in the past.

Cárdenas: The Revolution Fulfilled

Let us admit at the outset that it is difficult for an American writer to wax enthusiastic about Lázaro Cárdenas (even Mexican writers put on a poor show of being properly moved). It is not that Cárdenas kicked out the American oil companies—that was admirable; or that later he accepted the Stalin Peace Prize rather than give his American critics the satisfaction of turning it down—that was understandable. It is rather that Cárdenas had none of the tragic flaws and weaknesses that make a hero human; not even any of the foibles that make good copy. To one with romantic inclinations (and what writer has none?), he seems too good to be true. Without being

[5] *A Mexican Ulysses.* Vasconcelos was of course describing the Baja California of the twenties.

patronizing about it, he was always on the side of the poor and the oppressed, functioning practically and without publicity on their behalf. He never revenged himself upon his enemies. He did not enrich himself. He acted upon principle. And he retired decisively when his allotted term had ended, though he continued his good works as a private citizen, or as a public servant when called upon to do so. No one ever doubted Cárdenas' physical courage or denied that he was *muy macho*. What writers found repellent in his personality was the lack of a sense of humor, the almost saintly modesty, the puritanism, the campaigns against alcoholism and gambling, perhaps the deliberate *patience* with which he had bided his time as a faithful Callista in order to accomplish within the framework of the law what had to be done.

Having said as much, it must be admitted that Cárdenas' grim austerity, like Juárez' a century before, was exactly what Mexico needed. Nor did the fact that his early career was in uniform rather than in a law office make Cárdenas' beginnings any less prosaic than his great predecessor's. He was born in 1895 in Jiquilpán, a village of Michoacán halfway between Morelia and Guadalajara. He joined Villa's partisans in 1915 but defected to the Carranzistas, presumably because constitutionalism was more to his liking than banditry. Calles, who received him at Agua Prieta, christened him *El Chamaco* (The Kid) and put him to work in the raffish Sonora border town suppressing prostitution, gambling and the liquor traffic. He was also put to work taming the rebellious Yaquis, learning perhaps that Indian grievances were not to be settled with arms. Under De la Huerta he became a general (at twenty-five, the youngest) and provisional Governor of Michoacán, but in the Delahuertista Rebellion he sided with Obregón and Calles. Assigned to Tampico by President Calles, he learned by whom and for whom the oil was being extracted. (It was hard to say whether the company officials were more nonplussed by his refusal to take bribes or by his insistence on eating with the Mexican help.) Returning to govern Michoacán late in 1928, he gave the *cristeros* a greater shock by talking with them instead of hunting them down. But probably Calles received the greatest shock of all when, after allocating a million pesos apiece to the three generals sent out to put down Mexico's last big revolt (that of General Escobár in 1929) Cárdenas returned 700,000 pesos to the Treasury.

In Michoacán, Cárdenas built schools, constructed irrigation canals, and when the *hacendado* of a big sugar plantation punished his recalcitrant peons by burning their houses, distributed the land to them—though at first they were so frightened to receive it that he had to threaten giving it to peons from another state! He also erected a monument to Morelos, higher than the Statue of Liberty and uglier, on the island of Janitzio in Lake Pátzcuaro. And when Calles asked him to take the War Ministry in the cabinet of his third puppet, Rodríguez, Cárdenas had the temerity to refuse (later, when his term as Governor was completed, he accepted the offer).

Why Calles agreed to the choice of the already independent-minded Cárdenas to succeed Rodríguez is a moot question. Perhaps it would not have been good politics to defy the left wing of the PNR; or perhaps he assumed that Cárdenas was controllable. What he thought of the radical Six Year Plan on which Cárdenas campaigned, or of the unprecedented seventeen thousand miles the candidate traveled throughout Mexico to win the support of the people, or of the 2,268,567 votes by which his friend was elected, over 24,690 for Gen. Antonio Villareál—is not recorded. But Calles' self-confidence was not shaken. When the President-elect came to his ranch in Sinaloa to pay his respects, Calles kept him waiting in the hall while he finished a poker game.[6]

It was one of the dictator's last pieces of effrontery.

Cárdenas made an initial mistake by taking Garrido Canábal into his cabinet. He admired the socialism and prohibitionism of the little Tabasco dictator, but he finally broke with him over his anticlericalism. "It is an error to try to fight against fanaticism," said the President in removing him, "with antireligious fanaticism." Cárdenas had already given a hint of the new austerity by attending his inauguration in street clothes, moving out of Chapultepec Palace, cutting his own salary in half. Smoking and drinking were frowned upon. Cárdenas never attended a bullfight. But an order was immediately circulated that anyone in the country with a grievance could telegraph the President about it free of charge.

Meanwhile Cárdenas was enforcing the minimum-wage law and encouraging the radical Lombardo Toledano, who had visited Russia, to set up a new confederation of labor. The CTM (Confederación Trabajadores Mejicanos) soon rivaled Morones' CROM. Jurisdictional strikes broke out. There were cries of "Communism!" from the frightened businessmen.

On June 12, 1935, Calles published his "Patriotic Declarations" in the two largest newspapers of the capital, hinting that Cárdenas was about to go the way of Ortiz Rubio. Conservatives took heart, but

[6] William Cameron Townsend, *Lázaro Cárdenas: Mexican Democrat.* Ann Arbor, Michigan, George Wahr Publishing Company, 1952.

they slumped back in their swivel chairs two days later when it was discovered how quickly and quietly Cárdenas had retaliated. First he had secretly polled the state governors and his cabinet ministers on their allegiance. Then he had dismissed the cabinet, and in a new one cleverly replaced Canábal with the radical but staunchly Catholic strong man of San Luis Potosí, Gen. Saturnino Cedillo. Then he had placed the conservative ex-President Portes Gil in charge of the PNR.

In Cuernavaca, seeing that he had been outmaneuvered, the *jefe máximo* was reported to have exclaimed: "What an ass I am! I am the slave of my own device—institutional government!" A few days later Calles was on his way to California and for the first time in Mexico's history a dictatorship had been ousted without bloodshed. Cárdenas celebrated the occasion characteristically by picnicking unarmed and unguarded among the gun-slinging *campesinos* of Morelos.

Early in 1936 a glass workers' strike in Monterrey that threatened to become the focus of a right-wing rebellion gave Cárdenas an opportunity to show business where he stood. The President went to Monterrey and gave the contestants a fourteen-point program for settling labor disputes. The last two points read significantly:

13. Capital should be very careful not to continue provoking agitations because these would come to constitute a rallying point for political interests, and this would bring on civil warfare.

14. The industrialists who do not wish to operate because of the demands of the unions can turn over their industries to their laborers or to the government for it to operate. This would be a patriotic step, but simply to close down the factories would not be.

At the same time, however, Cárdenas warned: "Hereafter there must be no antireligious propaganda in the classrooms. All our attention must be concentrated upon the great Cause of social reform." During his first year in office Cárdenas had already distributed one fourth of all the land the landless peasantry had received since 1915. (During his whole term he distributed 45,330,000 acres among 1,020,594 peasants.) Since as late as 1923, according to Frank Tannenbaum,[7] 2,700 families still held one half the property in the country,

---

[7] *Peace by Revolution.* With drawings by Miguel Covarrubias. New York, Columbia University Press, 1933.

this was a long-overdue move to give the peasant majority some stake in the economy. But Cárdenas didn't merely give the peasants the land and leave it at that. Rehabilitation embraced the whole village. Townsend describes the village in which he himself lived, Tetelcingo in Morelos, before and after:

> ...It had no electricity, only one water hydrant, no playground, little land to farm, and only a ramshackle schoolhouse. Cárdenas spent less than one hundred thousand dollars and gave the forgotten town an agricultural school with a good building, implements, some stock, a brick kiln, and a playground; he doubled the tillable soil, planted thousands of fruit trees, gave the town a eucalyptus grove for firewood and posts; provided a good water system with tanks, watering troughs, and hydrants in four sections of town; established a hospital with a doctor and two nurses; introduced a paved highway, built homes for the homeless; and installed electric lights in most of the streets.

This is what Cárdenas was doing from one end of Mexico to the other during the 673 work days he spent outside the capital during his six years' in office, covering 54,695 miles by train, car, horseback, steamship, bus, and on foot.

What brought Lázaro Cárdenas into the world's headlines, however, was not what he was doing for the humble Mexicans but what he did to the arrogant Anglo-American oil companies. It will be recalled that under Díaz the rich oil fields of Tampico had been virtually given away; Edward L. Doheny alone bought 300,000 acres at a little over a dollar an acre. The reassertion of Mexico's rights to its own subsoil in the 1917 Constitution had been a scrap of paper as far as the foreign companies were concerned; they didn't even pay royalties to the government, and until Cárdenas gave labor its head, the workers in the oil fields were exploited mercilessly. Between 1901 and 1933, 53,039,412 barrels of oil had been shipped out of Mexico at stupendous profit.

In December of 1937, when Shell was negotiating for new concessions, Cárdenas agreed to them, provided a royalty be paid and labor's wage demands be met. To save itself a paltry million dollars, the company took its case against the union to the Mexican Supreme Court. The move backfired. It was revealed that the oil companies were charging *Mexicans* as much as 350 percent more for their products than foreign consumers of Mexican oil were paying, and that workers were receiving less than half what was being paid in the United States. On March 1, 1938, the Supreme Court rejected the companies' appeal.

The companies' plan was to cripple Mexican industry by stopping the flow of oil, and then wait until either Cárdenas fell or the American government intervened. Cárdenas did not wait. Without prior warning, he seized the properties of all the foreign oil companies on March 18 and announced that the former owners would receive proper indemnification in due course. This bold stroke did more to unite the Mexican people than anything since Madero took Ciudad Juárez in 1910. On March 23, 200,000 people, carrying banners hailing Mexico's "Declaration of Independence," flowed through the Zócalo. They promised the President support to counter whatever the companies might come up with. They contributed everything from wedding rings to chickens to pay for the expropriated property. The British were expected to send warships but instead meanly retaliated by demanding immediate payment of a back debt; Cárdenas paid it—and broke off diplomatic relations with Great Britain. In a letter to Josephus Daniels, the friendly American Ambassador, the President expressed gratitude that President Roosevelt had not seen fit to intervene on behalf of the oil companies, placing his Good Neighbor Policy ahead of their interest; but the official American hands-off attitude was tarnished later by Secretary Cordell Hull, who came to the aid of the oil companies by suddenly demanding ten million dollars for lands taken over in the agrarian reform program and acquiescing in a boycott of oil purchasing—which only had the effect of forcing Mexico to sell to the fascist powers, whose military buildup Cárdenas had been trying to stall by a united Pan-American boycott ever since the Spanish Civil War started.

Meanwhile the oil companies in desperation turned to Cárdenas' one surviving enemy in Mexico, Gen. Saturnino Cedillo, who still maintained a private army as Governor of San Luis Potosí following his ouster from the cabinet and Cárdenas' crackdown on his anti-Semitic Gold Shirt Movement. Cedillo, supported by the German agent Baron von Merck, was in the back country beefing up his private army with the help of contributions from the Church, the landlords and the oil companies. On May 18, 1938, Cárdenas took a train to the state capital and gave another of those demonstrations of personal bravery which endeared him to the courage-worshiping *mestizos*. Disdaining the protection of federal troops, he walked into the crowd of fanatical Cedillistas and mounted the steps of the Governor's palace, where he accused his former cabinet member of treason and demanded his surrender. Then he broke up forty-eight local haciendas, giving the land to the very peasants who had been recruited by Cedillo, and instead of the old-time promises of death before the firing squad offered amnesty to all who would surrender. Support for Cedillo melted away. On January 11, 1939, the rebel Governor was ambushed in the mountains with a tiny remnant of his followers. Exactly one year later the radical Cárdenas, first President in Mexican history to retire from power voluntarily, turned over the reins of government to Manuel Ávila Camacho, a conservative.

Conservative Backswing: *Ávila Camacho and Alemán*

Cárdenas' last months in office were so taken up holding the line against the demands of the oil companies—they finally settled for $40 million instead of the $350 million based on "future" profits they had originally demanded—that he could do little to arrest the tide of conservatism sweeping the country. He did manage to push through a high excess-profits tax and procedures enforcing the constitutional amendment providing for socialistic education, but these measures were swept away by the two administrations that followed. Cárdenas would have had the popularity among peasants and labor to lead a personal crusade for his programs in 1940. He could have backed Gen. Francisco Mújica, who had been responsible for the radical articles in the 1917 Constitution, but he didn't, and Mújica dropped out. Cárdenas preferred to see an orderly transition of power.

Gen. Juan Andreu Almazán had the backing of business and the Church and was popular in the capital; he even had the support of Diego Rivera, who made the switch of the century, deserting the Trotskyites to back him. Almazán announced that he would head an armed revolt if "robbed" of the election. Few would contend that the official count of 2,265,199 votes for Ávila Camacho over 128,574 for Almazán was unrigged, but Cádrenas stayed out of it. President Roosevelt threw his weight on the side of stability by announcing that Vice President Henry Wallace would attend Ávila Camacho's inauguration. Almazán's revolt did not materialize, and Ávila Camacho, with a large assist from World War II and its demands, proceeded to bring Mexico the conservatism that seemed to be in order.

The new President's first move was to take the railroads away from the unions, which had operated them under Cárdenas, and restore them to government control; under the unions they had been plagued by strikes, poor service, and a number of major wrecks. Union ownership had been a major Cárdenas mistake. Cárdenas' attempt to place the dominant political party as much under the control of peasants and workers as of the middle class and military, failed too, probably because the Mexican people were far too bound by traditional cacique-ism to be capable of acting independently in their own interests. Ávila Camacho quickly restored the party's institutional control to the politicians and generals who had always controlled it in fact. As a good Catholic, Ávila Camacho also wasted no time in putting an end to socialist education; first he appointed a right-wing Catholic Minister of Education, but when that aroused too much protest, he chose a Minister, Jaime Torres Bodet, who properly concentrated on teaching 1.5 million adult Mexicans how to read. No more *ejidos* were created, and those established by Cárdenas were split up, little by little, into small farms. Labor was still given free rein, but the radical Lombardo Toledano was removed from the leadership of the now dominant CTM.

There were frequent predictions that Cárdenas would intervene to arrest this swing to the right, but he refused even to be interviewed. In fact, only when his successor asked for help during World War II did he consent to command the Pacific military district and serve as Defense Minister. Mexico not only ranged itself solidly with the United States after Pearl Harbor, but on Independence Day of 1942 symbolized its national unity by putting all six living ex-Presidents on the balcony of the National Palace while Ávila Camacho rang Hidalgo's bell of Dolores.

The war brought many problems to Mexico. One was inflation. Denied its overseas markets, the United States began buying the products of Mexican mines, henequen and oilseed fields; spent $30 million rehabilitating the broken-down Mexican railway system; invested in real estate for the first time since Porfirio Díaz' epoch; sent tourists flooding across the border. Overnight Mexico became a creditor nation. Millionaires by the dozens sprouted in the capital. In token of the morality of the new largesse, the President's brother was quoted as saying, "If you build a road for 75,000 pesos and pocket 1,000, everybody will howl. But if you build a road for 75,-000,000 pesos and knock back a million, nobody will notice."

Meanwhile rising prices and scantiness of domestic food production wiped out whatever gains in land tenure the Revolution had brought to that three quarters of the population which was still peasant: Their buying power dropped to less than half of what it had been *in the Díaz period!* One result of this was that political rebellion in the backlands, with no legal outlet through the one-party system, was diverted to the illegal Sinarquista Movement secretly financed by the old Catholic-landlord alliance that had gone underground in the Cárdenas period. Right-wing demonstrations reached such a peak after federal troops killed 27 rioters and wounded 247 during a riot in León on January 2, 1946, that Ávila Camacho's successor felt obliged to give the state election in Guanajuato to the Sinarquistas—the first (and last) opposition state government in all of Mexico since the Revolution.

Another result of the war economy was the migration of labor in vast numbers across the northern border to supply, at wages ten times higher than those prevailing in Mexico, the labor shortage in the United States caused by the draft. Those crossing legally were called *braceros,* those entering illegally (i.e. swimming the Rio Grande at night) were the so-called wetbacks. The *braceros* returned to spend their money in Mexico, created a demand for consumer goods, and generally helped to break down xenophobic tendencies in both countries. But this good work was undone by the wetbacks, who revived in the United States the traditional stereotype of the Mexican as an indolent fellow with criminal tendencies, and in Mexico the corresponding stereotype of the "typical American" tyrannizing over his "cheap labor" with racial prejudice and guns.

Miguel Alemán, who had managed Ávila Camacho's campaign in 1940, became his successor in 1946. Since he was the first civilian to occupy the presidency since Madero, and since both the internal stability which characterizes Mexico from now on and the actual accomplishments of Alemán's presidency were made possible by the uncontestable power of the state party machine, this is the time to comment on the nature of the PRI.[8]

Octavio Paz defends the PRI against those critics who have compared its monolithic character to that of the Communist Party in Russia. Its "human" waywardness and lack of a fixed "ideology," he points out correctly, have saved it "from the spiritual aridity of a closed system with a syllogistic, police-state morality." [9] Paz does not deny that there have been violence, caprice, arbitrariness and brutality associated with PRI's rule, but he ascribes these to passion and chance rather than to fanaticism or deliberate intent. It is impor-

[8] Party of Revolutionary Institutions, the third and presumably final name by which the Party of the Revolution was called.
[9] *The Labyrinth of Solitude, Life and Thought in Mexico,* translated by Lysander Kemp. New York, Grove Press, 1962.

tant to bear in mind, however, that from now on no other political or economic organizations in Mexico exercise any autonomous power. The PRI dictates the Presidential choice of the electorate, and of all but a handful of the Deputies and Senators. The Congress is a rubber stamp for the party. The trade-union movement, which so far had generally won the decisions in its struggles with capital, did so only because (and so long as) it was subservient to the party. The peasant leagues which owed their very existence to the land which the government expropriated for them from the *hacendados*, had become, in Frank Tannenbaum's words, "creatures of the State; they are dependent upon it." [10] Leslie Byrd Simpson, another friend of revolutionary Mexico, summed up the situation during the Alemán years thus:

> By the end of the Cárdenas regime the term "revolution" had been wrenched out of its ordinary context. *The* Revolution is now a glittering edifice contrived of all the notions of the Party planners. The Party has become the Revolution, and, as its spokesmen say quite openly, but not altogether exactly: "The Revolution *is* Mexico." The Party of the Revolution has become a vast bureaucracy with endless proliferations, and each cell is presided over by a functionary who owes the Party his loyalty and his livelihood. The president is the titular head of the official family and is bound by the same discipline as any other functionary. He is the front of a monolithic hierarchy and he has to obey its dictates. For better or for worse, Mexico has become a welfare state under the direction of the Party, and it is the president's job to make its program work and see that the Party gets the credit. He is given flattering titles, and his name and picture are never absent from official publications, but everything he does must be "revolutionary" (in the Pickwickian sense). The busy Party propagandists see to it that everything, from the opening of a new dam or factory, to the discovery of the bones of Cuauhtémoc, is turned into a Party triumph. This unfailing self-praise makes Party literature singularly dull reading and, rightly or wrongly, awakens a feeling of wariness in the reader. This wariness applies particularly to statistics.[11]

[10] *The Struggle for Peace and Bread*. New York, Alfred A. Knopf, Inc., 1950.
[11] *Many Mexicos*. Berkeley, California, University of California Press, 1952.

The statistics issued by Miguel Alemán had many a glittering visual symbol to enliven them from one end of Mexico to the other, and there was nothing dull in the person of the new President. He was handsome and he was young. At forty-four, he already had behind him an impressive record as Governor of Veracruz and as Ávila Camacho's Interior Minister. He loved parties and he loved people—not the humble people Cárdenas loved, but the "in-people," builders and industrialists, promoters and playboys, hotelmen with swimming pools and beautiful women by the planeload to sit by them. Yet no other President save Cárdenas got so much done. He had visions and he carried them out, not ruthlessly but by persuasion, charm and money. His vision was of great dams and irrigation systems; of *viaductos* and *pereféricos* circling the capital, of four north-south highways; of a toll speedway linking the capital with Cuernavaca and Taxco, and on to Acapulco; and of great resorts (Acapulco could almost be called Alemán's creation) that would attract the "in-people" of all nations, especially of the United States. Alemán managed to get loans of almost $400 million from the Export-Import Bank in Washington—loans with which he reclaimed land, built hydroelectric plants, and completed the rehabilitation of the railroads. He envisioned a Mexico in the year 2000 with 200 million people (the population was already well on its way to 35 million) and said that without industrialization these multitudes would have nothing to live on. And he built as the proudest visual symbol of all this progress University City. Costing $25 million, this gaudy extravaganza was designed to accommodate twenty-five thousand students on its three-square-mile campus. Its sunken stadium was designed by Diego Rivera, its Cosmic Ray Pavilion was engineered by Felix Candela, its colorful relief mural was conceived by Siqueiros, and its great mosaic-walled library was the creation of Juan O'Gorman.

Beginning with University City, it is easy—perhaps too easy—to question the content behind the impressive physical patrimony Miguel Alemán bequeathed to Mexico. Only a dozen faculty members at the University devoted full time to their students; lawyers, physicians and other professional men gave occasional lectures for about the cost of taxi fare from their downtown offices.[12] The unruly student body, in the Latin-American tradition, tended to run the show to its taste, sacking professors who insisted on passing grades, stoning political enemies from the rooftops. The library, Juan O'Gorman pointed out to me, was equipped with everything but

[12] Hubert Herring in *A History of Latin America*. New York, Alfred A. Knopf, Inc. 1955.

books: "Even the poet Alfonso Reyes has a better collection in his own home." [13] Similarly in rural education, millions more were appropriated than ever before, and schools were built at a tremendous rate; but with teachers receiving less in *real wages* than day laborers— who wanted to teach? Many schools were abandoned for lack of a staff, and those teachers who did stick it out tended to be the least capable.

President Alemán did give Mexico a giant boost toward self-sufficiency in food by putting millions of new acres into cultivation with his irrigation projects—by 1948 only wheat was being imported—but the *cost* in diverting water from once fertile areas, and in deforestation, never showed in the statistics. The Valley of Mexico, turned into a dust bowl after centuries of insane and costly effort to drain the lakes that once made Tenochtitlán a paradise, was resupplied at least with drinking water by the construction of the multimillion-dollar Lerma Aqueduct that opened in 1951, but what effect this gigantic diversion had upon the Lerma River Basin was not revealed. Lake Cuitzeo, north of Morelia, still appears on the maps as the largest body of water within a hundred miles of the capital, but when dams were built to favor agriculture in Michoacán, the rivers feeding the lake disappeared, and the nine ancient villages of Tarascan fisher-men-weavers vanished from the shores of what had now become a swamp.

The paradox of the whole process of industrialization in Mexico, Simpson and Tannenbaum pointed out, was that it was based upon the premise of low wages. "Business activity was increasing," Tannenbaum noted, "investments in business were growing, there was more unemployment, a middle class was developing, and the country was showing evidence of industrial progress. But it was doing so at the expense of those who could least afford it—the industrial and agricultural laboring population." By 1950, some 63 million acres had been distributed to the *ejidos*, but only where the *ejidos* had been turned into huge, mechanized collective farms was agriculture functioning with anything like the efficiency of the 200,000 "small proprietors" who in 1947 on their 5,700,000 acres were producing 70 percent of all Mexico's crops. Zapata's ideal of the "proud and independent small farmer" had been scrapped, Simpson pointed out: "The individual *ejitario* has not, for whatever reasons, produced a surplus and therefore cannot become a consumer of industrial products." In effect, the bill for industrial development was being paid for by the 70

[13] Selden Rodman, *Mexican Journal: The Conquerors Conquered.* New York, The Devin-Adair Co., 1958.

percent of the population that could least afford it. Between 1941 and 1949 the peso lost 70 percent of its purchasing power. It was devalued from 3.60 to the dollar in 1933 to 8.65 in 1948 and to 12.5 in 1955.

To be sure, the middle class was growing slowly, and a vast Social Security system was developing rapidly to take care of the fluctuations of unemployment surrounding the urban industrial complexes, but the growth of the population toward 45 million—to say nothing of the 200 million the President envisaged by the year 2000—was beyond anything the industrialized welfare state could keep up with. Miguel Alemán was only accelerating a process long under way. Until some way could be found of turning the majority of Mexicans from peasants into consumers, industrialization could only profit the industrialists and their close beneficiaries.

By 1952, with a new election coming, it was inevitable that this wide-ranging dissatisfction be diverted by the Party into a harmless channel. The "scandal" of the fun-loving President and his cronies, the new millionaires, was a perfect blind. Alemán acceded gracefully by passing the baton to the one member of his official family who could not be implicated in the grafting, whose reputation of living on nothing but his salary was as unique as Cárdenas' had been in the thirties. The party nominee, Adolfo Ruiz Cortines, was famous for his frugality. During the Revolution he had been an eagle-eyed paymaster. As Alemán's successor as Governor of Veracruz he had moved to a 25-peso single room to save money, and for recreation he played dominoes.

The campaign, with Alemán and his friends flying to Europe for a vacation, made the most of the outgoing administration's spending spree. The Party charged, probably with exaggeration, that Alemán & Company had drained the country of $800 million, banking more than half of it abroad. One cabinet member was accused of making an $8 million fortune by letting building contracts to the highest briber. Another member was accused of setting up his own companies to contract with his department. A third was asked to account for acquiring a bank, a sugar mill, several capital skyscrapers, and four palaces—one containing a $58,000 Italian marble fountain, gift of a favored contractor. An official of the Federal District, by such devices as landscaping the streets with flowers at a thousand pesos a blossom, had acquired mansions, yachts, $200,000 airplanes, and "dresses to cover the sinful bodies of his lady friends." Another Alemán henchman was charged with taking $40 million out of the Treasury through his manipulation of the Foreign Trade Bank.

Alemán himself had been more circumspect. His acquisition of princely properties in Acapulco and along his new superhighway to that booming resort could be considered coincidental. Many of his sumptuous ranches throughout Mexico, like the one in Baja California with its 40,000 almond, olive and prune trees, air-conditioned house, bar, and kidney-shaped swimming pool were gifts from local merchants and ranchers who hoped for irrigation works in their areas.[14]

Government by Compromise: Ruiz Cortines, López Mateos, Díaz Ordas

Alemán surely expected that the parsimonious friend and fellow Veracruzano he had picked to succeed him would satisfy the public clamor for a degree of austerity, but he must have been shocked by the zeal with which Ruiz Cortines clamped down on official corruption. He began, following his inauguration in December of 1952, by selecting a cabinet that contained none of his predecessor's cronies, and announcing that government-protected monopolies must end. "I will demand strict honesty from all. I will be inflexible with public officials who are not honest." Then he published a complete list of his own assets, amounting to $34,000, and demanded that all 250,000 government employees do the same—warning that their figures would be rigorously audited before and after their terms in service. Twenty-nine generals were dismissed or transferred.

The President's full-scale assault on the monopolies began with an order that all Treasury payments be stopped while government contracts were reexamined. First to feel the ax was Jorge Pasquel, czar of the Alemán newspapers and of the scandal-ridden Mexican baseball league, who had built a fantastically tasteless castle for himself near San Luis Potosí, complete with a runway for his $2 million super-Constellation. Control of oil distribution in the capital was promptly taken away from Don Jorge. Antonio Díaz Lombardo, Alemán's social-security chief who had made $40 million as boss of the bus lines, was next to be dethroned, followed by Aaron Saenz, the multimillionaire sugar king. In the capital the police-protected brothels and the clogged drains in the disease-infested slum areas were cleaned out. The ring of middlemen who had been jacking up the price of corn, rice and beans was eliminated—resulting in a 10 percent drop in food prices by September.

[14] *Time*, September 14, 1953. Their hopes, the magazine reported, were "fully justified."

Ruiz Cortines was too prudent to bring the industrialization of Mexico to a halt—even if he could have. But he was sensible enough to make the big Alemán innovations pay off in terms of public service. The dams were equipped with pipelines and irrigation canals to reach the parched fields. The arid northwest was turned into a productive area rivaling Arizona and southern California. Furniture, and even a few teachers at modest salaries, were provided for the showcase schools and University. But Ruiz Cortines was beset by difficulties. Alemán had committed the income from Ruiz Cortines' first year to his own last year, with the result that the Treasury had a deficit. Prices dropped following the Korean peace, a drought in 1953 reduced agricultural output, and tourist revenues descended from $400 million to $200 million. The peso had to be devalued to 8 cents. Wetbacks—as many as a million a year, according to some estimates—were still entering the United States illegally, draining Mexico's labor pool in the northern states, driving down wage rates in the United States, and generally causing strained relations between the two countries with a border too long to police. By the time Ruiz Cortines retired from the presidency in 1958, austerity was no longer popular, venality was creeping back into public life, and everyone expected the new President to be a freewheeler.

Adolfo López Mateos, Ruiz Cortines' Labor Minister and a long-time champion of the unions, surprised everyone by being the first post-Revolution President to break a strike. Inflation had overtaken the cost of living, and a general strike had been intended to keep wages up at the expense of capital and the middle-class consumer. López Mateos, mobilizing the government forces to move against the unions, seemed to be saying that from now on no sector in the economy was to receive favored treatment.

The new President was as strikingly handsome as Alemán had been, and because he ruled fairly and without ostentation, became very popular. Calling himself "Left within the Constitution," he nevertheless cracked down on Communist activists like Siqueiros and Filomeno Mata—and got along famously with President Eisenhower. With his wife, who set a precedent by involving herself directly in institutions for deprived children and relief of flood victims, he toured Mexico indefatigably in a successful effort to make the welfare state work.

At the end of his term, visibly exhausted and suffering from cancer, López Mateos summed up the accomplishments of his administration. The population had increased 3.1 percent (to 38 million in 1962), but the gross national product had advanced more rapidly for the first time—by 4.8 percent. Wages had gone up 17 percent while the cost of living had been held to a 1.8 percent increase. Social security now covered 5,260,000 Mexicans, 500,000 more than before. The largest item in the budget, $246 million for education, significantly included $82 million for free text books.[15] In matters of health, malaria was almost totally eliminated, and the incidence of polio and tuberculosis severely cut down. In land reform, five million acres were distributed to the landless in a single year—in this President's six years, almost a third as much land was distributed as in all the years since 1915—though 700,000 agricultural workers still remained without land. Moreover, the obsolescent *ejido* system was now being slowly turned into an effective system of producers' cooperatives, and this, together with the billion dollars spent for dams, farm-to-market roads, farm implements and livestock, may in time be considered to be López Mateos' most enduring achievement.

Gustavo Díaz Ordas, who succeeded López Mateos in the presidency in 1964, was expected to initiate a swing to the Right in accordance with Party policy. He was a native of the state of Puebla, always a Catholic stronghold. As López Mateos' Secretary of Government, it had been he who had crushed the railroad strike in 1959 and jailed the Communist agitators; on the other hand, he held out alone in the cabinet, and successfully, against breaking relations with Castro following the Cuban Missile Crisis.

In his first four years of office, Díaz Ordas has confounded expectations by steering a middle course. The López Mateos programs have not been permitted to lapse. Even the Communist-affiliated Partido Popular Socialista swung to his support—and with good reason, for Díaz Ordas made it a policy to include representatives of both the leftist PPS and the rightist Catholic PAN in the Congress, stretching the proportional representation law to seat sizable

[15] Irene Nicholson (*The X in Mexico*, Doubleday, 1966) compares the 21.7 percent of the 1963 budget devoted to education and the 10.8 percent for defense with 1920, when 62 percent went to the military, as against a mere 0.9 percent for education. She notes properly, however, that higher education in the University of Mexico continued to be farcical, with an indiscriminate enrollment of unprepared students, and leftist student organizations continuing to make discipline impossible. By comparison only the National Polytechnic Institute, the National School of Agriculture, the Colegio de Mexico, and the various American schools were providing effective higher education.

According to another recent study (*Mexico: The Struggle for Modernity* by Charles C. Cumberland, Oxford, 1968), more Mexicans are illiterate today than ever before—a statistic that doesn't take account of the enormous increase in population, of course, but is still disturbing if accurate.

delegations of both, including their leaders Vicente Lombardo Toledano and Adolf Cristlieb. PAN had won unprecedented mayoralty elections in the capitals of Sonora and Yucatán, and it may have been felt that to keep this largest of opposition elements isolated in the provinces would be unwise.

President Díaz Ordas criticized the American intervention in the Dominican Revolution—but he permitted no demonstrations in the capital to protest it. He also openly praised the Alliance for Progress, as López Mateos never had. He extended Social Security into rural areas. He moved to diversify crops in Sonora and Yucatán. He encouraged joint United States–Mexican "border industries" along the Rio Grande. He gave large grants of land to the *ejidos;* but he also recognized that this now traditional policy was causing an atomization of land holdings (15 acres per person was the average) and a class of "owners" legally unable to obtain needed bank loans by mortgaging or selling their holdings; he therefore made loans available at very low interest rates for the purchase of fertilizers and livestock.

Two of Díaz Ordas' major undertakings were innovations in the field of agrarian reform. To correct the growing imbalance between city and country—the average urban annual income was $630, as compared to $125 on the farms—the new President directed no less than 90 percent of the funds earmarked for government public investment in the 1965 budget *to the provinces.* This decentralization was not only good economics; it was good politics. PAN's followers in the provinces far exceeded those who had elected the mayors of Mérida and Hermosillo. In 1966 there had been a muffled uproar within the leadership of PRI itself when Carlos Madrazo, former Governor of Durango, was ousted as party chief for proposing that nomination of state and local officials take place at the grass-roots level. In a widely publicized speech to University students two years later, Madrazo called for a liberal front, indicating his belief that PRI (to which he still pledged loyalty) was losing contact with the Mexican people.

Díaz Ordas' other innovation was in his revival of CONASUPO (Compania Nacional de Subsistencias Populares), an organization founded during World War II to regulate the price of domestic commodities. Under the imaginative leadership of Hank Gonzáles, CONASUPO took visual shape all over Mexico in clusters of conical silos designed to keep the peasants' grain from rotting—and being stolen. From its subsidized resources CONASUPO bought corn, wheat, beans and rice in order to keep the price of these basics within the means of the farmer-consumer. CONASUPO bought so much wheat in 1963, in fact, that it became the sole exporter of wheat that year. Later it expanded its activities from grains to shoes, oil, eggs, school uniforms, and farmers' clothes, buying from suppliers and selling without profit to those housewives formerly exploited by middlemen. Except for that 20 percent of the population still too poor to buy or sell anything, CONASUPO was helping to bring subsistence-level Mexico into the national economy at the expense of the taxpayer.[16]

The student rioting that erupted at University City and elsewhere in the fall of 1968 was a consequence of two weaknesses in the Mexican system that have been alluded to frequently in these pages:[17] the failure to provide adequate education above the grade-school level, and the failure of the aging one-party bureaucracy to provide effective representation for unorganized workers, peasants, ethnic minorities, and the youth. In 1968, 50,000 students were registered at the University of Mexico, and another 44,000 in the preparatory schools run by it, and the $40 million budget was so inadequate that out of 8,000 teachers only 1,000 were being paid to work full time. Dropouts ranged from 20 to 60 percent of every entering class, and only a minority of those being graduated were sufficiently well trained to find jobs. The rioting students, with every Communist faction represented in their strike committee, were not stressing their educational neglect, however; what they were demanding, primarily, was abrogation of that part of the Penal Code punishing acts of "social dissolution" (subversion); the release of all political prisoners; the firing of Mexico City's police chief; elimination of the special riot patrols; and "indemnity" for "government aggression." Mexico's failure to provide democracy,

[16] Actually, of the *small* taxpayer; because one of the abiding failures of the Revolution has been its unwillingness to institute a progressive personal income tax. Urban workers at a bare subsistence level pay as much as 40 percent of their income in taxes, while the rich businessman pays little or nothing.

The "imbalance," according to Cumberland (*Mexico: The Struggle for Modernity*, 1968), has widened since 1940, with 1 percent of the gainfully employed population enjoying 66 percent of the total national income. Of the half of all Mexicans who remain rural, only 8 percent earn more than $80 a month, and 54.93 percent of the agricultural income is monopolized by 2.58 percent of the people involved in agriculture. The 708 Mexicans owning more than 800 hectares of land claim 35.1 percent of that 54.93 percent.

[17] See this chapter, pp. 140–141. Premonitory violence, at San Luis Potosí (1961) and Morelia (1966), and the government's stern countermeasures, are described in the Travelogue, pp. 193–194 and p. 200.

in other words, was playing into the hands of leftists who would abolish *all* democratic institutions if permitted to govern.

If Díaz Ordas yielded to these demands—which was most unlikely —Mexico would once again be in the throes of another period of revolutionary anarchy, with the end result this time a dictatorship of the Left. If the government suppressed the outbreaks without rectifying either the educational or political failures that led to them, a dictatorship of the Right, indistinguishable from those obtaining in such Latin American countries as Brazil, would ensue. A middle course, democratizing the autocratic PRI, providing much more self-government in the states, and allocating a larger share of the federal budget to effective higher education, would be more in line with Mexico's enlightened progress from 1925 to the present.

Post-Revolutionary Arts: Painting, Architecture, Literature

Mention has already been made of the achievements of José Clemente Orozco and Diego Rivera in Revolutionary mural paintings, of Mariano Azuela and Martin Luis Guzmán in the Revolutionary novel; nothing was accomplished in architecture during the twenties because the country was too drained by the great conflict to build. Under Cárdenas, Orozco was given a commission to decorate the Library at Jiquilpan, the President's birthplace; but his greatest works, the frescoes in the Hospício Cabañas, the University Theater, and the Government Palace, in Guadalajara, were all commissioned locally by the Governor of Jalisco—virtually at the cost of the artist's materials. Siqueiros also painted a ground-breaking fresco in that period for the Electrical Workers' Union in Mexico City; he used the montage technique which Griffith and Eisenstein had already developed in the cinema. Under Ávila Camacho, Rivera completed his lyrical masterpiece at the Agricultural School in Chapingo.

In the fifties, with Orozco dead and Rivera alternately succumbing to the blandishments of turgid Communist propaganda and bland capitalistic portraiture, the mural renaissance faltered. By the square yard, more murals were being painted than ever before, but with two exceptions they were the work of academicians in a debased tradition. Siqueiros' earlier experimentations with plastic paints, violent foreshortening to make the "action" envelop the spectator, and billowing surfaces, began to bear fruit. His mural in the La Raza Hospital is probably his finest work. Rufino Tamayo's images of alienation, cleverly synthesizing Mexican folk art and Picasso, had already been acclaimed in New York and Paris; the gifted colorist now painted two glowing evocations of Mexico's past for the Bellas Artes Museum in the capital.

In the early sixties there was a brief, inconclusive struggle between "Mexican" figurative humanism and "International" abstract formalism. The most interesting artists to emerge from it were José Luis Cuevas, a draftsman of magical talent whose grotesques were supremely nihilistic; Artémio Sepulveda, a potential Orozco lacking walls; Francisco Corzas and Rafael Coronél, romantic mannerists of considerable subtlety; and Francisco Toledo, like Tamayo a Zapotec Indian whose sophisticated fantasies pleased Paris more than they did Oaxaca. Art galleries multiplied in the capital, and many artists from abroad—Mathias Goeritz, Arnold Belkin, Leonora Carrington, Toby Joysmith, Maxwell Gordon, Lucas Johnson—contributed their talents to the happily dislocated Mexican art scene.

Architecture, rather than painting, became the dominant Mexican art in the fifties and sixties. (It is a curious fact that—folk artists excluded—not a single creative sculpture has been produced in Mexico since the Conquest.)

Four distinct types of architecture emerged. Least original and most ubiquitous was the Mexican adaptation of the International Style—"one of the most fatuous expressions of our uncivilized times," Juan O'Gorman calls it, "—these glass and concrete monstrosities into which cold, heat and light enter with equal belligerency." Its pioneers, back in the thirties, were José Villagrán García and O'Gorman himself. Its most effective practitioner was Mario Pani, whose approach to building the capital's vast housing complexes was sociological. Pointing out that the index of the birth rate in Mexico "is higher than in India, China, Indonesia" and that "by the year 2000, we Mexicans will number 120 million, with Mexico City growing all the time twice as fast as the rest of the country," Pani proposed to house the millions already crowded into the capital and "now living like animals" into high-rise apartments, and to "keep the traffic moving." [18] Under the circumstances it seemed "insane" to Pani that the average height of the proliferating capital's buildings was one and a half stories. His housing complex at Tlatelolco, which houses seventy thousand on 198 acres in the heart of the city, has its own parks, medical and dental clinics, schools, pools,

[18] Clive Bamford Smith (ed.), *Builders in the Sun: Five Mexican Architects.* New York, Architectural Book Publishing Co., Inc., 1967.

parking lots and movie theaters. The imaginative use of exterior color, sometimes in mosaic, is what gives these adaptations of the International Style their distinctive Mexican look.

Seemingly as utilitarian, but structurally more original and visually more poetic, were the various warehouses, churches, filling stations and outdoor restaurants designed by Felix Candela, a refugee from the Spanish Civil War whose concrete-shell "umbrellas" now cover 4 million square feet in the capital alone. "My principal task," says this engineer, who refuses to call himself an architect, "has been to simplify, to convince people that success does not depend upon building extravagant forms but only, on the contrary, upon making simple ones, and studying the details with care and love. Structural design has much more to do with art than with science." [19] Building without conventional props, ribs or stabilizers, Candela's discovery has been stat strength resides in shape. His ally, as in the case of the builders of the pyramids and the Gothic cathedrals, has been the almost inexhaustible supply of cheap labor: It takes hundreds of men building wooden molds and pouring concrete to make Candela's sun-shields soar like butterflies.

A genius as rare and contradictory is that of Juan O'Gorman. Like Frank Lloyd Wright (they were friends and admired each other), he stands alone, with no real disciples and little to show for his passionate conviction that Mexican architecture must be "organic" rather than "functional," keyed to the barbaric splendor of the Mexican landscape and the pre-Columbian past. O'Gorman's one masterpiece is his home in the capital's Pedregal, a "cave" hacked out of the black volcanic rock and embellished with the same heraldic stone mosaics in natural colors that are the glory of his otherwise conventional University Library.

The varieties of modern Mexican architecture are rounded out by a fourth category—private homes in simplified adaptations of the severe but opulent "Spanish" style—a category in which Ignácio Díaz-Morales (see pp. 196–197), Luis Barragán and Manuel Parra are the most brilliant exemplars. Landscaping on a grand scale is Barragán's forte. Before moving into the Pedregal development and transforming it magically for its millionaire homeowners, Barragán had been a successful real estate operator. But he had already acquired his vision of adapting Ferdinand Bac's Mediterranean gardens to Mexico while attending Le Corbusier's lectures in Paris in the early thirties. With Le Corbusier's theory of "machines for living" and the Gro-

---

[19] Smith, (ed.), *op. cit.*

pius-influenced architecture at the University, Barragán, with his "emotional" and mysteriously shaded patios filled with cacti, rock flowers and gnarled *palo bobo* trees, has no sympathy:

> Why should architecture be only for use? Why not for pleasure? Why should glass dominate buildings? Why should doors be two meters, sixty centimeters high? My spirit *needs* this height. I want to be at peace when I come in out of the traffic of Juárez and Madero! The complete human being is not just physical. The architecture magazines have been a bad influence. Modern architecture looks fine in photographs—but can you live in it? A landscape has less value when seen through a plate of glass; through familiarity, by your own constant presence, you reduce its value. I enjoyed Michelangelo's dome most when I saw it once, through a keyhole. So why open a whole wall to bring a garden into a house? The sense of mystery is important for life, for everyday living, as it is for love. The sense of discovery, of adventure, promotes life. Only primitives, or very cultivated people, are concerned with beauty; the others want comfort, security, order, likeness. But all religions make their propaganda through beauty. Architecture today reflects the loss of privacy in modern life. In public the opportunity to think and to reflect is lost. Houses have become *clubs* where people are no longer alone. The good architectect must counter all this.[20]

Manuel Parra, whose philosophy is similar, counters all this by building homes with subtle adaptations of Tarascan and other pre-Columbian motifs, rooms eccentrically shaped, vaulted ceilings whose ribs never symmetrically join the walls at a corner or over a door. Commenting to me in Cuernavaca on a photograph I had taken of the traffic tunnel that winds in and out of Guanajuato, Parra said: "You know what these celestial balconies are, spotted here and there on that wall with such apparent aesthetic inevitability? They are the toilets at the back of the streetside houses that once overhung that sewage ditch. I want to build like that, effortlessly; to let things grow in the right places."

Literature in the post-Revolutionary period has been less "engaged" with life than architecture but perhaps is more "Mexican" than the painting in relating the intellectual's feeling of alienation

---

[20] Quoted in the author's *Mexican Journal.*

to his local condition. From a Revolutionary point of view, the modern poets and novelists are reactionaries; not that they yearn for the old order, but that they are less concerned for the masses' advancement than for the individual's (or their own) salvation.

In poetry, the break with Iberian modes came at the turn of the century when the Nicaraguan poet, Rubén Darío, turned from Madrid to Paris. Darío had explained the title of his influential first book, *Azul*, "Blue," as an "attempt to capture the color of dreams, of art, Hellenic, Homeric." A tone of deliberate frivolity, elegant and hedonistic, characterized his efforts to carry further Verlaine's pale burden of "Music above all else, and after music, shade." Darío's most brilliant followers in Mexico, Alfonso Reyes and Carlos Pellicer, are as cool and elegant as the Nicaraguan expatriate but not at all decadent. Reyes brought a Hellenic spirit to Mexican letters—Olympian, yet always engaged in behalf of his aspiring juniors. Pellicer treats the pre-Columbian themes of death and flowers with a Rilkean sensivity but with more wit than the German symbolist.

In her first novel,[21] Rosário Castellanos presents a depressing picture of a hacienda's expropriation during the Cárdenas period. The landlords are weak and vacillating; the Indians sullen and mean-spirited; one would never guess that the flame of illuminating aspiration had ever crossed this dark terrain. A brooding compassion is this novelist's saving grace; and the same could be said of Juan Rulfo, whose view of Indian Mexico is even deadlier. The characters in this writer's major novel,[22] in fact, *are* dead. Rulfo, like Orozco, views history as a tragic circus in which evil impresarios betray clowns by making them believe in their own masquerade; but whereas Orozco's villains and victims are larger than life, Rulfo's seem to have no reality at all and only the sick can identify with their fate. Pedro Paramo drifts from one evil to the next, dragging the weaker souls in his village along with him—not from any heroic propensity to override convention, but because he is an animal. Nothing good is expected of him, and he suffers not from remorse but from unrequited lust. The parable is a vehicle for the style; and only the style survives.

Style is very important to Carlos Fuentes, too; but Fuentes' canvases of post-Revolutionary Mexico are much broader than Rulfo's

[21] *The Nine Guardians*. Translated by Irene Nicholson. New York, The Vanguard Press, Inc., 1960.
[22] *Pedro Paramo*. Translated by Lysander Kemp. New York, Farrar, Straus & Cudahy, 1959.

or Castellanos'. His characters think as well as feel. They are aware
of the depths of their depravity, and to this extent have a tragic
dimension. In Fuentes' first and so far best novel,[23] the chief characters are a revolutionary-turned-financier and a desperate poet.
"One does not explain Mexico," the poet remarks, "one believes in
Mexico, with fury, with passion, and in alienation. . . . Mexico has
never had a successful hero. To be heroes they had to fail. . . . Good
may not be identified with victory, nor evil with defeat. For otherwise the United States would be good and Mexico evil." But unfortunately when the poet tries to answer the question what Mexico
is to do if it is to continue its search for material progress, escape
the "leprosy" of Americanization, and at the same time identify
its own image, his thinking becomes vague. Fuentes himself is aware
of this lack of concreteness. "We destroy ourselves," he notes, "in
order to make and find ourselves in a desert no richer than our
own skin and words."

Octavio Paz, the major poet of the period and probably of all
periods, states the same thought constantly:

> . . . my thoughts that gallop and gallop and get no farther
> also fall and rise, and turn back and plunge into the stagnant
> waters of language.[24]

But for all his preoccupation with words and a melancholy passivity akin to T. S. Eliot's, which urges him to insist that "the
time is past already hoping for time's arrival"—the melancholy of
the deracinated scholar-diplomat—there is a grave nobility in Paz.
It links him in spirit to the "classical" Orozcos of the National
Preparatory School cycle and to the inspired selflessness of the
true Mexican heroes from Morelos and Hidalgo to Juárez and
Madero. It breaks through symbolism to affirmation:

> The mind at last is incarnate in forms,
> its enemy halves are reconciled
> and liquefy the conscience-mirror,
> again become fountain, fabled spring:
> Man, tree of images,
> words that are flowers that are fruits that are acts.[25]

---

[23] Carlos Fuentes, *Where the Air Is Clear*. Translated by Sam Hileman. New
York, Ivan Oblonsky, Inc., 1961.

[24] "The Endless Instant," translated by Denise Levertov, in *The Muse in
Mexico: A Mid-Century Miscellany*, edited by Thomas Mabry Cranfill. Austin,
Texas, The University of Texas Press, 1959.

[25] "Hymn Among Ruins," translated by Denise Levertov, in *op. cit.*

Part II
ILLUSTRATIONS

PLATE 1. Wrestler. Olmec Culture, *c.* 850–300 B.C. National Museum of Anthropology and Archaeology, Mexico City.

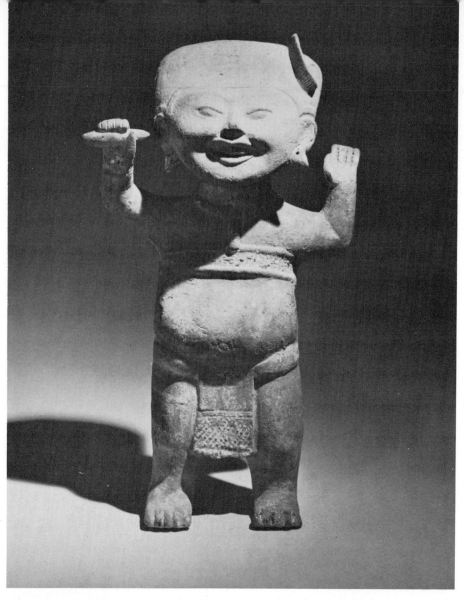

PLATE 2. Boy with smiling face. Totonac Culture, *c*. 200–800 A.D.
André Emmerich Gallery, New York City.

PLATE 3, *left* Musician. Nayarit Culture, *c.* 800–1000 A.D. Stavenhagen Collection, Mexico City.

PLATE 4, *top right* Stone Head. Totonac Culture. Stavenhagen Collection, Mexico City.

PLATE 5, *left* Ceramic Head of Girl. Zapotec Culture, *c.* 800–1000 A.D. Howard Lee Collection, Oaxaca.

PLATE 6. Ceramic Figurine. Maya Culture, Jaina Island, *c.* 600–900 A.D. André Emmerich Gallery.

Photo: Ruth D. Lechuga

PLATE 7.   Temple of the Sun, Palenque. Maya Culture, *c.* 600–900 A.D.

PLATE 8.   Relief, Bonampak. Maya Culture, *c.* 600–900 A.D.

Photo: Ruth D. Lechuga

Photo: Giles G. Healey

PLATE 9. Lacandon Indians with "god pots" at Bonampak the day the murals were discovered in 1946 by Giles Greville Healey.

PLATE 10. Captive. Detail of fresco, Bonampak. Maya Culture, *c.* 600–900 A.D.

Photo: Giles G. Healey

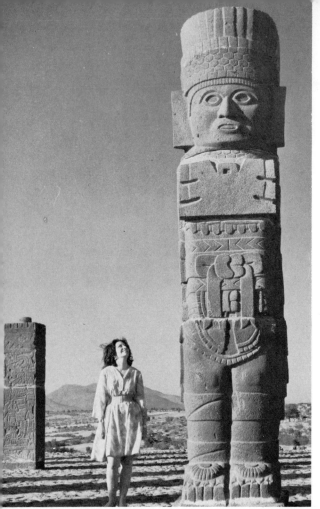

Photo: Author

PLATE 11. Guardian Warrior. Tula Citadel. Toltec Culture, *c.* 1200 A.D.

PLATE 12. Tlaloc (rain god). Ceramic Incense Burner, Mixtec Culture, *c.* 1000–1200 A.D. André Emmerich Gallery.

PLATE 13, *left* El Castillo, Chichén Itzá, Yucatán. Maya-Toltec Culture, *c*. 1200–1300 A.D.

PLATE 14, *top right* Sacred Cenote with dredging raft, Chichén Itzá.

PLATE 15, *bottom left* Ruins at Tulum, Quintana Roo. Late Maya-Toltec Culture, *c*. 1400 A.D.

PLATE 16, *right* Chac Mool. Stone sculpture at Temple of Warriors, Chichén Itzá.

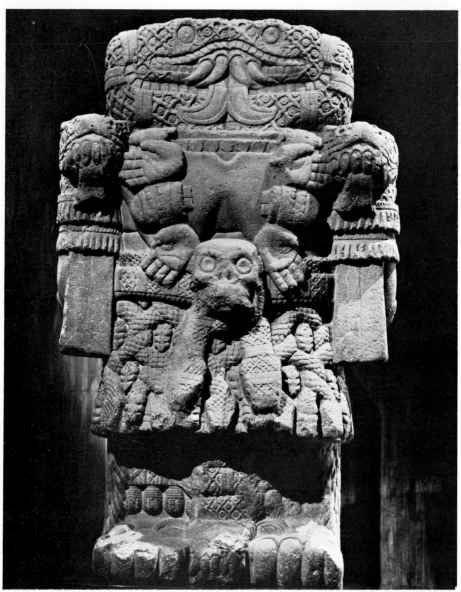

PLATE 17.   Coatlicue. Fertility-Death effigy in stone. Aztec Culture, *c*. 1300–1500 A.D.

PLATE 18. The Conquest of Mexico. Detail of fresco by Diego
Rivera in the National Palace, Mexico City.

PLATE 19. Franciscan and Indian. Fresco by José Clemente Orozco.
National Preparatory School, Mexico City.

PLATE 20, *left* Indian carving on arches and capitals of Franciscan Open Church at Tlalmanalco.

PLATE 21, *top right* Free-standing facade in ruined apse. Augustinian fortress church, Octopán.

PLATE 22. Fortress monastery of Atotonilco, near San Miguel de Allende.

PLATE 23, *right* Crosses with peasants. Chamula, Chiapas.

PLATE 24. *Voladores*, Cuetzalan.

PLATE 25. Augustinian courtyard (now post office) and church, Querétaro.

PLATE 26. Detail of angel playing mandolin, Augustinian Church, Querétaro.

PLATE 27. Detail of flying buttress, Tresguerras' Santa Rosa de Viterbo, Querétaro.

PLATE 28. Tresguerras' Santa Rosa de Viterbo, Querétaro.

PLATE 29. Ash Wednesday Fiesta, Chalma.

Photo: Author

PLATE 30. Under the Virgin of Guadalupe. Peasant family in photographer's booth, Iguala.

Photo: Ruth D. Lechuga

PLATE 31.   Cathedral of Mexico at night. Zócalo, Mexico City.

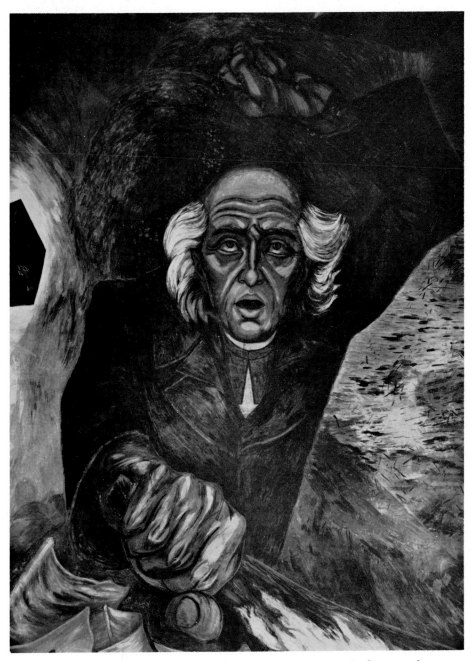

PLATE 32. Hidalgo at the Alhóndiga leading Mexico's first revolution (1810). Fresco by José Clemente Orozco in the Palacio de Gobierno, Guadalajara.

PLATE 33. Morelos. Fresco by Diego Rivera in Cortés' Palace, Cuernavaca. (The scratch across Morelos' shins is the work of a vandal.)

PLATE 34. Antonio López de Santa Anna. Photograph apparently made during his visit to New York in 1866.

Courtesy Library of Congress

PLATE 35.   Gen. Winfield Scott.
Courtesy of the Library of Congress

PLATE 36. Juárez rejecting Princess Salm's plea for Maximilian's life. Wax group in Town Hall, San Luis Potosí.

Photo: Rogaciano Mendez A.

PLATE 38. Porfirio Díaz, the year before his overthrow and exile in 1910.

Photo: Casasola Archives

PLATE 37. Execution of the Emperor Maximilian at Querétaro. Painting by Édouard Manet, Louvre, Paris.

Photo: Casasola Archives

PLATE 39. President Francisco I. Madero reading a speech at the American Embassy in 1912 while Ambassador Henry Lane Wilson looks on.

PLATE 40. Gen. Victoriano Huerta, Madero's successor after *coup d'état*.

Photo: Casasola Archives

PLATE 41. Young revolutionary, appropriately outfitted in Texas, poses for camera before recrossing the Rio Grande to join Villa's army.

Photo: Casasola Archives

Photo: Casasola Archives

PLATE 42. Revolutionary execution, *c.* 1914.

Photo: Casasola Archives

PLATE 43. Gen. Francisco Villa, in presidential chair, talking to Gen. Emiliano Zapata. National Palace, Mexico City, December 6, 1914. The officer on the left is Tomás Urbino.

PLATE 44. Warriors of three wars. Left to Right: Álvaro Obregón, Francisco Villa, John J. Pershing, (reputedly) George F. Patton, Jr. International Bridge, Ciudad Juárez, August 27, 1914.

Photo: Casasola Archives

PLATE 45.   President Plutarco Elías Calles.

PLATE 47.   President Lázaro Cárdenas.

PLATE 46. José Vasconcelos, pointing with cane at the spot in the Ciudadela where Gustavo Madero was lynched.

PLATE 48.   President Miguel Alemán.

PLATE 49. Tree of Death. Ceramic from Metepec (Toluca).

PLATE 50. Dance of the
Devils. Modristlán, Guerrero.

Photo: Donald Cordry

PLATE 51. Dance of the
Archers. San Pablito, Nayarit.

Photo: Donald Cordry

PLATE 52. Las Estacas, Morelos.

PLATE 53. El Salto, San Luis Potosí.

PLATE 55, *above* Cabo San Lucas, Baja California.

PLATE 54, *left* Acapulco, Guerrero.

PLATE 56. Market Woman from San Andres, Cuetzalan.

PLATE 57. Huichol Indian gear, Nayarit.

PLATE 58. Ceramic painted figurines, Guerrero. Collection Robert Brady, Cuernavaca.

PLATE 59. Young *chinela* dancer at ease, Tepoztlán, Morelos.

Photo: Author

PLATE 60. Vehicular traffic tunnel, Guanajuato.

PLATE 61, *right* Automex Towers, Toluca. Designed by Mathias Goeritz.

PLATE 62. Cosmic Ray Pavilion, University City. Designed by Felix Candela.

Photo: Author

Photo: Author

PLATE 63. Diego Rivera: Self-Portrait. Detail of a fresco in the Ministry of Education, Mexico City.

PLATE 64. Diego Rivera: "Nude." Agricultural School, Chapingo.

PLATE 65. José Clemente Orozco: Chained Slave. Detail of a fresco in the Chamber of Deputies, Guadalajara.

PLATE 66. José Clemente Orozco: "Self-Portrait." Museum of Modern Art, New York City.

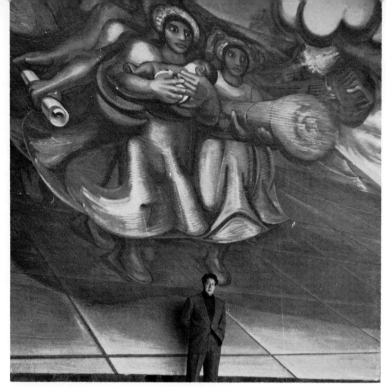

Photo: Author

PLATE 67.   David Alfaro Siqueiros, 1956.

PLATE 68.   Octavio Paz, 1956.

Photo: Author

Part III
TRAVELOGUE

MEXICO is too vast, and its tourist attractions are explored in too many current guidebooks, to make a comprehensive survey in this appendix sensible. What I propose to do instead is to relate to the foregoing history some of the landscapes and landmarks, and to describe in detail works of art, primitive villages, and places of great natural beauty that have been neglected.

Since my first trip to Mexico in the thirties, when good roads hardly existed and time was measured by breakdowns on the Revolution-ravaged rails, all but the most remote mountain regions have become accessible to comfortable travel. As Minister of Tourism, ex-President Miguel Alemán has even provided a fleet of trucks, the "Green Angels," that offer gas and repairs free of charge to motorists in distress on the main highways. An ordinary car will get you to all the principal cities; a Volkswagen will get you anywhere an ox-cart can go, and to park in the clogged capital or slip in and out of traffic on the dizzying *glorietas* (rotary intersections), this vehicle is unrivaled. A good road now links the Yucatán Peninsula to the rest of the country, and there is even a car-ferry from Mazatlán to La Paz in Baja California in case one prefers not to fly. Puerto Vallarta alone of the major resorts is accessible only by plane, though a Pacific highway linking Acapulco with Mazatlán is nearing completion.

The North: Four Roads to Mexico

The half of Mexico which lies north of the Twenty-second Parallel—crossing the country just below Tampico and San Luis Potosí and just above Aguascalientes and Tepic—is virtually without interest for travelers. Most of it is desert and mountains. The border cities, from Tijuana to Ciudad Juárez in the west and Nuevo Laredo to Matamoros in the east, are tawdry and Americanized. The cities of the interior—Hermosillo and Chihuahua, Durango, Saltillo, Torreón, and Zacatecas—are grimy industrial centers, and until the Mexican Government rehabilitates General Villa's reputation and marks the sites of the great battles he fought near them, they will have no romantic associations for most travelers. The cities near the West Coast—Culiacán and Ciudad Obregón—and Tampico on the Gulf of Mexico, are industrial too. Only Monterrey and San Luis Potosí have more than their flourishing industries to recommend them.

Visitors entering from California or Arizona will travel the West Coast highway south as far as Tepic before turning east to Guadalajara and central Mexico. There are good hotels, attractive beaches and excellent fishing at Guaymas (Sonora) and Mazatlán (Sinaloa), and these are the recommended places to stay. Alamos, southeast of Ciudad Obregón, is the only remnant of colonial Mexico in the west and worth detouring to see. A ghost town for centuries, it is being restored and has been declared a national monument.

There are four highways from Texas into Mexico. The westernmost, originating at Ciudad Juárez, is by far the longest and least interesting, passing through Chihuahua, Torreón, Zacatecas and Aguascalientes. The easternmost, from Brownsville–Matamoros, leads to Ciudad Victoria, and from there through the tropical Huastec country between Tampico and San Luis Potosí, before slicing through the mountains around Pachuca to the capital. Between Ciudad Victoria and Ciudad Valles lies the most spectacular waterfall in Mexico, and one of the two most memorable swimming holes in the country. "El Salto" is threatened by a nearby hydroelectric project, but unless the jungle river is entirely diverted, the column of water will continue to fall through ferns and lianas two hundred feet and then gently descend from lip to lip of a series of daisy-fringed turquoise basins, each of which serves as a natural swimming pool, deep enough to dive into. El Salto is a jog to the north off Route 80 running west of the highway. Ciudad Valles, a hundred miles south on the highway itself, has fine swimming pools of its own at its roadside motels.

Whether entering Mexico from central Texas at Del Rio or Laredo, stop-offs at Monterrey and San Luis Potosí will introduce the
two most attractive cities of northern Mexico.

Monterrey, the capital of Nuevo León, is Mexico's leading industrial city, and after the capital and Guadalajara, third in population with 350,000. It is the most Americanized of Mexican cities—
modern factories and churches, quick-lunch rooms and curio shops,
hotels with pools and TV, broad avenues clean to the point of ste-
rility. But the setting is grandly dramatic. Stone mountains ring the
valley. One of the peaks (Silla de Montár) has been carved by the
howling winds at eight thousand feet into a profile of haunting in-
tensity.

There are many things to do in this city as big as Baltimore. The
Cuauhtémoc Brewery, which makes "Carta Blanca" and "Bohémia"
(both superior to any American brand), serves free beer to visitors.
There are theaters and vaudevilles and local art shows worth taking
in. And there are caves, like the beautiful Grutas de García, twenty-
seven miles from the city off the Saltillo road. Canyons and fishing
streams abound in the nearby hills. The Cathedral has a fine Baroque
facade, but its interior was badly damaged during Zachary Taylor's
sack of the city in 1847 (see p. 76). The so-called Bishop's Palace,
west of the city, was not only the scene of heroic resistance to the
American invasion but harassed the French in 1864 and was stormed
by Pancho Villa in 1913. Its museum contains the printing press
which Padre Mier brought to northern Mexico in 1813. The "Ca-
rapán" folk-art gallery displays some of the best buys in Mexico;
its proprietor, Umberto Areliano y Garza, employs a dozen Huichol
Indians to make eye-catching abstractions out of colored yarns on
waxed wood. The smaller squares-within-squares, "eyes of God,"
made by these peyote-chewing primitives from the states of San
Luis Potosí and Nayarit use exactly the same color tricks exploited
by Josef Albers, the father of Op Art.

San Luis Potosí, except for its outlying motels and a glass sky-
scraper with a nightclub atop, is not Americanized at all. It is also
rich in history—the wax tableau of Juárez and Agnes Salm has already been mentioned in Chapter 3. Its many Baroque churches in
the local brown stone are handsome but unspectacular. The great
Huastec sculptures in the museum are *copies* of the originals carted
off to the National Museum of Anthropology and Archaeology in
the capital—though the labels don't say so.

The circumstance points up the city's traditional hostility to federalism. It erupted in violence as recently as September of 1961,

when a street demonstration protested "fixed" voting machines in the defeat of a popular native-son candidate for Governor by the "official" PRI nominee from the capital. The demonstrators were machine-gunned by federal troops, and scores of them were killed. There were no repercussions, except that the new Governor—who turned out to be a good one, allocating 50 percent of the state's pitifully inadequate federal funds to teachers' salaries—was socially ostracized by the city's proud upper class, never being permitted to enter their homes, their country club, or their exclusive dancing pavilion, La Lonja.[1]

I visited the home of one of these aristocrats in 1968. Portraits of Santa Anna, Iturbide and Cortés were prominently displayed. The old gentleman regarded Porfirio Díaz' dictatorship as Mexico's Golden Age. He did think that López Mateos and Díaz Ordas were "good" Presidents in the sense that they kept "hands off business" and provided an atmosphere of peace "without the all-out thieving of such bandits as Cárdenas and Alemán, our real rulers even today."

Central Mexico I: The Outer Ring

Guadalajara, Pátzcuaro, Morelia, Uruapan

Guadalajara, a very long day's drive west of the capital, but a short day's drive from Tepic and San Blas on the Pacific Coast, may be Mexico's second city (population, 400,000) and the one in which Americans feel most at home in terms of climate, cleanliness and sports, but in a spiritual-aesthetic sense it is Orozco's city.

Returning here to the land of his birth in the late thirties, the great Jaliscan painter invented forms to match his content, creating as he did so entirely new color harmonies, on a scale and with a violence of imagination comparable to Tintoretto's or El Greco's. Their "story line" was the Christian mythos; Orozco's was the Mexican Revolution (1810–1939). Like them, he didn't exactly "accept" his mythos, rebelling against its inconsistencies and excesses as they did; yet it remained for him, as Christianity did for them, the supreme experience.

Picasso is the only other modern painter whose powers of inven-

[1] An interesting sidelight of this state of affairs is the case of La Virreina, one of Mexico's outstanding restaurants, whose proprietress happened to be a PRI adherent in 1961. The restaurant is boycotted by the aristocrats—except when a VIP comes to town; then a big party with wines, Scotch and liqueurs is thrown for him at La Virreina, following which the aristocrats walk out without paying the check!

tion are as awe-inspiring, yet beside the mighty Hidalgo cycle in Guadalajara's Palacio de Gobierno, such a cerebral fantasy as the "Guernica" seems like a clever assemblage of cutouts. The subject is the same—the horror and pity of war—but whereas Picasso felt compelled to invent visual symbols related to little in the common heritage, Orozco was able to take a number of perfectly familiar historical events (familiar to Mexicans) and on that "story line" magnify the human material into universal images.

As one ascends the stairs of the noble building that dates from 1643, one's eyes are carried up and back to the gigantic effigy of the revolutionary priest, brandishing his torch directly overhead. From its flame, the color symphony of the surrounding areas takes shape. Below the white heat enveloping the prophet's head (flying splinters of burnt wood give the head a palpable dimension), are the swirling bodies of the masses that stormed the Alhóndiga. Differentiated are Pípila bearing his gravestone; a towering central figure with arms outstretched, throat pierced by a blade; a child draped over a cross. Below them lie the shattered bodies of the dead and dying. To offset the curves of their anguish, stacks of bayonets bristle like cacti.

And then the side walls! Gradually, as one ascends, they come into focus, perhaps forty feet high and wide. The one on the left is a prodigious still life, dominated by a blocky cross and red bishops' miters against the white-hot sky. On the left is hell itself, snarled and smoking. The bearers of swastika, fasces, hammer-and-sickle and dollar signs stomp over the violated emblems of culture. And at the bottom of this maelstrom, Karl Marx, a pompous bearded head set upon a dwarf body, is making a speech.

At the University of Guadalajara Theater the big wall at the back of the stage is another tribute to man's capacity to suffer and endure. The photographs of the concentration camps that shocked the world in 1945 had yet to be seen; which goes to prove that life follows art—if the artist is bigger than life. With upraised arms the victims drive their cowering oppressors across a chasm into the flaming "paradise" they have prepared for humanity. The oppressors, as they flee, point to legal precedent in law books spattered with blood. On one of the side walls is a haunting image of a father and son standing over the broken body of a child. On the other, facing this scene, is a brutalized Mexican soldier backing up two bloated, bird-brained revolutionists, their hands on their pistol holsters, their feet on stacks of rifles and law books. In the shallow dome, high-keyed colors, distortion and swirling movement contrast effectively with the somber hues of the stage panels. Here the artist is paying his respects to science—admiringly, the Mexicans say, but to my mind with tongue in cheek. A five-faced head, a trepanned (empty) skull, entrails receiving shock treatment—these give no very reassuring vision of the miracles the professors have in store for those who put their trust in physical therapy.

But the climax of Orozco's art is the Hospício Cabañas. I was lucky to visit it, in 1956 and 1964 with Orozco's friend, Ignácio Díaz-Morales; and especially lucky the first time because the architect was then supervising the repair of the dome, which had burst its 1803 iron hoop: it was possible to see the dome murals from close up, as even Orozco had never seen them. The artist, Díaz-Morales recalled, had been provided with a primitive scaffolding that obscured everything except the area directly in front of his brush. In fact he had never seen the work as a whole except from the rotunda of the Orphanage Chapel 106 feet below—and then only when the work was completed. Even in the Sistine Chapel, working conditions could not have been so difficult; and indeed the images of "Wind" and "Water," with fingers not quite touching, can only be compared with Michelangelo's somewhat similarly posed "Creation" group. Orozco does not suffer by the comparison. The head of "Wind," its features loosely composed to suggest a blowing apart of the facial structure, could only have been carried off by the Florentine master—if he had been familiar with El Greco. There could be a reference in this figure to Quetzalcoatl, creator among the Indian gods, who was also a symbol of the wind until the day Tezcatlipoca, god of night, assumed a tiger's form and pulled him down to earth.

Eight years later, when the repair work was over, I stood under the dome looking up. Encompassed by the orchestration of those seventy intricately modulated frescoes of arch, lunette, vault, squinch and cupola frame that build up to that climactic *coda* of blues, reds and grays, Díaz-Morales told me of the visit Orozco had made to Guadalajara a few days before his death in 1948. "We stood in this spot and I said to him, 'Maestro, you should be buried here!' He hated monuments, memorials, panegyrics, praise, but he replied, 'Yes. That would be wonderful.' And then he looked at me with that ironical smile of his and added: 'I would be laughing here for all eternity with my *monos* (monkeys).'"

Díaz-Morales has left a worthy masterpiece of his own to Guadalajara. This is the Plaza de la Liberación. The cathedral and palaces surrounding this focal point were of course already there; but it was Díaz-Morales who swept away the clutter between them, planting the trees and designing the fountains. The result is a gathering place to linger in serenely. As in the noble concourse of New York's Grand Central Terminal, one never feels lost.

Guadalajara has many other attractions. In addition to being spacious and clean, it is a progressive, open-hearted city; and last but not least, its women are beautiful. The suburbs of Tonolá and Tlaquepaque, where the affluent Tapatian relaxes on warm evenings at his summer residence, are pottery towns. In them descendants of the Tonaltec Indians still make high-glazed and painted earthenware figures, each family handing down its secret formula from generation to generation. The thing that impressed me most during my first visit to Guadalajara, however, was the pair of larger-than-life seated sculptures flanking the gates to the city. The one to the right is Mariano Azuela, the pioneer social novelist. The one on the left is José Clemente Orozco. *Both heroes of culture had been alive ten years before*. In Guadalajara, they were already immortal. Where else could this happen?

Chapala and Pátzcuaro are the great lakes of Mexico, and the country around them is mostly Michoacán, a state with such a variety of attractions, talented people, and romantic landscape that visiting it is like visiting a separate country. Chapala, where D. H. Lawrence wrote *The Plumed Serpent* in 1923, is less interesting than smaller Pátzcuaro. Around the lovely town of the same name, where Vasco de Quiroga tried to build his cosmic church, ancient ash trees still shade Gertrudis Bocanegra Square, and Juan O'Gorman painted his gay mural in the Library honoring that heroine. In the village clustered about the lake, Mexico's finest pottery is still painted and glazed. The townsmen still fish with butterfly nets, and weave the finest serapes west of Toluca. And here, every November 1, when *calaveras* (candy skulls) are sold in the streets, the little island of Janitzio lights up at midnight with ten thousand candles.

General Cárdenas, a native of Michoacán, endowed Janitzio with its huge statue of Morelos that dominates the lake. When he was President Cárdenas also employed Orozco to paint the formidable, mostly black-and-white murals in the Gabino Ortíz Library at Jiquilpan, across the street from the house in which Cárdenas was born. If the General expected the Revolution to be romanticized, he must have been disappointed, for the scenes at Jiquilpan are of firing squads, mounted *caudillos,* and faceless mobs carrying red flags, in the artist's most disillusioned (and convincing) realism.

Between Jiquilpan and Pátzcuaro, the road branches south to

Uruapan. I've never been in China, but I continuously had the feeling that this must be what it is like at its best. The terrain rolls sensuously from the gently truncated pyramids of ex-volcanoes, pagoda-shaped and densely green with conifers, that stud the plain, to much higher mountains with sharp peaks purple in the haze of distance. The plain itself varies in texture from the shimmering pale-green of wheat to the rich black or contoured umber of fields newly prepared for planting; and among the fields the wind, stimulated by some uneasy turbulence in the huge saucer of varying altitudes, builds twisters, miniature dust devils, of the dry soil. These swirl crazily like tops until miles away, attenuated to great heights, they suddenly, like Aladdin's jinni, vanish.

Perhaps the impression of China comes from the stone walls that divide the fields. They average six feet high, with uneven tops, and are built only to the thickness of a single dusty rock; consequently they are full of holes through which the light leaks, giving the appearance, from a distance, of black lace. Perhaps the impression comes also from the houses of the Tarascan peasants. These are built of unfinished logs, or squared timber, with the ends crossing unevenly to protrude at the angles. The walls and high-pitched roofs are shingled black; and the gates in the stone walls are covered with little peaked "hats" of black shingles too, like the garden shelters of the philosophers in Sung painting. The more substantial houses of adobe have red tile roofs with an overhang of almost three feet, dentiled and sometimes gaily painted.

Perhaps, though, the insistent impression of China comes from the Tarascan Indians themselves, with their Mongoloid features, broad-brimmed flat-crowned sombreros, and serapes of black wool, sparsely sprinkled at the corners with diamonds of deep red and blue.

Uruapan is a pretty little town on the banks of the green Cupatizio River. And around its square, shaded with cedars and *fresnos* (ash trees), are the factories where the famous lacquer trays and boxes are made. Chinese again! Some believe this art was introduced directly from China long before the Conquest. But federalism once more has stepped in to drain the province of its glory: The best examples are now to be found *only* in the Museo Nacional de Artes and Industries Populares in the capital, where they are for sale. One can still pick up, fortunately, some of the finest guitars at Paracho, a few miles to the north, where Quiroga introduced this instrument in the sixteenth century.

Twenty-two miles northwest of Uruapan, on a road that was once bad enough to cost me a steering gear, is a sight no traveler to Michoacán should miss. This is the buried church of San Juan de Parangaricutiro, with its spire and altar rising above a field of solidified lava. Without warning on the morning of February 20, 1943, the world's newest volcano sprouted in the cornfield of Dionísio Pulido. In a matter of days Parícutin had become a mountain from whose cone flames and fiery rocks illuminated the countryside—and Dr. Atl was painting it by day and by night.[2] In a matter of months Parícutin had subsided, and the surrounding villages were returning to their normal (though from now on, blackened) existence. To see the church's defiant steeple and the white marble of its unscathed apse poking above this landscape of hell is to have thoughts about religion's miraculous survival, or its vulnerability to disasters, natural and man-made—depending on one's point of view.

Morelia lies in a lovely valley a little to the northeast of the Uruapan-Pátzcuaro area, halfway between Guadalajara and Mexico City on the main highway. The word "picturesque" could never be applied to its stately splendor. Entering from the east, one passes the 254 arches of a ruined eighteenth-century aqueduct. In a little square facing the Church of the Roses, there are ancient trees braided with vines whose roots are as thick as the tree trunks. Bronze effigies of Cervantes and Don Vasco de Quiroga face each other in the leafy shade, enclosed on all sides by peach-colored palaces with cast-iron balconies. Then walk to the Alameda....

The Cathedral, between the two squares of this central park, took 104 years to be built, and its intricately carved rose stone facade and wooden organ case brought the Plateresque Style to full flower. From the 210-foot towers, all the domes and steeples of Morelia march to this climax. But it was not from here, but at eye level, that the Alameda was designed to be seen. This surely is one of the architectural wonders of the Western World. Everything is of a piece. The broad arcades supported by Doric columns give rhythm to the more static facades of the palaces, their wide areas of simplicity accented by the richness of elaborate balconies, the rows of delicate brackets, the complex dentiled cornices, the funerary urns of stone profiled against the blue sky. Small, widely spaced rosettes adorn the architraves and pendants. Corinthian pilasters do not clash with the severer orders beneath them, nor do the window pediments decorated with stone drapery ever seem to sag. Black gutter spouts, two feet long, protruding like cannon (to which in some cases

[2] *El Parícutin: 1943–1950. Como nace y crece un volcán. Obra escrita e illustrada por el Dr. Atl.* Mexico, 1950.

copper pipe extensions have been added) give another note of serial, brazen discipline to the stone symphony that fills the park. The buildings can be seen only one, or at most two, at a time. The planting of the plaza, and its particular furniture, provide still another harmony. The benches are of stone, long and pierced at their backs by cloverleaf "windows." The bandstand, a gift from Cárdenas' brother Damaso, who was Governor of Michoacán in 1952, harmonizes perfectly, being constructed of cream-pink trachyte like the buildings that surround it. It is encircled by miniature Doric columns, set widely apart and beautifully pitted by the weather. There are just enough trees of every height and shape; just enough flowers. The water in the circular marble basin is black and motionless; and along the borders of the grass beds, cut in elegant patterns, stand rows of very high, square columns crowned by truncated obelisks. The iron lanterns which hang from these columns illuminate—but don't defy—the night.

Lest anyone think Morelia is all sweetness and light, the University is notorious for its Communist strikes and violent demonstrations. In 1966, three hundred students were arrested in a disturbance arising over a 10-centavo increase in the bus fares. When one of the students was accidentally killed, the students seized and burned the buses, paralyzing the city for three days. President Díaz Ordas let the Governor, an old political foe, sweat it out for three days, then released a regiment of federal cavalry who rode right into the buildings of the supposedly "autonomous" campus, arresting the three hundred students, and seizing what they described as "tons of Communist propaganda with the Russian Embassy's label on it." Two years later a "Freedom March" started out from Dolores Hidalgo to march on Morelia and release the still-imprisoned student leaders; it swelled so ominously along the way that another regiment of cavalry had to be brought in to break it up at Valle de Santiago. "There hasn't been so much excitement here," an official told me in 1968, "since our students burned down your Bi-National Center in 1961 to protest the Bay of Pigs."

Guanajuato, San Miguel de Allende, Querétaro

These three cities of surpassing beauty and historical interest lie in a mountainous region west of the main north-south road from San Luis Potosí to the capital, and they are easily accessible *from* the capital now that a toll road to Querétaro has been completed. But they may also be reached by driving straight north from Morelia to Guanajuato. This road passes over what is left of Lake Cuitzeo (see p. 141) and through Yuriria and Salamanca. In Yuriria, by the lake of the same name, stands one of those massive convents built by the Augustinians, with a wonderful vine-wreathed facade and a severe cloister featuring Corinthian columns and griffin-rainspouts. McAndrew called it:

> ... unsurpassed even by the luxurious Augustinians in its scale, its profusion of carved ornament, and air of magnificence. In their attack, the Chichimecas gained the atrio but failed to break into the church. Mistaking a statue of St. Nicholas (or St. Augustine?) at the top of the facade for a living person, so we are told, they shot at it until an arrow lodged in the stone. With no machines of war more menacing than the bow and the atl-atl, or throwing stick, and with no force able to throw their arrows as high as the top of the tower, the attackers could do little harm. [Nothing really hurt this church until its own priest made it a furnace to smelt the gold leaf from its rich *retablos* in 1815. The pious women of the town got the fire out, but couldn't keep part of the vault from falling.] ... Thought out of date in his day, Father Grijalva found it "the most superb building imaginable" and could say of it "what Tertullian said of the theatre which Pompey built in Rome: that it was surpassed only by the spirit of him who made it." [3]

I can recommend a visit to Salamanca as highly, for different reasons. Only in the Jesuit churches of Pomata and Juli in southern Peru have I seen anything to compare with the enormous golden Churrigueresque *retablos* of St. Joseph and the Virgin in the transepts of the convent of San Augustín. This is flowering gold leaf at its most inventive and impressive.

Guanajuato *is* picturesque; in fact, it is the most picturesque city in Mexico. Of course, there will always be champions of Taxco, Mexico's other silver town, but Taxco has become so overrun with tourists that you sometimes have to climb their backs to see Santa Prisca's pink facade. Unlike Taxco, which perches on top of a hill, Guanajuato nestles in a 7,000-foot-high valley—or, more accurately, a confluence of *barrancas*. When you pass over the city in a plane, the view is staggering: a spider web of converging creases into which some celestial architect appears to have poured liquid marble.

[3] John McAndrew, *The Open Churches of Sixteenth-Century Mexico*. Cambridge, Massachusetts, Harvard University Press, 1965.

But when you enter it in a car, you will pass through The Tunnel (see p. 151).

When Adolfo López Mateos became President of Mexico in 1958, the State of Guanajuato, like all the other states, elected a new Governor. But Governor Juan José Torres Landa was not like any of the others. He built new roads and bridges, attacking decaying cities like Celaya and León with fleets of bulldozers, slicing great boulevards through them, placing the half-buried churches on axes that made them visible miles away. The Governor's enemies called him ruthless. A wealthy citizen of Celaya complained that his house had been cut in half and his taxes doubled, to which the Governor is supposed to have retorted: "Of course. You are now situated on an improved road!"

For centuries the Guanajuato River had run through the town, with the people building their houses over it, and dumping into it). After a terrible flood in 1905, a huge trough was cut along the riverbed to divert the overflow from dams outside the city; soon it became the principal sewage outlet for the city—and of course it stank. Governor Torres Landa had his engineers build a large sewage tunnel *under* the old trench. Then he diverted the river and built a two-way concrete boulevard, half of it running in floodlit stretches beneath the domed archways. Every few hundred yards the road emerges into sunlight and the driver can imagine that he is in the midst of a well-preserved medieval castle. Simultaneously the Governor had solved the hopeless traffic problem of Guanajuato, many of whose streets are as narrow as knife blades and some of which must be mounted by ramps or stone steps. He named his celestial tunnel for Miguel Hidalgo.

The Alhóndiga, which Hidalgo's revolutionaries stormed in 1810 (see p. 48) will always be the great historical attraction in Guanajuato. Its interior is now a museum embellished with frescoes by José Chavez Morada, and with one of its rooms devoted to mementos of Diego Rivera, a native son.[4] The best view of the city is from the Pípila Monument with its somewhat sinister inscription: THERE WILL BE MORE ALHÓNDIGAS TO BURN! Some visitors will enjoy most the Juárez Theater, inaugurated in 1903 with a lavish performance of *Aida*, and embellished along its skyline with

---

[4] Curiously, the painter looked like a frog and sometimes depicted himself carrying one—curiously, because the town's name is derived from the Nahuatl words for Frog Hill! The museum contains an interesting letter from Justo Sierra, recommending to Porfirio Díaz that the artist be given a scholarship abroad, and enclosing a Cézanne-like sketch.

eight allegorical figures in bronze, the work of one W. H. Mullen, of Salem, Ohio. Others will prefer the crypt of the cemetery on the Cerro del Trozado with its macabre collection of corpses, mummified by the dry heat, and its guide who sobs: "All my friends are down here." Still others will prefer the abandoned silver mines, the dozen or two splendid churches in and around town, or the pleasures of Marfil, a decayed suburb of palatial homes and gardens that have been tastefully restored for American expatriates.

From Guanajuato, the road southeastward to San Miguel de Allende passes through Dolores Hidalgo and by the vast Augustinian Sanctuary of Atotonilco. Dolores, where Hidalgo rang the bell for Independence in the parish church with its majestic Churrigueresque facade, has been blessed (or cursed) with a colossal monument on the edge of town which resembles a stalled lunar rocket. Atotonilco is badly crumbling, the "popular" murals that swarm over the walls and vaults are in danger of falling off. They are said to be the work of one Miguel Antonio de Pocosangre, who painted them in 1740–48, some sixty years before Hidalgo's "army" made its first stop here.

San Miguel, surnamed "de Allende" after Hidalgo's general, is almost as pretty a hill town as Guanajuato, and with as many fine churches and public buildings. The colony of American art students and Sunday painters grouped around the Instituto Allende give the town its brassy tone—but they are also responsible for the town's prosperity and the spit 'n' polish with which its treasures are displayed. The Instituto serves more than a thousand students a year, the vast majority from the United States and Canada; few Mexicans deign to accept the scholarships that are offered, though once upon a time Siqueiros, Tamayo and Carlos Mérida lectured here. Presently the *maestros* are James Pinto and Fred Samuelson, and the very able director (as always) is Sterling Dickinson.

There are many handsome churches in San Miguel—San Francisco with its Churrigueresque *Las Monjas* with its dodecagonal dome, the Oratorio of San Felipe, the Capela Santa Casa de Loreto—but the most impressive is an out-and-out fake that turned out to be a work of genius. This is La Parroquia on the plaza, a "Gothic" masterpiece superimposed on a Franciscan chapel in the gay nineties by an illiterate Indian mason (Ceferino Gutiérrez) who based his design on a postcard somebody had sent him of Cologne Cathedral. (I, for one, prefer the imitation to the original.) The tradition of inspired innocence is being carried along inside by the current parish priest, José Mercadillo, a self-taught painter who as a boy once cleaned Diego Rivera's brushes in the National Palace.

A sixteen-mile-long lake is projected to irrigate the semiarid valley above which the hillside town perches. But the place to swim is sulfuric Fuentes Taboada, a few miles down the hill, with its oblong warm pool and circular hot one.

Querétaro, capital of the small state of the same name, is a much larger city than San Miguel or Guanajuato, and as rich in history and architecture, but curiously neglected. The fault is in the guides and the guidebooks. The guides rush tourists to the Hill of Bells, the dingy spot marked by an Austrian-donated chapel where Maximilian and his generals were executed (see p. 87)—and let it go at that. The guidebooks say little or nothing about the great Augustinian patio or the Convent of Santa Rosa de Viterbo, two of the masterpieces of Baroque architecture in Mexico.[5] Nor are the townspeople helpful in locating them.

The patio of the Church and Monastery of San Augustín may be identified from the engraving on the Mexican 20-peso note. Presently it serves as the city's main post office. It's a staggering sight, this double-tiered square of arches, the upper tier punctuated where the springers join the piers by colossal caryatids with hands upraised, waterspouts projecting from their arrogant mouths like cigars. Through these arches the exquisite segmented dome of the church may be seen; blue glazed tiles in geometric patterns, and at the corners of the polygonal drum on which it rests, stone musicians. These sculptures, surely the work of untutored Indians who somehow escaped the dead hand of the colonial academy, are as exuberantly inventive as anything cut in stone since the Conquest, their plumed helmets and barbarous bone instruments calling to mind the dancer-priests of Bonampak and Palenque.

Santa Rosa de Viterbo, on the southwest edge of the city, is the masterpiece of Francisco Eduardo Tresguerras (1759–1833), whose works in architecture, painting and sculpture adorn his native Celaya as well as Querétaro:

> In the white and gold church of El Carmen of Celaya, which he planned and decorated single-handedly, the neo-classical orders are used with a buoyancy worthy of the rococo *rocailles*. Austere pediments, architraves, metopes, and triglyphs combine astonishingly to express pure joy.

---

[5] Even *Terry's Guide to Mexico* (1965 edition revised by James Norman; Doubleday) the handsomest and most detailed compendium of travel information, dismisses the patio with a perfunctory sentence and fails to mention the great dome with its spectacular sculptures.

Playful angels, roughly chiseled, perch on cushioned clouds that settle on fluted columns like foam on steins of beer. Already both architect and sculptor, Tresguerras turned painter to fill scalloped *trumeaux* with vapors and childish forms, baby angels adoring the Holy Baby. Equally dimpled grown-ups smile to God, receive stigmatas, or fly in golden chariots pulled by horses as mild as poodles.[6]

In the Sacristy at Santa Rosa in Querétaro, Tresguerras painted his largest mural, occupying the whole end of the barrel-vaulted room; nuns instructing their pupils in a garden and lambs carrying white roses from the Virgin to the feet of Christ to be turned red by His blood. In the church itself he designed a gold-leaf explosion of Churrugueresque. Outside, the dome, the bell tower with its Moorish cap, and the flying buttresses are his. And what flying buttresses! Beauvais and Chartres have nothing to compare with them. The piers are staggered courses; then come the huge volutes like coiling stone springs; and on top of that, purely decorative urns resembling bishops' miters or fancy perfume flasks. The play of sun and shadow among all these Tresguerrian surfaces is a photographer's dream.

Querétaro has other architectural treasures—the eighteenth-century aqueduct with its seventy-four arches culminating in Tresguerras' Neptune Fountain, a handsome Parroquia on the Plaza Obregón, the splendid seignorial mansion of the Marqués de la Villa del Villár del Aguila on the flowery Plaza de la Independéncia, and the Church and Convent of Santa Clara with another of Tresguerras' glazed-tile domes and some prized colonial sculpture inside—but Santa Rosa and the Augustinian Post Office are the chefs-d'oeuvre not to be missed.

Puebla, Cholula, Cuetzalan

Eighty-six miles southeast of the capital on a plain at the base of the Sierra Madre and in full view of Mexico's three snow-capped volcanoes, lies Puebla, Mexico's fourth city population-wise, and its first culturally—according to the *poblanos*. Many agree with the prideful inhabitants, but not this author. For one thing, Puebla is the most difficult city in Mexico to find your way around in; the street names were "simplified" by some mad numerologist—16 Poniente 535, 24 Sur 1612, 8 Norte 5875 Oriente, etc., etc.—with

---

[6] Jean Charlot, *The Mexican Mural Renaissance: 1920–1925*. New Haven, Connecticut, Yale University Press, 1963.

the result that even the natives wander about in a mathematical daze and when asked directions smile guiltily and send you to the part of the city farthest from where you are standing. (It once took a *Mexican* an hour to drive from the center of the city to the largest hotel, a distance of about a mile; by the time he arrived he had circumnavigated Puebla three times.)

Checkerboard-square Puebla is a bland city architecturally—unless you like tiles. There are tiles everywhere you look, on the churches and private houses, in kitchens and privies, up staircases and in sidewalks, all over the celebrated Casa de Alfenique (Spanish for almond cake) on 4 Oriente 6 Norte—enough for a show-biz wedding cake. The Zócalo is famous for its high trees, fountains and arcades, but even tolerant *Terry* gags over the Cathedral which flanks one side of it:

> Its exterior exhibits a well-ordered stateliness, marred only by the fact that the twin towers stand too far apart and are too tall, and by a gloomy feeling imparted by the rather lifeless blue-gray stone ... a dreary effect added to by the barren stone terrace upon which the cathedral is built, and the surrounding iron fence surmounted by winged angels.

Which is not to say that in Cincinnati, Ohio, or Atlanta, Georgia, the Puebla Cathedral wouldn't look very good indeed, but only that in Mexico there are so many better ones. Its *campanario*, erected in 1678, has looked down upon some stirring scenes. Here Father Motolinia, and probably Cortés before him, walked. Here in 1847 Col. Thomas Childs, with the wounded from Cerro Gordo, held off Santa Anna's army for thirty days in plain view of the eighty thousand townspeople until reinforcements arrived from the American fleet in Veracruz. Here Gen. Ignázio Zaragoza whipped the French on *Cinco de Mayo*, 1862, and five years later Gen. Porfirio Díaz did it again, making Maximilian's curtain scene in Querétaro possible.

There are other churches, eighty in all, of which Santo Domingo, two blocks from the Zócalo, is the most resplendently furnished; but the Secret Convent of Santa Monica in the northern part of the city attracts the most tourists for its romantic associations. The push button behind a vase of flowers in a second-story parlor was discovered in 1934 by federal officers, thus terminating a clandestine retreat for nuns that had functioned off and on ever since Juárez' Reform Laws abolished such establishments in 1857.

The eighty churches of Puebla, however, are as nothing compared to the reputed 365 of Cholula and its environs, nine miles west of the larger city. Cholula was a holy city in Toltec and Aztec times, and its most important Christian shrine, Nuestra Señora de los Remedios, is built directly on top of the gigantic Tepanapa Pyramid, buried at the time of the Conquest either by the Indians or the Spaniards. It has since been "mined" with electrically illuminated galleries, so that a double attraction is offered—neither of them aesthetically inspiring. Cholula itself is a depressing town, flat, hot, poverty-stricken and dusty, except during one of the many religious fiestas celebrated here, when it jumps—and explodes with fireworks. Particularly disappointing is the Moorish Capilla Real adjoining the Franciscan Church of San Gabriel, with its 49 domes supporting a forest of columns.

Actually the region's most interesting ecclesiastical architecture, more *colorful* than any in the world, is spotted all over the landscape. Ancient (1525) San Francisco at Huejotzingo, nineteen miles northwest of Puebla, the Ocotlán Sanctuary in Tlaxcala nineteen miles north with its polychrome Indian statuary, and San Francisco Acátepec's dazzling facade are outstanding. But the little domed chapel at Tonantzintla, a few minutes out of Cholula, is unique. The whole interior is filled with a blizzard of angels, saints, *putti*, dolls and grotesques in brightly painted and gilded high relief. It was the contribution of the Indians of the village. Painted in yellows, azure blues, metallic greens and crimsons, with the highlights in white or gold leaf, the effect is entirely different from the usual Churrigueresque *retablos*. The little gnomes and dwarfs that climb the pilasters have a definitely secular look, with their bold, saucy expressions, tripartite banana tongues and brandished grape clusters; nor do the angels in mini skirts, with Kewpie-doll faces, inspire a reverent mood. It's pagan, and it's great fun.

But more interesting than any of the churches of Puebla—because it's alive and because you will have it all to yourself nine chances out of ten—is the village of Cuetzalan. A leisurely day's drive through the peach orchards of Amozóc and Oriental, it perches at the absolute end of Route 125. There may be (and very likely are) lovelier Indian villages in Mexico than Cuetzalan, with costumes as bizarre, but this author has never found one, and surely there is no other such left on a macadam road—with a *pensión* sleeping *two* for sixty cents.

Cuetzalan is a hill town with cobbled and stepped streets. The wooden cornices on its whitewashed tile-roof houses overhang the narrow streets by so many feet that they sometimes actually touch. The town overlooks the jungles stretching away to Poza Rica and Veracruz. An hour's ride away on horseback is Yogualichal, a windowed Totonac-Aztec pyramid surrounded by smaller *ruinas*. Much closer are the hamlets of San Andrés and San Miguel, where the women still wear their hair piled high and entwined with purple and brown wool yarn above a white coif with densely embroidered corners. The rest of the costume—almost puritanical compared to some of those worn in Guatemala—consists of a white *huipil*, with a band of pink or blue embroidered birds about the neck and cuffs, an angle-length white skirt, and a broad red sash embellished with tufts of wool in many colors and a swatch of lace down the center glittering with sequins. These women, whose beauty and arrogant coiffure make them dominant in Cuetzalan's Sunday Market, are camera-shy and understandably reluctant to part with any of their ornaments.

Central Mexico II: The Inner Ring

Tlalmanalco, The Snow Volcanoes, Chapingo

The finest and one of the oldest "open chapels" in Mexico adjoins the Franciscan church at Tlalmanalco. It is not easy to get to, returning from Puebla, for the *autopista* has no exit at Chalco and you have to drive as far as Ixtapalapa into the capital, pay again, and retrace your way to the Cuautla spur. From Chalco, as desolate and windblown a town as Cholula, it is another six miles to Tlalmanalco. The ancient fortress church with its one tower splendidly canted, as if to catch the stone music of its adjoining arches, leans against the atrium. The open chapel is to the left of the church behind a picket fence. Umber-colored columns supporting the shallow arches are richly carved by the Indians with monkeys, bunches of fruit and death's-heads. Between the cloister and the church is a small chamber filled with rubble. After climbing to look through the single lunette window, one is rewarded with a stunning view of Ixtaccíhuatl, the Sleeping Maiden, on her glacier, with rivulets of ice for her hair. Did the good Franciscans thus intend to domesticate the magical Aztec lady by putting a frame around her? It is known that Moctezuma's people looked with awe upon the two volcanoes. The Brothers built their shrine as close to this one as they could get without freezing. Popocatépetl, which still fumes, was active enough in those days to make proximity hazardous.

Ixtaccíhuatl, five hundred feet lower at 17,343 feet, is harder to climb. In fact, an expedition of mountaineers was lost in one of her crevasses as recently as the winter of 1968. Popo is best climbed from Amecameca, where guides are available and alpine equipment may be rented. Dr. Atl, before Parícutin suddenly appeared (see p. 199) made Popocatépetl his domain, and the story I like best about the mountain is of the time when the old volcanologist and painter was at the crater, looking down benevolently at a small Indian boy and several barking dogs below. The boy turned to the dogs and pointing to the white-bearded Atl said to them: "Don't you know you mustn't bark at God Almighty?"

It was Atl (Gerardo Murillo) and José Guadalupe Possada, the great popular engraver of the Porfiriate, who gave the muralists their earliest inspiration. Atl had been in Europe just before the Revolution, and he insisted that Diego Rivera leave Paris to study the techniques of fresco and encaustic in Italy. In Chapingo, the Agricultural School eight miles beyond Texcoco, Diego painted his most Italianate work, and his masterpiece, in the little chapel. The eccentric shapes of the little domed chamber forced the artist to be inventive, and the earthy nudes which he deemed appropriate for an agricultural school brought out a strain of sensual lyricism which his didactic Marxism couldn't blunt. Emiliano Zapata in his grave, fertilizing the new growth, is a great image; and Manuel Ávila Camacho, the hapless *patrón*, is handled with just enough satirical subtlety to be funny.

Teotihuacán, Tula, Actopan, Tepotzotlan

Thirty-one miles northeast of the capital on a new superhighway lies the ceremonial center of the all-Mexican civilization that preceded the Toltecs and the Aztecs (see pp. 6–7). The village of San Juan Teotihuacán replaces its lost name and "Pyramids of the Sun and the Moon" serve as the popular identification for its principal physical features, whose actual significance time has also buried. A few miles east, at Otumba, Cortés turned on his Aztec pursuers and fought the desperate delaying action that almost ended in disaster. Bernal Díaz del Castillo was with the stragglers who marched past the largest single man-made edifice in the Western Hemisphere without apparently ever noticing it! The Pyramid of the Sun is 210 feet high and its base covers 540,000 square feet. Its steps were originally coated with stucco. The adjoining Temple of Quetzalcoatl was built much later by the Toltecs, who took over the ceremonial site; it is adorned with collared serpent heads and fearsome effigies of Tlaloc that look like gas masks. Excavations in an earlier temple beneath it revealed a treasure in sculpture and some of the finest of pre-Columbian frescoes. The Pyramid of the Moon and many other temples in the complex remain unexcavated. (Acolman, on the road to the ruins, contains a splendid Gothic fortress church built in 1539 by the Augustinians.)

Tula, the Toltecs' homesite, which was discovered and restored much later (see p. 9), lies somewhat to the northwest of Teotihuacán in the state of Hidalgo, a little off the main toll road connecting the capital with Querétaro. Here, before they conquered central Mexico and later migrated to Yucatán, the Toltecs left temples, ball courts, and some of their characteristic sculpture—reclining Chac-Mools to invoke the rain, just like the ones found earlier (but made later) at Chichén Itzá; stone caryatids, male, menacing and monumental, that resemble similar sentinel figures found at Tiahuanacu in Bolivia and Kardassy in Egyptian Nubia. The ones at Tula, about twelve feet high, are carved out of separate superimposed drums of stone. Their breastplates are stylized butterflies and their pitilessly staring faces are framed in square earplugs and circular feathered helmets. It was a brilliant idea of the Mexican archaeologist who discovered them to place them on top of the principal pyramid, dominating the arid landscape.

The nearby town contains a massive monastery-church built by the Franciscans in the mid-sixteenth century. Its presence in so unimportant a locality was one of the clues leading the archaeologists to the ruins: Clearly the brethren must have been laboring to offset some shrine sacred to the early Indians. Near the town is a memorial of sorts to later history: a freight train of Revolutionary vintage on a siding that has been ingeniously turned into a housing development, its windows gay with geraniums.

Actopan, on a winding continuation of the branch road to Tula and not far from Pachuca, is another impressive early fortress church. It was built by the Augustinians for their mission among the fierce Otomi tribes. The tower is Moorish, the cloisters are Gothic, the portal is Plateresque, and to one side is an extraordinary wall pierced with holes, capped with urns, and framed in half-dome opening, that no one seems able to identify.

Tepotzlan (not to be confused with Tepoztlán, the Indian village near Cuernavaca with a fine church of its own (see p. 221), is the site of one of the great churches of Mexico, the Jesuit Seminary of San Martín. The pink facade and tower of this beautifully proportioned church, erected about 1750, is a marvel of intricate stone sculpture, and the Churrigueresque interior is as breathtaking a golden fantasy as Salamanca's.

Toluca, Metepec, Valle de Bravo, The Hot-Bath Resorts, Malinalco

Moving counterclockwise about the capital's ring, the next main road leads due west to Toluca. On the way is the Automex factory with two imposing decorative towers designed by Mathias Goeritz. The city itself almost as high and chilly as the capital and backed up by the snowy extinct Toluca Volcano, is commercial and clogged with traffic. But the Friday market in the middle of it is not to be missed. A good bargainer, with taste, can find the handsomest serapes in Mexico here, as well as a fine assortment of multicolored wool sweaters, huaraches, sombreros, and carved wood boxes.

About a ten-minute drive from Toluca is the village of Metepec, renowned for its gaily painted ceramic figurines, candelabra and bells. Ten years ago the best examples of this work were to be found in the homes of the individual craftsmen. Today, if there are any good examples left, they are being exported. The many sidewalk stands that have sprung up in the village are stocked with routine fare.

Valle de Bravo, south of the main highway leading from Toluca to Morelia, and San José de Purua, farther west along the highway itself, are summer resorts popular with Mexicans from the over-crowded capital. Valle de Bravo, now part of Mexico City's far-flung water and hydroelectric system, is a cold lake surrounded by piny mountains. The water is not clear, though from a distance its opaque green color is attractive. Reeds growing along the shallow margins make swimming difficult; fishing, sailing and water-skiing are more popular sports.

San José de Purua is a typically Mexican resort hotel, big and sprawling, and surrounded by overmanicured parks, circular duck ponds and artificial waterfalls that clash with the natural beauty of the steep mountain valley. The establishment was built by the con-tractor for the Guadalajara road who saw Indians relaxing in a muddy spring; asking why, he was told that from time immemorial its waters had cured their ailments. The brown water is piped directly now into the hotel's swimming pool, and into other nearby pools, where those who can't afford the swank hotel are brought in by bus-loads every Saturday and Sunday, bathing and feeding at their snack-bars out of sight of the well-heeled customers.

Another such hot-bath resort, in slightly better taste, is Ixtapán de la Sal, off the road that descends south from Toluca to Cuerna-vaca. It has its own complex of hotels and public baths. One of the latter, under a shed, is divided into an oblong pool of 104° F. brown water for the hoi polloi, and private chambers, each one of which is equipped with a king-size sunken tub of its own, backlighted by cheap stained glass with artificial flowers growing against it, piped-in music, and a pair of sheeted beds. These chambers are suggestively named Madame de Pompadour, Venus de Medici, Princess de Lam-balle, etc.—and the brochure handed to customers, headed "RE-VITALIZE! RECUPERATE! REJUVINATE!!!" explains that the waters are good for "nervous breakdowns, insomnia, business strain, some feminine irregularities, and a sure activation of the sexual glandular system, both feminine and masculine."

A little farther along this road, on the border between the states of Morelos and Guerrero, are the Grutas de Cacahuamilpa, enormous limestone caverns which in 1968 were being equipped with an elec-tric railway for the convenience of Olympic Games visitors. On one of the walls Maximilian's Empress wrote, "Carlota reached this far," under which, eight years later, Juárez' successor added: "Sebas-tián Lerdo de Tejada went farther."

At Tenancingo, between Metepec and Ixtapán de la Sal, a fifteen-mile dirt road to the east leads to Malinalco. Here again the pre-Columbian priesthood and the mendicant orders confronted each other. In the town is the Augustinian monastery. High on the cliff overlooking it, half an hour's walk up, is the ruin of a Toltec-Aztec pyramid. Under a thatch roof, defying the weather and photography, is a jaguar's head (its eyes long since removed), surrounded by three very large flat eagles carved out of the living rock. Sitting cats guarded the entrance to this temple once, but nothing remains now save their tails and haunches. Over the mountain lies Chalma, a one-street village that plays host to thousands of pilgrims, staggered throughout the year, who come on foot or by bus to pay homage to the "miraculous" life-size Crucifixion, "El Señor de Chalma," and to take a "purifying" bath in the pool near the shrine that was con-sidered sacred long before the Christians arrived in Mexico.

Central Mexico III: The Capital

Historically, and scenically as well, there is no avenue in the world to compare with the Paseo de la Reforma. Its terminals are Chapultepec Castle and the Zócalo. When a spring of fresh water gushed from rocky Chapultepec in pre-Columbian times, an aqueduct carried the pure drinking water across the lake to Tenochtitlán, the island capital of the Aztec Empire. Ever since Tenochtitlán fell to Cortés, the Zócalo (which rose upon the ruined plaza) has been the governing center and the religious nexus of New Spain, the empires of Iturbide and Maximilian, and the Republic of Mexico. And where the aqueduct leapfrogged the shallow lake waters, the Paseo gradually assumed its present splendor. First it was filled in to become a carriage path for the viceregal coach. It was hardly more when the *niños heroes* died at their cannon, and the future commanders of the American Civil War, who had taken Chapultepec, rode down it to raise the Stars and Stripes over the Zócalo. Empress Carlota broadened it two decades later to get an unobstructed view from her window in the Castle, they say, of Maximilian's projected infidelities, as he rode down it every morning to his office in the National Palace. Twenty-five years later, Porfirio Díaz' *cientificos*, bemused by the boulevards of "rational" Paris, gave the Paseo its five-fingered, tree-lined spaciousness, and set up the diminutive bronzes along its bordering park. Twenty-five years later still, the noble Francisco Madero rode down it bravely to the Zócalo and his terrible fate, to be followed shortly by the Zapatistas with their crossed bandoliers and broad-brimmed sombreros, and the *dorados* of Pancho Villa's *division del norte*. Here the urban proletariat assembled to pour into the Zócalo on March 23, 1938, for the tumultuous affirmation that greeted Lázaro Cárdenas when he recovered for Mexico the imperial domain of the foreign oil companies. And here ever since, the millions of foreign visitors (who have reclaimed, in a sense, that domain) pour in and out of the hotels and restaurants and shops and museums that now border it. They circle the magnificent *glorietas* from the Diana Fountain at the entrance to Chapultepec Park, pass the Golden Angel on its towering column, the bronze Cuauhtémoc defiantly brandishing his spear, and Manuel Tolsa's equestrian "Caballito," now placed at the intersection of the Paseo with its extensions: Avenida Juárez passing the Alameda, and Avenida Madero, which leads into the Zócalo.

By 1968, Greater Mexico City had grown to six million inhabitants, by far the largest city of Latin America, and close to New York and Los Angeles in the hemisphere. If such a sprawling metropolis can be said to have a geographical center, it is the Cuauhtémoc Monument on the Paseo. Avenida Insurgentes crosses the Paseo at this point. Insurgentes cuts the capital in half, running north and south. Its southern terminus is in the suburb of Tlalpan, where it connects with the toll road to Cuernavaca and with a *viaducto* leading northeast to the Airport and to the Puebla *autopista*. Insurgentes' northern terminus is at the Shrine of the Virgin of Guadalupe and the entrance to the toll road leading to Teotihuacán. A branch road, somewhat north of the Cuauhtémoc, leads to the toll road to Querétaro. Between its southern terminus and the Cuauhtémoc, Insurgentes passes Xochimilco to the east, the Pyramid of Cuicuilco, University City, the Pedregal Gardens, Coyoacán (with its Frida Kahlo Museum and, somewhat to the south, off Calzado Tlalpan, Diego Rivera's Anahuacali), the country's largest bullring, and a long line of restaurants, theaters, banks and shopping plazas. Close to the northern extension of the avenue are the National Normal School and the La Raza Hospital (with murals by Orozco and Siqueiros, respectively) the Polytechnic Institute, the Central Railway Station and the vast López Mateos housing development. Around the Cuauhtémoc itself are some of the largest tourist hotels in Mexico and the principal art galleries and antique shops.

Returning to the Paseo and its extensions, all of the capital's sites of major artistic achievement lie along this axis.

The most recent ranks first. The National Museum of Anthropology and Archaeology, designed by Pedro Ramírez Vásquez and Rafael Mijares, lies on the north side of the Paseo in Chapultepec Park. It was dedicated in 1964. Covering 430,000 square feet, its central exhibition room contains the masterpieces of all pre-Columbian periods, and its wings contain sculpture from the particular cultures—Teotihuacán, Huastec, Maya, Toltec, Aztec, etc.—displayed against painted backdrops and maps that relate the past to the present. The rectangular court between the wings is covered by an aluminum "umbrella," 269 by 177 feet, that sprouts from a carved concrete post to which it is invisibly tied with girders and tensor cables and from which "rain" falls from time to time. The "summary" chamber contains such monumental works as the fearsome Aztec mother symbol, Coatlicue; the so-called Calendar Stone of the Sun, found under the Zócalo; the 22-foot-high effigy of Tlaloc found near Texcoco; and the mammoth Stone of Tizoc. A scale reproduction of the little temples at Bonampak, in which the great Classic Maya frescoes were discovered in 1946 (see pp. 232–233), is in the garden, with the murals themselves faithfully copied inside.

The quality of the art of today suffers appallingly in contrast with the pre-Columbian work, if one steps across the Paseo to inspect the contents of the linked glass circles that constitute Mexico's Museum of Modern Art. This is not the fault of the artists. Politics, unfortunately, has been the only criterion here. The buildings are handsome enough, but wildly inappropriate to the hanging of pictures. The sculpture in the gardens round about is "garden sculpture" of the most slavishly imitative sort. The Permanent Collection not only contains no single example of modern art from abroad, but not a single first-rate picture by Orozco, Rivera, Siqueiros, and Tamayo,[7] and among the exhibitions of current work by the younger artists amateurish and tasteless pictures so predominate that an occasional work of quality is seen to great disadvantage. Identification of pictures (if they are identified at all) is perfunctory and sometimes inaccurate.

In Chapultepec Park, besides the botanical gardens, the zoo, the presidential residence and the Molina del Rey (where the Americans and Mexicans fought a fierce engagement after Contreras-Churubusco), there is the famous Castle, now a museum. It contains murals by Orozco, Siqueiros, O'Gorman, and others, not among their best, and a collection of historical trophies.

Walking up the Paseo past the "Cuauhtémoc" and turning right on Juárez at the "Caballito," one passes the Alameda Park on the left and the Del Prado Hotel and the Museo de Artes Populares on one's right. Behind the latter two is the old part of the city where the firing between the Maderistas and the conspirators holed up in the Ciudadela took place during the Ten Tragic Days (see pp. 105–109). In the Del Prado there is a fine mural by Diego Rivera depicting a "Sunday Afternoon Walk in the Alameda" during the Porfiriate. The Popular Arts Museum is actually a display of Indian handicrafts for sale—excellent examples, and from all parts of the country. In the corner of the Alameda formed by Juárez and the San Juan de Latrán stands the sinking pile of "French" marble which Porfirio Díaz had erected as an opera house and which now serves as the Palace of Fine Arts. It contains frescoes by all the important muralists, galleries for exhibitions of international importance, and a theater for concerts and the dance.

Orozco painted his fiery, apocalyptic "Catharsis" in the Bellas Artes at the same time (1934) that Rivera was making his copy of the blandly rationalistic "Man at the Crossroads" which Nelson Rockefeller had destroyed in the lobby of New York's Rockefeller Center in 1933, when he discovered that it contained a salute to Lenin. For the first and last time, while these two murals were

---

[7] Admittedly the first three are primarily muralists, but at least their drawings could be shown. There are several good pictures by Rivera from his Cubist period in Paris, but in this genre he stands in the second echelon, below Picasso and Braque.

being painted, Orozco and Rivera confronted each other—in their works and *at* work. A story of that confrontation, which I received from an eyewitness, reveals as much of their personalities as the two frescoes do of their ideas and art. One day as they were working on their scaffolds, back to back, a dozen students drifted in and called up to Diego that they had sketches to show him. He lumbered down, ordered drinks for all of them, called their sketches "very promising," even bought one. Then they turned to Orozco. "Maestro . . ." Annoyed at being interrupted in what to him was a very private struggle, Orozco glanced down at the students and their sketches and said, "Art, gentlemen, is like parachute jumping. Sometimes the parachute never opens. In art, this is almost always the case. You are parachute jumpers. Your parachutes have not opened." And back to work he went.

The great early epics by both artists are a few blocks to the northeast of the Bellas Artes, down Avenida Madero to the Zócalo and three blocks north along Calle Argentina. (There is an early Orozco in the House of Tiles [Sanborn's Restaurant] on Madero itself, but it is an overly classical allegory.) The Orozcos in the National Preparatory School and the Riveras in the Department of Public Education are seminal works. In the Preparatory School Orozco moved cautiously from classical subject matter and draftsmanship toward the expressionist style fully developed later in the Bellas Artes fresco and at Guadalajara. In the ground-level patio, one fresco—the so-called "Maternity"—remains of the original classical set. The others treat Revolutionary themes, tentatively but with great power and dignity. "Cortés and Malinche" in the vault of the stairwell is a marvelous evocation of the mythical significance of these figures. In the second story Orozco made his first move toward expressionism, lashing out at his critics (and Vasconcelos' reactionary foes) with the arsenal of satirical weapons he had accumulated while cartooning for the Carranzista press. But on the third floor, the artist returned to the more contemplative style of the ground level and the stairwell; these are compassionate elegies to the victims of the civil war.

Rivera made his start in the Preparatory School, too, painting a derivative and unpromising "Allegory" in hot-wax encaustic in the Bolívar Theater. Then he moved down the street to Vasconcelos' Ministry and began to fresco its vast patios and stairwell with record-breaking industry. With a few exceptions, none of these frescoes of the nineteen twenties which celebrate the expatriate artist's sudden conversion to Indian Mexico and the Revolution compare with the Chapingo chapel, which followed (see p. 209). The finest group, in the stairwell, has yielded to faulty chemistry and the weather. Yet the cumulative effect of the 235 separate panels in the arcades [8] is overwhelming.

There are other important frescoes by the two masters in the heart of the capital, notably those by Orozco in the Supreme Court Building and the Hospital-Church of Jesús Nazareno, both on Piño Suárez, and the extensive Rivera decoration of the stairwell and upper arcades of the National Palace in the Zócalo. The Orozco sets are in the master's post-Guadalajara style, which I find strident, complicated, and unpleasant to look at, but many consider them his finest work. No one would call Rivera's heavy-handed propaganda in the Palace that prolific artist's best work, but they are ingenious storytelling. The depictions of Cortés as a syphilitic cripple are ludicrous.

Rivera's Anahuacali south of the Zócalo and the Frida Kahlo Museum in Coyoacán have already been mentioned. The Anahuacali, a neo-Aztec "tomb" which the artist designed in his last years, contains his extensive collection of pre-Columbian sculpture, including some of the finest Nayarit ceramics to be seen anywhere. Frida Kahlo was Diego's second wife, and a talented surrealist painter in her own right; the little museum in Coyoacán contains some of her best work.

The northern section of the capital contains two sites of interest. The Lagunilla Market at Avenidas República de Chile and Perú is not what it used to be when it was popularly called The Thieves' Market, but it still offers for sale a variety of antiques, *retablos* on tin and wood, and pre-Columbian figurines (mostly fakes). The Basilica of Our Lady of Guadalupe is an immense eighteenth-century church in Tepeyac (Villa Madero) which enshrines the cloak of the Indian Juan Diego on which Bishop Zumárraga in 1531 was the first to see the "miraculous" imprint of the Dark Virgin (see pp. 39–40). Here, every December 11, humble penitents from all over Mexico assemble, making the last lap on their knees, while ambulances, their sirens screaming, carry away the fallen. Crowding with them into the Basilica, dense with the mingled smells of incense, sweat, cook-

[8] Sixteen hundred square meters, according to Virginia and Jaime Plenn in their *A Guide to Modern Mexican Murals* (Ediciones Tolteca, 1963). Their figure includes the few panels Diego permitted his "collaborators"—Montenegro, Mérida, Charlot, De la Cueva, Amero and O'Gorman—to paint.

ing fat, and guttering wax candles, one is literally catapulted on a wave of bodies into the darkness of the nave, and then out again into the floodlit plaza where costumed "Aztecs" dance to savage drum rhythms.

"Almost all the writers who have dealt with the culture and problems of Mexico (of whatever religious or economic persuasion) are agreed that the one factor that has created and preserved Mexico as a nation has been the apparition and veneration of Our Lady of Guadalupe." [9] Thus Donald Demarest, and the evidence to bear him out is not only here. Her image is everywhere—in the buses and taxis, in stores, on postcards, in the homes of rich as well as poor, tattooed on arms, woven into matadors' hats, chalked on mountainsides, flowered in public parks, outlined in neon. Politicians have acknowledged her as the only unifying force in a country immemorially divided by geography, race, language, revolution, poverty and persecution. Indianists have conceded that nothing else could have arrested the cultural disintegration that overcame the Indians elsewhere. Above all, the very fact of the survival of Roman Catholicism in Mexico—a survival in the teeth of the most virulent and systematic antireligious campaign of modern times outside the Iron Curtain—must be attributed to the efficacy of this symbol. And what visitor familiar with the halfhearted lip service prevailing in the United States among Catholics, no less than Protestants, can doubt that it *more* than survives? The crowds in the innumerable churches, even on weekdays, testify to it. The solitary Indian before his tiny shrine along the loneliest road, his arms outstretched in the sign of the cross, bears witness. The phenomenal mass demonstrations at Tepeyac confirm it.

Southern Mexico

Cuernavaca, Tepoztlán, Taxco, Acapulco, Puerto Vallarta

I have lived in Cuernavaca on three occasions, longer than I have lived anywhere else in Mexico, but I find it difficult to describe. Dozens, perhaps hundreds, of rich Americans, some of them socialites, some of them celebrities in the theater, some dilettantes or hangers-on, some convalescents, some tennis players, live here. But Mexican millionaires, and celebrities from the political and art

[9] Donald Demarest and Coley Taylor, *The Dark Virgin: The Book of Our Lady of Guadalupe*. A documentary anthology. Freeport, Maine, Coley Taylor, Incorporated, 1956.

worlds, have second homes in Cuernavaca too. Their worlds never mix, and seldom touch. Nor will they have anything to do with the young artists, Mexican and American, who come to Cuernavaca weekends. Then, of course, there are the natives, who live off all of these intruders—some well, but most poorly; surely detesting their affluent guests, but rarely showing it. Before the 1950's, when the high-speed toll road knifed into Cuernavaca (and beyond to Iguala, and finally to Acapulco) Cuernavaca was an end in itself. But now that the highway is completed, Cuernavaca is for many a place where the Jet Set and the tourists stop for lunch, take a quick look at the Riveras in the Palace of Cortés, and pass on. Which is too bad. For Cuernavaca (Cow's Horn) with its perfect climate, its leisurely pace, and its tropical-garden houses sprawling up and down the *barrancas* is one of the most attractive small cities in the Americas.

Eccentricity flourishes in a climate like Cuernavaca's. In the century between Maximilian Hapsburg, who chased butterflies in the Borda Gardens, and Mathias Goeritz, who paints his sidewalk orange to conform to the color of his house, men with unusual talents from abroad have found Cuernavaca to their liking. There may be no better way to convey the town's ambience than to describe three of these acclimated foreigners in their habitat.

Manuel Suárez is a Spaniard who has made a fortune selling concrete water tanks to the Mexicans and would now like to sell them Hernándo Cortés. He goes about this well-nigh impossible task by displaying an effigy of the Conqueror (the only one in all Mexico) in bronze on a rampant charger; it stands at the entrance of Suárez' Casino de la Selva, a complex of bungalows, bowling alleys, swimming pools, overhead kiddie cars, and razzle-dazzle art works that caters almost exclusively to the week-ending Mexican middle class. But he makes his apologies to the Indians by filling a garden with little pre-Columbian replicas, and to the intellectuals by offering a bronze of Dr. Atl, larger than life. In 1967 Suárez brought Siqueiros to Cuernavaca, putting him on a princely retainer to create two relief-murals, each the "largest in the world." One is for the Casino and the other for a new hotel Suárez is building in the capital. It seemed perfectly predictable that neither Suárez nor the Mexicans saw any irony in the fact that Siqueiros' entire life as an artist has been devoted—when not engaged in threatening capitalists like Suárez for the Communist Party—to making romantic heroes of Cortés' victims.

Ivan Illich, of Russian-Jewish extraction, is a Catholic monsignor who directs a school in Cuernavaca to train missionaries to carry the social revolution to Latin America. In Cuernavaca he is not notorious because there are two other padres at least as iconoclastic: Gregorio Lemercier, who got into a hassle with the hierarchy several years ago when he proposed using psychoanalysis to weed out pederasts and other misfits taking orders to resolve their sexual problems—"The Church is not afraid of Freud," the Spanish-language *Life* quoted him saying recently, "It is afraid of sex"; and Bishop Sergio Méndez, who hired Goeritz and other artists to modernize the Cathedral and who conducts mariachi Masses there and encourages the communicants to embrace each other fraternally during the ceremony.

Illich is tall, rawboned, handsome and dynamic and he likes to dress in a serape and huaraches. He speaks nine languages perfectly, including Yiddish, which he picked up in New York while working for Cardinal Spellman, and his admirers insist that he is in line for the papacy itself. Although he is intellectually arrogant, making no effort to conceal his disdain from those he considers stupid, his program for changing the Church from a complacent, self-perpetuating bureaucracy of theologians and alms collectors into a loose federation of self-propelled "missioners" working for the regeneration of the exploited and landless is in tune both with Christ's teachings and with the Mexican Revolution. Expelled from Puerto Rico, where he savagely attacked American missioners to Latin America for ignoring Hispanic culture and acquiescing in American business and foreign-policy ideals, Illich finds Mexico a perfect base for his far-flung operations. As one of his Cuernavaca admirers put it, "The PRI would never permit him to subvert *Mexicans*, but it's delighted to have him train missioners to overthrow the governments of *other* Latin Americans—which is typically Mexican, isn't it!"

Robert Brady is an American painter–interior decorator from Des Moines, Iowa, who has spent a fortune turning one of the broken-down palaces of colonial Mexico into a superbly appointed private museum of Mexicana. The palace is part of the Cathedral compound, with its entrance two blocks from the Zócalo on the severely high-walled street called Netzahualcoyotl. Passing through the studded oaken portal that pierces that eyeless rampart, one enters into adjoining patios lush with giant trees, flowers, vines, pools, sculpture niches, and romantic balconies. In the tower hangs a chandelier that once graced the Cathedral in Puebla. The white adobe walls are hung with tapestries or used as a setting for Pátzcuaro plates, Michoacán masks, Guerrero figurines, or candlesticks from Metepec.

One hopes that the city will inherit this treasury—as it did not inherit Fred Davis' unrivaled collection of folk arts in a similarly restored colonial mansion a few blocks away.

All around Cuernavaca are delightful places for a day's outing. The pyramid of Xochicalco is one. It is not far out of town, on the same road that passes Ixtapán de la Sal on the way to Toluca. The elaborate reliefs around the base of the one structure so far uncovered are classified "Toltec"; they look much more Mayan, and if they should turn out to be, the archaeologists will be in trouble. Farther up the same road are the Grutas de Cacahuamilpa and the branch road to Malinalco described elsewhere (p. 212). Hacienda Vista Hermosa, farther south, is an ancient sugar mill that has been turned into a resort hotel in a setting of beautiful gardens and pools. Lake Tequesquitengo, in this general neighborhood and not far from the Acapulco speedway, is a small body of murky water popular for water-skiing but not attractive to swim in. The place to swim—the best in Mexico, probably, though ignored in all the guides—is Las Estacas, off the road to Cuautla. Acres of rolling lawns and cushioned peninsulas form the banks of a stream so pure that a depth of twenty feet looks like two. The source of the river is a circular pool perhaps thirty feet across with a perpetually rolling bubble of water at its center. To plunge into this bubble and try to keep from being tossed to one side is a deliciously cleansing sensation. The painter Lucas Johnson, who claims to have conquered its centrifugal force, says that inside the waterspout is a dry, smooth-sleeved "eye" from which the earth's bowels may be seen straight down, darkly.

The conventional day-long excursions from Cuernavaca are to Tepoztlán and Taxco. Tepoztlán is an Indian village in a valley off the Cuautla road that has been so visited and written about that it retains little of its original charm. There are Indian motifs brilliantly carved into the portal of the church. There is an ancient shrine to the Aztec god of pulque, whose fiesta is still celebrated every September 8, on a pinnacle above the village. And there is a small museum of pre-Columbiana put together by the poet Carlos Pellicer. The best time to visit Tepoztlán is on one of the three days preceding Ash Wednesday, when the *chinelas* in their painted robes and lamp-shade hats cavort in the square, and a band of Humpty-Dumpty figures with suggestive masks satirizing demagogues bounce in and out.

It is regrettable to have to call Taxco a tourist trap, but that is what it is. It is the artificial creation of two Silver Kings, José de la

Borda, an eighteenth-century mining magnate who gave the town its lovely parochial church ("God gives to Borda and Borda gives to God") and William Spratling, a twentieth-century dilettante from New Orleans who revived the handcrafting of silver in Taxco and with the proceedes amassed a collection of local (Guerrero) and Veracruz sculpture. Borda's contribution is relatively intact. Santa Prisca, completed in 1751 at a cost of eight million pesos, is a late Baroque masterpiece in pink stone with superbly carved twin towers, an imposing glazed-tile dome, and inside a wealth of Churrigueresque altars, *retablos,* and colonial paintings. Its site on the steep hillside crowded with the quaint plazas, winding alleys, and red-tiled houses that are Taxco's features, is cloyingly picturesque. Spratling's contributions have been a dubious blessing. The dozens of silver shops that have sprung up in the wake of his original Taller de las Delicias, far from providing "bargains" in this tourist commodity, as claimed, display the most overpriced and (for the most part) vulgar tableware in Mexico. Spratling's collection of Remojadas pieces has become such a source of litigation between the town to which it was left and the grabby federal museums that three years after the donor's death it was still under lock and key.

All along the road south to Iguala, the city where Iturbide published his Plan (see pp. 56–57) that consolidated Independence from Spain, peasants hold aloft live iguanas for sale. There are several roadside stands that sell the painted ceramic figurines of women and fabulous beasts that are Guerrero's outstanding folk art. At Chilpancingo, birthplace of the Bravo brothers and site of Morelos' revolutionary Constitution of 1813, there are frescoes by Alfredo Zalce and others commemorating the city's proud history. A branch road east leads to Vicente Guerrero's birthplace, Chilapa, where attractive hand-loomed embroidered woolen *rebozos* are made.

Acapulco, with its hundred hotels, many beaches and Quebrada cliff divers, is too well known to require detailed description. A town of 20,000, it swells to 200,000 in season. Its glory is its harbor. Four hotels and as many nightspots do deserve special mention. La Perla, at the El Mirador Hotel, is the place whose "floor show" consists of the diving exhibition into the rocky tidal gorge below. The Acapulco Hilton has a most unusual pool: a meandering "moat" of jade-green water that surrounds an artificial island between the rooms and the beach; on the island under truncated cone pavilions fringed with palm shades are the dining room and cocktail bar; on the beach one may don a parachute and become airborne behind a speedboat—a sport for men who envy the birds, and who doesn't? Las Brisas is a cluster of two hundred pink-and-white stone cottages, each with its pink-and-white swimming pool, pink-and-white maid, pink-and-white surrey-fringed Jeep and pink-and-white garbage can, renting for a hundred dollars a day; perched on an almost perpendicular cliff strewn with giant pink-and-white boulders, Las Brisas has a very precarious balance: even a mild earthquake could substitute boulders for houses without disturbing at all its pink-and-white look. The Hotel Pierre Marques is the whim and plaything of the world's richest man (Paul Getty) who saw the site from his yacht off Revolcadero Beach and said, "Buy it and build there," without bothering to come ashore. The hotel, famed for its cuisine and sky-high prices, has a uniquely sterile waterfall—a sheet that tumbles from a slot on top of three "ruined" arches. It also has a magnificent beach with a strong undertow and many sharks.

The nightclubs and discotheques of Acapulco are more disappointing than the hotels. There are Tiberio's and Tequila à Go-Go, and Aku-Tiki with its Polynesian floor show, and the Jacaranda Room at El Presidente with its decor by Dali, and (for exclusivity and top cover charges), The Club, which has "real oil paintings" and Gothic windows filled with psychedelic flowers in stained glass. The Zona Roja (Red-Light District) is in a maze of dusty unpaved streets. Unappetizing tarts with rolled-up stockings sit on chairs tilted against the neon-lighted dives while pimps try to drum up trade among the clogged vehicles; the floor shows are remarkably tame and monotonous, but the price (of everything—including murder [10]) is reasonable.

Acapulco is as popular with most Mexicans as it is with American tourists—in part because it is a symbol of that "American Way of Life" the Mexican middle class aspires to, in part because it offers intellectuals the spectacle of Americans disporting themselves the way Americans are supposed to disport themselves—tastelessly and expensively. But vulgarity is catching; on one of their own beaches (Boca Chica) I have seen Mexicans plying a burro with rum punches and laughing at its antics as it staggered in the surf. Diego Rivera built himself a house here, the town's only work of art, covering

[10] Guerrero is famed throughout Mexico for its lawlessness, and Acapulco is the crime capital of Guerrero. Of the average 200 murders a month in the state, 60 take place in Acapulco, with its heavy traffic in marijuana, prostitution and guns. In 1968, when 33 people were killed in a union gun battle, the army had to be called in to restore order.

its walls inside and out with imaginative sea dragons in mosaic; it is falling apart, the only sign of the town's interest being a placard which reads "DANGER! IT IS FORBIDDEN TO ENTER!"

Puerto Vullarta, they say, was as unspoiled as a Breton fishing village in the days before Tennessee Williams discovered it and Elizabeth Taylor and Richard Burton gave it the forlorn notoriety of an abandoned movie set. A hotel brochure, in that ineffable dialect called Spanglish, says it all:

> Posada Vullarta will be, as prophesied by its owners, the ideal center of reunion which will challenge the jungle Martini in hand.... The secret of Puerto Vullarta is its dynamic past, present and future. Native women still wash their clothes by pounding it on the rocks.... Tour around the popular residential areas known as "Gringo Gulch" and "Golden Coast" where the house of the Burtons' (Liz Taylor's) is and ends in the commercial section of Vallarta with time allowed for shopping.... If you want someone to escort you along the rivers and toward the jungle just pay an extra horse for your guide and admire the exuberant foliage with its naturally saturated jungle noises.

Posada Vullarta, for all that, has the best-run luxury hotel in Mexico, with decor and landscaping in good taste, and an unforgettable cuisine. Only the beach is disappointing, grainy and gray, with considerable undertow. It's an expensive establishment, but things have to be expensive in a place *totally dependent on imported foods;* with no automobile highway, everything except fish ("–and we have no fishing fleet") must be flown in. Taxis charge $2.80 for the five-minute drive from the airport, and four times that for a minimum sightseeing ride. This ride includes such beaches as Los Muertos, where native fishermen cook delicious mackerel over bonfires of oily coconuts, Yelapa ("Instant Tahiti," says the sign), and the really heavenly Mismaloya between rocky headlands, where *Night of the Iguana* was filmed.

Puerto Vullarta is 140 mles due west of Guadalajara. Though there is no road connecting them yet, affluent Tapatians regard Puerto Vallarta as "their" resort. By the time the Pacific Coast Highway is completed, it will be everybody's resort, 150 miles from Mazatlán, 300 from Acapulco and from Mexico City. Will that make it a fleshpot indistinguishable from Acapulco? Perhaps. But there are so many "Puerto Vullartas" along Mexico's Pacific Coast—

Barra de Navidad is one, Zihuatanejo is another—that collectors of unspoiled fishing villages are not likely to be frustrated for quite a while.

Orizaba, Córdoba, Jalapa, Papantla, Veracruz, Coatzacoalcos, Villahermosa, Campeche

The direct road to Veracruz and the Gulf of Mexico is by way of Puebla and passes through the cities of Orizaba and Córdoba. There is a branch road from Córdoba north to Jalapa, the capital of the State of Veracruz, but Jalapa is more easily reached from Veracruz itself; and the northerly coastal highway from Veracruz passes through the heart of the Totonac country: Papantla, El Tajïn, Poza Rica and Tuxpan. To the southeast, the Gulf Coast highway passes through Coatzacoalcos, La Venta, Villahermosa and Campeche on its way to the Yucatán Peninsula.

Orizaba, in the heart of the tropical coffee country, is a manufacturing city of sixty thousand at a pleasant altitude of four thousand feet. Its cotton mills and the brewery that makes Moctezuma XX, Mexico's best dark beer, keep it humming—but at a leisurely pace. A strong early fresco by Orozco was painted in the industrial school, around an arched window. When I went to see it in 1956, it had been badly damaged by the weather, and when I asked the janitor why the window couldn't be glassed to protect it, he answered: "Because the glass wouldn't be cleaned and then no one could see the *view!*" He didn't remember who had painted the fresco.

But this is the special charm of Orizaba, and of Córdoba and Jalapa too: Because they are unmindful of art and history, and neglected by tourism, they never change. Córdoba is where Iturbide and Juan de O'Donoju signed their treaty recognizing Mexico's independence (see p. 57). Surrounded by its orchards and tobacco plantations and coffee bushes, the town hasn't changed much in the half century since the original Terry (T. Philip) described it as

> ...very ancient and time-stained. Antique Spanish-Moorish windows (*ventanas*) heavily barred with iron, quaint wooden balconies, massive colonial doors with iron knockers (*llamadores*) and studded with broad-headed hand-wrought copper nails are characteristic features. Most of the houses are low and are roofed with red tiles (*tejas*) which form a pleasing contrast to the luxuriant green of the tropical vegetation. The roofs are the favorite promenades of splendid peacocks. Somnolent *zopilotes*

(buzzards) constitute the street-cleaning department...
[In the plaza] old residents assemble and take the rest-cure
throughout the drizzling day. To the sound of squawking
parrots they sit around metal tables and smoke cigarettes,
criticizing the doings of the *metropolitanos* at the capital,
swap discarded political ideas, re-clothe jokes that came
over with Cortés and sip claret diluted with seltzer-water
squirted from blue-glass siphons encased in wire network.[11]

Jalapa, the "City of Flowers," is more substantial architecturally,
and on its seven hills with the peaks of Orizaba and Cofre de Perote
in the distance, it is majestically situated. With its university, superior schools, publishing house, experimental theater, art gallery and
symphony orchestra, it is one of the few provincial cities of Mexico
with a cultural life of its own. It has an important archaeological
museum, outside of which stand (if they haven't been moved to the
capital or sent home where they belong) several of the colossal
Olmec heads from La Venta. But it is the landscape and the vegetation in the Totonac country between Jalapa and Veracruz that
astonishes the American today just as it did the soldiers in Scott's
army as they advanced from the malarial lowlands to Cerro Gordo:

> Matted tangles of leafage spattered with gold, big tuli-
> pans gleaming in the shadows like a red rose in the hair of
> a Spanish dancer, blossoms like scarlet hornets that almost
> flew at one's eyes, and blooms like red-hot hair-brushes, the
> sight of which made the scalp tingle, were balanced with
> big, close masses of white throats and purple mouths, and
> with banks of the greenish-white cuatismilla, discharging
> invisible clouds of a fragrance that seemed to be locust
> blended with lily of the valley. Trees with tops like bal-
> loons, like corkscrews, and like tables, trees drained almost
> dry by starry parasites that swung from their branches,
> trees covered with strawberry blossoms—or what appeared
> to be strawberry blossoms—that were to graduate into
> coffee beans, trees bare of everything except great yellow
> suns, the Flower of God, that fascinated one's gaze—these
> and countless other surprises followed one another; and
> then would come a whole grove netted over with morning
> glories in full bloom.... Of all the places occupied by
> American troops in Mexico, the most delightful was Jalapa.

[11] Quoted in *Terry's Guide to Mexico*.

In fact, probably, a more delightful place is nowhere to be found. Spring was the only season.[12]

Papantla, sixty miles north of Veracruz on the coast, is the center of the vanilla industry and the Totonac Indians' ceremonial city. *Voladores* "fly" around their poles in many Totonac villages (Cuetzalan, pp. 207–208, among them) but for ten days during the May-June festival of Corpus Christi they put on their biggest show here. Dance groups in barbaric costumes, the Quetazles, the Negritos, the Moros, perform in the streets, but the climax is always when the flute player atop his pole dances on his tiny platform and sounds the invitation to be airborne; then the *voladores* in their red suits and feathered helmets fall backward, the ropes wound about their bodies and attached to the top of the pole unwind, and with heads down and arms extended like wings, they go around and around in the dazzling sunlight.

El Tajin, a few miles inland from Papantla in the orchid jungle, is the ancient Totonac ceremonial center; its calendric pyramid, with 366 windowlike niches, dates back to Olmec times (see p. 6). Cempoala, off the same coastal highway closer to Veracruz, has a less original pyramid of its own, but a more important one historically. It was here that Cortés made his first productive contact with the Indians, and later fell upon the unsuspecting Pánfilo de Narváez during a thunderstorm. (see pp. 18, 25).

Veracruz, associated not only with Cortés' arrival but with Santa Anna, Juárez, Maximilian, the French and American invasions, and Carranza, wears its historical notoriety lightly. A gay and swinging port it always was—and still is. The only substantial relic of invasion-prone Veracruz is the massive fortress of San Juan de Ulúa, built (from 1528) to be impregnable, but clearly not so. For political prisoners San Juan de Ulúa was monstrously effective. Some of its slimy dungeons are so small that only men in crouching positions could be inserted into them through manholes, and at high tide they must have sat chin-deep in saltwater. For tourists with cameras, the fort's frowning battlements and gun pits seem made to order. But the real charm of Veracruz is in its multicolored houses surrounded by almond trees and bougainvillea, and its pleasure-loving people. The beaches (Villa del Mar and Macambo are the best) are not outstanding, but the cafés in the portals around the Plaza de la Constitución with shrimp vendors passing and marimbas playing are

[12] Justin H. Smith in *The War with Mexico,* reprint edition. Gloucester, Massachusetts, Peter Smith, 1963.

wonderful; and Mardi Gras is more fun than in New Orleans and Rio for those who like a really spontaneous romp in the streets.

For travelers with enough time on their hands to *drive* to Yucatán, there are several places of considerable interest along the coastal highway that passes through the states of Veracruz, Tabasco and Campeche. Coatzacoalcos is not one of them. The recent discovery of vast sulfur deposits in the area have turned this once malarial port into a smoky agglomeration of chemical refineries and Pemex tanks behind the old banana-loading docks. On either side of Coatzacoalcos are archaeological zones renowned for their Olmec finds. Cerro de las Mesas, quite near Veracruz, contains the Hill of Altars, where seven hundred jade figurines of great beauty were found, and a vast complex of ruins still untouched. (The road south to Oaxaca from here passes the notorious Valle Nacional of Porfirian ill-fame described on pp. 91–92.) La Venta, in the jungle southeast of Coatzacoalcos, is the Olmec heartland, where the colossal "Negroid" heads were found by the American archaeologist Franz Blom when he became the first to penetrate this difficult Tabasco swampland in 1925.

La Venta is still a pretty messy place to get into. Fortunately the problem has been solved brilliantly by Carlos Pellicer, the poet (see p. 152). His outdoor museum of La Venta is two miles from the center of the city on the shore of the Lake of Illusions, and there the 20-ton heads, 30-ton altars and dozens of other major sculptures are to be seen in a setting resembling the original one. If the task of transporting them from La Venta seems impressive, think of the ingenuity of the Olmecs two thousand years earlier, who dragged the larger blocks of uncut basalt from the nearest quarry almost a hundred miles distant into their sacred swamp! The smaller Olmec pieces are displayed as brilliantly by Pellicer in the Museum of Archaeology in Villahermosa proper. This collection is almost as rich in Totonac, Maya and Aztec works, and contains scale copies of the celebrated Bonampak frescoes. Taken together, Pellicer's two museums in Villahermosa rival the capital's Museum of Anthropolgy and Archaeology as the greatest collection of ancient Middle American art in the world.

North and northeast from Villahermosa the highway to Yucatán hugs the coast as far as Campeche. To Ciudad del Carmen and beyond, there is a 250-mile stretch where the road leapfrogs two rivers and brackish "Lake" Terminos. Four ferries in all must be taken (in a high wind think twice about it), but Ciudad del Carmen, a shrimping town renowned for its *camarones empanados*, is a lovely place to linger. Campeche is better taken on the run. Capital of the province of the same name, it still has the forts that guarded against pirates, each turret dominated by a scavenger in black—*zopilotes jurídicos?* In Campeche, water is conveyed from house to house in blue barrels slung between wheels and drawn by donkeys. And the colors of the houses, mellowed to pastel by the salt spray, are attractive. But the museum has a hideous mural, combining the worst of Picasso and Tamayo—"Exploitation and Ultimate Triumph of the Indian"—and a glass case containing the bones, in fetal position, of a King of Jaina. "His name is unknown," says the label, "but he was 50 years old and measures 1 metre, 73 centimetres." *Sic transit...*

Palenque, Yaxchilán, Bonampak

The outstanding Classic Maya sites in Mexico—Palenque, Yaxchilán and Bonampak—are all close to Villahermosa in neighboring Chiapas —close as the crow files—but only Palenque is easy to get to.

Palenque, when I visited it in 1956, was accessible only by the Sureste, a narrow-gauge railway that connects Coatzacoalcos with Campeche. The train I was on tipped over short of its destination and I was obliged to complete the trip on horseback—the perfect way of entering a Maya ruin in the jungle. Today there is a good road from Villahermosa, and an airstrip with regular flights.

Cortés passed within a few miles of the ruins of Palenque in 1525 on his march to Guatemala without suspecting their existence; they had been ruins for centuries even then, the great civilization that built them long forgotten. I had read the account of the American traveler, John L. Stephens, who visited the site in the forties of the last century. Stephens had not been its discoverer—a French antiquarian, Dupaix, had visited Palenque a decade earlier—but Stephens was the first to appreciate its romantic beauty, and his traveling companion, the English artist Frederick Catherwood, embellished his account with some fine drawings of the temples and sculpture. Their visit took place during the rainy season. They were devoured by mosquitoes. Their Indian porters refused to spend the night in the ruins, which were reputed to be haunted. Half the population of the village had just been swept off by cholera. Stephens himself became the victim of ticks and had to be carried out of Chiapas in a litter. But the exaltation of the place stayed with him:

> We lived in the ruined palaces of kings; we went up to their desolate temples and fallen altars; and wherever we moved we saw evidences of their taste, their skill in arts, their

wealth and power.... We called back into life the strange
people who gazed at us in sadness from the walls.... In
the romance of the world's history, nothing ever impressed
me more forcibly than the spectacle of this once great and
lovely city, overturned, desolate and lost; discovered by
accident, overgrown with trees for miles around, it did not
have even a name to distinguish it. Apart from everything
else it was a mourning witness to the world's mutations.

Nations melt

From Power's high pinnacle, when they have felt
The sunshine for a while, and downward go.[13]

It was good to see Palenque, as Donald Demarest and I saw it that
late afternoon, in the eerie, ruined light. The jungle setting, the com-
pactness of the temples, the devastating power and purity of the
stucco reliefs led one to feel that everything at Palenque reached
perfection, and that with this thrilling achievement, this absolute
aesthetic pitch, things had to fall apart. As we stood on the roof
of the Temple of Inscriptions, a tiny native woman was drawing
water from the original aqueduct—precisely like the first, in her
bare feet, white *huipil*, and pigtails, except that the tin pail would
have been an earthenware jug.

But what use had the aristocrats and sorcerers who had built these
architectural masterpieces for the likes of her, or her prototype?
She planted the corn, bore and raised the children, perhaps carried
some of the smaller building blocks. The male slaves carried the
larger ones, including the marvelously reliefed five-ton plinth which
the archaeologist Alberto Ruz Lhuillier raised with windlasses and
jacks when he discovered the King's Tomb at the end of a long
secret passage under this temple in 1952. When the worker ants
weren't building for the celestial architects, they were providing
the cannon fodder.

Fortunately the archaeologists have not gone farther at Palenque
than to remove the best of the movable sculpture. Cropping the
jungle around the ruins and keeping it cropped (for the jungle moves
in, almost perceptibly) is of course a necessity, but it has added to
the beauty of these hilltop temples, whose steep steps have yet to be
excavated, providing them with velvety, emerald bases like so many
exquisite urns in a museum's cabinet.

[13] John Lloyd Stephens, *Incidents of Travel in Central America, Chiapas and
Yucatán*. New Brunswick, New Jersey, Rutgers University Press, 1949.

To the question whether the great arts of pre-Columbian Mexico meant anything to anyone before the restless eclectics of our time, I quote the testimony of Albrecht Dürer, who in 1520 saw the jewels and gold figurines which Cortés had sent to Charles V the year before. "These things," the great German artist wrote, "are so precious that they were valued at a hundred thousand gulden. But I have never seen in all my days what so rejoiced my heart. For I saw among them amazing artistic objects, and I marveled over the subtle ingenuity of the men in these distant lands." (The Spaniards, more impressed by the monetary value of Moctezuma's gifts, promptly melted them down.)

Today we take for granted the genius of the pre-Columbian artists but cannot fathom their motivation. The archaeologists tell us little. Pyramids, like those at Palenque, Xochicalco, Tajin, and Chichén Itzá, were probably erected to mark the lapse of time between some great event in the past and the (then) present. But why? Aldous Huxley, describing the mysteries of Copán, a Maya shrine 350 miles southeast of Palenque in Honduras, had this to say: "Time is unbearable. To make it bearable, men transform it into something that is not time, that has the quality of space." But he adds, "What causes a people, or at any rate the thinking part of a people, to become as acutely time-conscious as the priestly mathematicians of the Maya Old Empire? ... A man is born to whom, for whatever reasons, time is an obsession. It also happens that he possesses the kind of abilities which enable him to solve his problem—the problem of the intellectual mastery and transformation of time—in comprehensible quantitative terms." [14] It is an answer, but not *the* answer. The mystery remains. Best of all, the art remains. Nor do we have to be obsessed by time to be thrilled by it. The same qualities that appeal to us in Athens, in Chartres, in the Sistine Chapel, in the Hospicio at Guadalajara, appeal to us here. Perhaps this is the only constant in variable history. The wars, the social institutions, the dates, and the names are swept away. Art remains!"

For the Mexico traveler who wants to see a Maya ruin of the Classic Period as its discoverers found it, a trip to Yaxchilán or Bonampak is essential.

Yaxchilán, which lies fifty miles southeast of Palenque in a big bend of the Usumacinta River separating Mexican Chiapas from Guatemala, was discovered in the late 1880's by the British antiquarian A. P. Maudslay. Then, as now, a dying tribe of un-Chris-

---

[14] Aldous Huxley, *Beyond the Mexique Bay*. London, Chatto & Windus, 1934.

tianized Maya Indians, Lacandons, visited Yaxchilán periodically to burn copal in their "god pots" and worship the ancient deities whose very names had been forgotten. When I visited it in 1957 with Demarest, it was necessary to go to Tenosique by train, and from there charter a Cessna for a short flight in the jungle, from where dugout canoes for an ascent of the river were available. Overnight accommodations, food and hammocks slung between trees, were provided by the knowledgeable "guardian" of the ruins, Miguel de la Cruz. The ruins lie behind the pier on a high bluff overlooking the mighty river. The terrain has a floor of limestone, sharp and white with black markings amid rotted vegetation—a brown peat moss that looks and smells like that surrounding the roots of laurels in the New Jersey mountains surrounding my home. It's a slippery footing, and in many places we had to pull ourselves up by roots and lianas. How the ruins have survived the tentacles of this rankness of growth so many centuries is a wonder. Many haven't, of course. We found temple after temple, split by trees, the roof caved in, the gates filled with rubble. But at least four are more or less intact. One has fragments of rose-and-blue frescoes still clinging to its walls. Another still retains its intricately carved lintels. And a third has the center of its three doors blocked by the torso of a gigantic "king." The head of this stone figure has fallen and rolled to a spot fifty feet below, where it has assumed an upright position. The Lacandons make a pilgrimage here every year to see if the head still stands. If it did not, they say, the world would come to an end. "But we're not afraid of the world's end," they told Miguel, "when that time comes we'll be with all honest men (they never bring their women here, or mention them) in paradise, the place where men are without fever or consumption and have only two children."

Bonampak is fifteen miles southwest of Yaxchilán across the Usumacinta, deep in the Selva Lacandon. From fragments revealed by Miguel de la Cruz, Ruz Lhuillier and the discoverer himself, I reconstructed the drama of its revelation. Bonampak (Maya for "painted walls," a name suggested by Sylvanus Morley) remained a secret as long as the Lacandons had a chief. The last of these died in the early 1940's. In February of 1946, Lacandons took a party of Americans headed by Charles (Carlos) Frey to the site, but they missed the temple with the great frescoes. Then came Giles Greville Healey, an American photographer employed by the United Fruit Company in Guatemala, who on many earlier treks through Chiapas had compiled his own list of sites. He got along with the tribesmen. They showed him the murals. He photographed them in color, applying kerosene to the semiopaque deposit of calcium carbonate which had protected them since their painting (*c.* A.D. 730–820) when Classic Maya art was at its height. The kerosene brought out the colors and forms just long enough to permit flash photography. Painted on wet lime, and possibly a whole wall to a single sitting, since no joints show, the frescoes depict religious rites, bands of musicians, court scenes, battles in the jungle, triumphal processions with mutilated captives, and dance festivals. The colors are brilliant, and the handling of action is without precedent in its realism. In a flash, more was revealed of Maya culture than all the temples and sculptures had disclosed. The Mayas grew in stature as artists, but no one would ever again describe them as pacific.

By the 1960's an airstrip had been hacked out of the jungle and visitors can now be flown to Bonampak by charter in small planes, but weather has not been kind to the murals. The places to see them, as already noted, are the National Museum of Anthropology and Archaeology in the capital, and the Archaeological Museum in Villahermosa, where painters have created exact-scale replicas of the three decorated chambers from sketches made on the spot with the aid of infrared and ultraviolet photographs.

Oaxaca, The Isthmus of Tehuantepec, San Cristóbal de Las Casas

The Inter-American Highway into central southern Mexico may be picked up at Izúcar de Matamoros either by driving south from Puebla or east from Cuernavaca by way of Cuautla. From that point on to Oaxaca, and beyond Oaxaca to the Isthmus of Tehuantepec and across the wild mountains of Chiapas to the Guatemala border, there is so much hot desert, such a desolation of bristling blue cacti, and so many thousands of hairpin turns, that every time I traverse it I say to myself fervently, "Never again!" Yet there is no better way of getting to Guatemala, and the most Guatemalan town in Mexico, San Cristóbal de Las Casas. And there is no other way at all of getting overland to Oaxaca—one of Mexico's great cities. And hairpin turns, through some mental quirk which boggles at quantity, become converted by memory into *one* hairpin turn. And now there is another reason for taking this route: It is possible at last to *drive* into the Yucatán Peninsula, by way of the road already described—Coatzacoalcos, Villahermosa, Campeche—which is joined by a good road spanning the Isthmus.

On my third trip to Oaxaca, with Bill Negron in 1963, we decided to stop off at Acatlán and visit Herón Martínez. Our difficulty in locating him tells something of the change that has come over even this little-traveled part of Mexico in less than a decade. In 1956 Herón was making a unique kind of unglazed pottery and selling it in Oaxaca—animals with riders and acrobats, candelabra with little figures dangling from wire, all painted with an intricate design in blues, blacks, oranges and greens. Because he was uncelebrated locally, he was easy to find. But in 1963 an urchin took us by a roundabout way to a part of Acatlán I had never seen before. Herón had changed, and his pottery (glazed now) had a Texas look. Puzzled, I questioned him for some time and finally elicited the reluctant information that up the street there was "another Herón Martínez." There was, and not one, but several! We did find the original artist, finally, and his work hadn't deteriorated a bit, but he had a huge workshop now and was executing commissions for agents as far away as San Francisco at high prices. The whole town these days, he explained, was full of "fake Herón Martínezes" and to prove that he was the real one—though we assured him no papers were necessary—he showed us a framed diploma from Adolfo López Mateos, President of Mexico, authenticating his status as "Folk Artist of the Republic."

Oaxaca itself hasn't changed noticeably. On my first visit in 1937 I had watched Alfonso Caso and his assistants removing the last of the royal treasures from the newly discovered tombs on Monte Albán. Today the golden necklaces and earplugs are on display in the splendid Regional Museum of the Zócalo of the provincial capital; and the famous archaeologist, after moving up the political ladder to the Interior Ministry under Alemán, and then heading the Instituto Indigenista [15] which he founded, is now writing his memoirs. The Zócalo, with its jade-green arcades and giant laurel trees full of singing birds, is the same. Its dozens of tiny booths dispensing everything but pipe tobacco haven't changed, nor its army of vendors hawking serapes, nor the nearby Indian market, largest on the continent, with the famous gray clay bells from Coyotepec and children's whistles with the blowhole under the donkey's tail. The stall nearest the market still sells copal incense and witches' charms that haven't changed

[15] This wonder-working organization, which unfortunately receives so little federal support that it reaches only a fraction of the Indians it might serve, is nevertheless more enlightened and effective than its counterpart in the United States. It teaches the primitive tribes the advantages of cooperatives; offers elementary accounting and Spanish if the Indian wants them; supplies free medical and surgical care; installs pure, fresh water; and gives the aboriginal for the first time a sense that outsiders respect him for what he is and can do better than others.

since pre-Columbian times. And at the Hotel Monte Albán, *plumados* in sandals and feathered headgear still listlessly go through their cere- monial-dance paces under the dirty skylight. But at Cervantes' curio shop the best *huipils* are now displayed under glass in a "museum," and one has to go to the villages far in the surrounding mountains to find bargains.

Not many physical associations remain of the two great antithet- ical Oaxacans who affected Mexico's nineteenth-century history so indelibly. Only Santo Domingo Church and Monastery could be haunted by the ghosts of the Zapotec Indian Juárez, whose cavalry used it as a barracks during the Reform Wars, and by the Mixtec Indian Porfirio Díaz, who as a young patriot led a daring raid upon the monastery, which led to the city's recapture by the Juaristas. The interior of this massive Baroque church is as fine a repository of polychrome sculpture and gilded ornamentation as any to be seen in Mexico—the best that can be said for which was said long ago by the perceptive Charles Flandrau, "A little is pleasant, merely too much is vulgar; but a positively staggering amount of it seems to justify itself." [16]

The center of Zapotec civilization for two millennia was Monte Albán, a mountaintop four miles west of Oaxaca. Among the major archaeological sites in Mexico, it is the oldest, dating back perhaps to the fifth century B.C., and the only one continuously occupied until the Conquest.

The site covers twenty-five square miles. The central plaza is 1,000 feet long and 650 feet wide. Monte Albán's hieroglyphic writ- ings, its calendar, its numerals, and its observatory shaped like an arrowhead to face the winter solstice, antedate the Mayas, to whom these intellectual feats are usually ascribed. There are also indica- tions of a healthier, less caste-ridden culture. For one thing, the Zapotecs appear not to have become obsessed, as the Mayas were, with measuring time; time and space were identical in their thinking, and the stars were worshiped as symbols of permanence amid the flux of worldly ambitions. The proof of the success of their philos- ophy is the centuries of peace and uninterrupted commerce with the lands to the south and north—a unique achievement in the annals of Middle America. No weapons were found in the Monte Albán tombs. The famous Tomb 7, which Caso discovered in 1932 with its nine pounds of jewels, is of a very late date, probably just before the Conquest, and its craftsmen were the ultrarefined, less humane

[16] Charles Macomb Flandreau, *Viva Mexico!* Reprinted by Harper & Brothers, n.d.

Mixtecs who had by then taken over. To this day the Zapotecs, whose blood sacrifices went no further than puncturing the lobe of the ear, will have nothing to do with bullfighting.

The serenity of their culture is best expressed in the proportions of the Great Plaza at Monte Albán, its nobly stepped temples, and its gentle domination of the whole tropical valley.

Mitla, the Mixtec shrine, is an hour's drive on the road south, beyond Santa María del Tule where stands the immense *ahuehuete*, 162 feet in diameter, which was ancient when Cortés and his men took shelter under it. Mitla was the particular shrine of the god Xipetotec, a forerunner of the bloody Aztec idols, and Mitla's appliquéd geometrical abstractions in stone (perhaps symbolizing the birds' feathers and serpents' scales of Quetzalcoatl, who was also worshiped here) are forbidding. Penitents were sealed up alive in these walls, and one legend has it that Fray Francisco de Burgoa in the 1650's sent priests into the subterranean passageways until they encountered snakes and evil smells and a fierce wind which caused them to "wall up forever this back door to hell." It was this same good Dominican who secretly watched a pagan confession rite and was horrified to hear the confessor conclude: "Now you can be happy and sin again."

The late Miguel Covarrubias, who wrote a rapturous book about the isthmus of Tehuantepec, once told me that I didn't like this part of Mexico because I had had to change all four of my tires one morning in Juchitán. That may have been part of the reason, but there were others. The matriarchy of tall, haughty Tehuanas with ankle-length skirts, whom Diego Rivera glorified in the Education Ministry, was no longer to be seen—at least in the towns through which the Inter-American Highway passes. Salina Cruz, the Pacific port Porfirio Díaz had built to capitalize on trans-isthmian traffic, was put out of business when the Panama Canal was opened in 1914; its beach is a windblown desolation. Since it is now possible to drive between two of the most attractive cities in Mexico—Oaxaca and San Cristóbal—in a day, travelers rarely stop.

But perhaps it is only fair to give Covarrubias the last word. When he visited the city of Tehuantepec in the late thirties, male passengers still leaned from the creaky railway carriages that bumped along the riverbank to get a closer look at the bathing Tehuanas, and the swains of these beauties, climbing the Jaguar Hill that gives the town its Nahuatl name, pointed out remnants of the beasts which a legendary giant sea turtle had turned to stone to stop them from terrorizing the inhabitants. Juchitán, Tehuantepec's close neighbor and ferociously republican rival, was then a sprawling town of twenty thousand "pure or nearly pure" Zapotecs:

> A standard neo-classic *palacio municipal* faces the square, the whole of its ground floor taken up by arcades where the market is held, teeming with hard-working, outspoken *tecas,* coquettish *refresqueras* mashing pineapples, papaya, and guanabana to put into long drinks, or scraping ice to serve as *raspada,* soaked in a bright magenta syrup. Other women sell neat bouquets of flowers or strings of frangipani for the saints or for the dead, gilt chains, pendants, and silver coins washed in gold to replace the twenty-dollar gold pieces of former, better days. There are sellers of bread, of large baked corn wafers, of tamales, of live and cooked iguanas, of coconuts and fruit, of sweets, medicinal herbs, baskets, hammocks, and *xicalpextles* (lacquered and painted gourds). There are dealers in shrimps and dried fish, and great displays of water jars, a Juchitán specialty. As in Tehuantepec, the heart and soul of the town is the buzzing market, and its life and blood are its women, ever active, good-natured, but relentless in business, a fair match for the commercial cunning of the foreign merchants— Spaniards, Arabs, Syrians and Lebanese.[17]

Beyond Juchitán, the Inter-American Highway leading to Guatemala splits. The southern branch parallels the narrow-gauge railway (but out of sight of the Pacific) to the frontier city of Tapachula, center of a rich coffee-, cocoa-, cotton- and banana-producing area. The northern branch climbs the mountains to Tuxtla Gutiérrez, Chiapas' capital, San Cristóbal de Las Casas, Comitán, and the border at Ciudad Cuauhtémoc, gateway to the dazzling Guatemala Highlands.

San Cristóbal, surnamed Las Casas for the conquistadors' priest who became the Indians' fiery advocate and first bishop of Chiapas, still has the air of a frontier settlement. Between my visits in 1956 and 1964 it had hardly changed. It was still the most Indian city in Mexico, and it will always be the coldest place in the tropics north of La Paz, Bolivia, though its altitude (7,454 feet) is only 106 feet higher than Mexico City. The women of the Chamula and Zinacantán tribes still pad into town on their leathery bare feet, carrying packs of firewood and babies on their backs, their black homespun

[17] Miguel Covarrubias, *Mexico South: The Isthmus of Tehuantepec.* Cassel & Co., Ltd., n.d.

huipils with rose stitching pulled over their mouths to keep the "consumptive" night air from their lungs. Their men, in white wool shorts and high-heeled sandals, still come to the market to buy new black-banded flat straw hats with long pink tassels. Señor Humbres' La Segoviana still sells the best embroidered shirts, belts, leather bags, sandals and bronze knockers north of Guatemala. And at the pension Español, three Indian seven-year-olds in woolen burnooses still build an aromatic fire of cedar chips in a corner of the room before one turns in, and another fire first thing in the morning. Only two things had changed. "Pancho" Blom had died. And the Instituto Indigenista seemed to have abandoned the Indians.

Franz Blom was one of those old-time Americans—like Spratling, Fred Davis, Anita Brenner—who "went Mexican," and in the process saved a bit of Mexico that the Mexicans hardly knew they had. Between San Cristóbal and the Usumacinta River lies the untracked Lacandon Forest. Untracked, that is, by anyone but Giles Healey and Franz Blom. Blom tracked it all, mapped it, made friends of the suspicious, miserable Lacandons. Indians from all over Chiapas brought him gifts—priceless sculptures and iron grave crosses, old *huipils* and musical instruments, and with these he made of his handsome, ancient house a museum. On my second visit to it, I asked an attendant what had happened to Gertrude Duby, the easygoing archaeologist's formidable German wife. He pointed to a "Voluntary Contributions" box on the wall, over which I read this much of a printed warning:

> In droves and in herds you come ringing my bell
> My impulse is always to wish you in hell
> For my peace you disturb,
> My garden you trample . . .
> For all you took and you took and you took
> Leave something more than your name in my book.

Showing a color film he had taken of the Chamulas stamping out a blazing ritual field with their bare feet, Franz Blom once said to me: "I'm glad I'll be dead when all the Indians are in overalls and all the tourists are in Indian costume." It hadn't happened yet, but a pall of hostility hung over the marketplace. The village of Chamula, which was full of color and pride and friendliness in 1956 when the Instituto was giving the Indians the feeling that their customs and crafts were worth preserving, had yielded to bureaucracy—and anti-gringoism. The door of that wonderful candle-lit church that had been jammed with worshipers kneeling in the pine needles years before was locked. And a surly attendant (in overalls) impounded cameras and handed out printed forms entitled—"Voluntary Contributions."

It would be dishonest to pretend that there are no gems of the Mexican diadem that this Mexican traveler hasn't seen. There are many. And one is the Montebello Lakes, a two-day trip over rough roads southeast of Comitán. The twenty-thousand-square-mile sector of the Lacondon Forest in which the lakes lie was made into a National Park by the government in 1960. *Terry's Guide to Mexico* calls these lakes "unquestionably the most beautiful and isolated in Mexico" and adds that "each seems to glow with different colors of the rainbow." (I take their description on faith, as I hope they will take mine of Cuetzalan and Las Estacas.)

The Yucatán Peninsula

Shaped like a thumb, jutting into the Gulf of Mexico between the Isthmus of Tehuantepec and Central America, Yucatán's history has been entirely shaped by its isolation from the rest of Mexico and by its peculiar terrain.

The isolation of Yucatán had political consequences in pre-Columbian and modern times alike. Maya civilization was enabled to survive here long after its ceremonial centers in Honduras, Guatemala and Chiapas had been destroyed or abandoned. The Maya outposts in Yucatán were in turn conquered by the Toltecs of central Mexico in the twelfth century, when the Toltecs' northern enemies gave up their pursuit short of the isolated peninsula. The Spaniards in turn encountered great difficulties subjugating Yucatán in the sixteenth century; a tribe of the Toltec-Mayas (the Itzás) escaped altogether until late in the seventeenth century, and the remaining aboriginals were never wholly assimilated. For a century following independence from Spain, Mexico was constantly engaged in attempts to suppress rebellions against federal authority. Porfirio Díaz' conversion of the peninsula into a virtual slave state administered by a few henequen planters and repopulated with Yaquis from Sonora (see p. 91) was the last attempt to cope with the problem by violent means. But even today, with a highway finally connecting Yucatán to the rest of Mexico, the state's hostility to federalism survives in such phenomena as the peoples' insistence upon calling themselves *yucatecos* rather than *mexicanos* and in Mérida's refusal in 1964 to elect a PRI mayor.

Topographically and in terms of its economy, the Yucatán is also quite unlike the rest of Mexico. Except for some very low hills in the east and south, the whole peninsula is a limestone table covered with scrub jungle and watered entirely by subterranean rivers. Where these rivers approach the surface, there are open "wells" (*cenotes*); in other, populated places, like the capital, Mérida, the underground water is tapped by windmills. The coastal north, which contains most of the population, is fanned by cooling ocean breezes; almost daily light showers, except in the rainy season (June through September), are a further blessing. But in the jungles bordering the state of Campeche on the west, and in Quintana Roo—the virtually unpopulated and unexplored eastern Territory bordering Belize (British Honduras) to the southeast—it rarely stops raining.

In the old days, if one is to believe the chronicler of Chilam Balam, the Yucatán was an earthly paradise. "There was no sickness; they had then no aching bones; no high fever; no burning chest; no abdominal pains; no consumption; no headache..." What happened?

> With the true God, the true *Dios*, came the beginning of our misery. It was the beginning of tribute, the beginning of church dues, the beginning of strife with purse-snatching, the beginning of strife with blow-guns, the beginning of strife by trampling on people, the beginning of robbery with violence, the beginning of forced debts enforced by false testimony.... This was the origin of service to the Spaniards and priests...while the poor people were harassed.[18]

The peninsula is dotted with ruined ceremonial centers of the old days, paradisal in architecture at least. Mayapán, Sayil and Labná, Ekmul, Kabáh, and Dzibilchaltún (the oldest) are all accessible; but Uxmal, Chichén Itzá, and Tulum (in Quintana Roo) have most to offer the traveler who is not an archaeologist.

Uxmal and Chichén Itzá

Uxmal is the most compact of the three famous ruins, and the "purest" in the sense that its Maya structures all date from the Late Classic Period (A.D. 700–1000), with very little influence from the Toltecs who occupied them thereafter. Puuc-Chene is the name

[18] Ralph L. Roys (ed.), *The Book of Chilam Balam of Chumayel*. With an Introduction by J. Eric S. Thompson. Norman, Oklahoma, University of Oklahoma Press, 1967.

given to the local variation of the Maya style which flourished here
—long, low palaces, their openings divided with squat columns, sur-
mounted by "combs" and carved masks, and decorated with vertical
bands of friezelike stone ornamentation. The casual disarray of centuries of neglect, the action of wind and sun and gravity, have
produced a fine conglomeration which, happily, Stephens, Blom,
and Sylvanus Morley, Uxmal's early explorers, did nothing to restore. Eager tourists climb the almost perpendicular steps of the
Pyramid of the Magician, hanging precariously onto a rusty chain as
the footing splays out from under their feet; or pose against the
orange-and-black striations of the Palace of the Governor, the trian-
gular shadow of whose opening, punctuated by a single brutal
column, frowns upon them with an almost sexual emphasis.

Uxmal is fifty-eight miles southwest of Mérida in rolling country;
Chichén Itzá is seventy-five miles east of the capital on the feature-
less plain. The site was brought to the world's attention by Stephens,
who visited it in 1841 on the same safari which led him to Palenque.
Early archaeologists then visited it. But in 1900, Edward Thompson,
American Consul General in Yucatán, bought the hacienda on which
the ruins stood and, employing a diver and a dredge, extracted from
the Sacred Cenote a wealth of gold, jewelry, copper plaques, and
bone and jade ornaments, some originating from as far away as the
Valley of Mexico and South America. He sold them to Harvard's
Peabody Museum—a loss of the national patrimony which every
Mexican Government since has understandably resented—and in 1968
the Cenote was being "mined" again, this time by a team of scuba
divers in the pay of *Look* magazine, and presumably under the
control of Mexican archaeologists.

The treasures of the Sacred Cenote were offerings to Chac, the
rain god. From the rim, almost two hundred feet in diameter, to
the jade-green waters sixty feet below, virgins doped with copal
were also flung as offerings. "It was their belief that they did not
die," Diego De Landa reported, "although they were never seen
again. They also threw in many other things, precious and highly
prized." De Landa was the first Bishop of Yucatán, the recipient of
mixed feelings on the part of the archaeologists, since he destroyed
the most important Maya codices, and at the same time left a record
(*Relación de las Cosas de Yucatán*) which is the bible of all Maya
studies. The Cenote is also associated with Hunac Ceel, the ruler
of Mayapan in the twelfth century who drove the Itzás out of
Chichén Itzá; he established respect for himself here, it is said, by
descending into the Cenote's fearsome depths and coming up with

the "prophecy" of Mayapan's domination of the peninsula—a domination that was to last until the Conquest.

The most interesting of the many well-preserved structures at Chichén Itzá are the Castillo, the Temple of the Jaguars, the Ball Court, and the Temple of the Warriors—all grouped around the avenue leading to the Sacred Cenote; and across the highway, in "Old Chichén," the Caracol (Observatory), the Nunnery and the Church.

El Castillo, a pyramid 75 feet high with 365 steps, served as a fort during some of the campaigns the Spaniards and Mexicans were obliged to wage against the recalcitrant Mayas. Under the outer pyramid archaeologists found an inner one whose temple contained a recumbent Toltec rain god (Chac Mool) and a limestone throne painted bright red, with eyes and spots of green jade. Both are still to be seen—if the gallery isn't locked and its guard "gone for the day," my experience on two of three visits to Chichén Itzá.

The Temple of Warriors is an imposing Toltec structure with hundreds of sculptured pillars, colonnades, courtyards, pyramids, and a fine Chac Mool of its own.

The Temple of the Jaguars once contained important Maya frescoes recording the Toltec conquest. They were in poor condition when Stephens first described them, and are almost indecipherable now. From drawings and tracings left by Maler, LePlongeon, and others, a battle scene has been reconstructed thus:

> It is a strange battle—no horror, no death; it is more like a battle ballet. . . . Lines of warriors, weaving back and forth and up and down, easily carry the eye into each section of the panel, balance and counterpoise directing the movements. Long, straight, flying spears, repeated diagonally, unify the pyramidal composition. Two leaders on the right side of the panel are armed like the rest, but above their heads rise snakes with darting tongues; a chief on the opposite side also has his protecting serpent. In the center of the lower section a timekeeper kneels before a calendar wheel. [19]

The Ball Court is an enclosure as long as two football fields placed end to end. The goals, through which the ball had to be aimed, are like doughnuts projecting from the side walls at right

[19] *Painted Walls of Mexico: From Prehistoric Times Until Today.* Text by Emily Edwards. Photographs by Manuel Álvarez Bravo. Foreword by Jean Charlot. Austin, Texas, University of Texas Press, 1966.

angles. Through these rings, no more than a foot in diameter, the contestants tried to propel a ball by motions of their hips and elbows, to which pieces of leather were attached. (The fact that the ball is known to have been made of rubber is cited as one proof that the Mayas were deeply indebted to their more ancient Gulf Coast cousins, the Olmecs.) Judging by one of the nearby reliefs, losers, instead of being traded or returned to the minor leagues, were executed.

The Caracol, the astronomical observatory which stands seventy-five feet above the plain on a base consisting of two terraces, is named after its spiral staircase. Small openings point to cardinal directions and fixed stars. The silhouette of the Caracol is magnificent; and so is the roof-comb of the tiny "Church" not far from it, bristling with stone masks of the rain god, turtles, armadillos, snails and crabs.

Mérida, Isla Mujeres, Cozumel

Mérida, the base for visiting all the Yucatecan ruins, and also for trips to Cozumel Island, Isla Mujeres, and Tulum, is an attractive city, justly renowned as the cleanest in Mexico. Its streets are numbered—*oriente* and *poniente*, the even numbers *norte* and the odd *sur*, as in Puebla—but less confusingly, since all the important buildings and hotels are centrally located near the Plaza Mayor. The Cathedral is handsome in its simplicity and the color of its buff stone, but revolutions have stripped its interior bare. The Montejo Palace, also on the Plaza, is the finest sixteenth-century mansion in Mexico. Its Plateresque portal is richly carved, the armored knights with their feet on the bowed heads of Indians symbolizing very well the fate of Yucatán in the centuries that followed. Less brutally frank about their despotism, the henequen *hacendados* of Porfirio Díaz' time went to France for their taste in home-building and furnishing. A particularly beautiful example of these town houses is across the street from the Panamericana Hotel, designed *c.* 1910–14 by Manuel Amábilis. The facade is shocking green, loaded with ornamentation and pilasters in appliquéd white stucco. The colonnaded patio inside and the spacious salons giving on it are beautifully proportioned. Louis XV furniture, chandeliers of blue and green glass, and enlarged family photographs complete the decor.

Isla de las Mujeres, a tiny fish-shaped island in the Caribbean off the northeast tip of the peninsula, and Cozumel, a larger island fifty miles south of it, are the best beach resorts on the Atlantic side of Mexico. Both are in the Territory of Quintana Roo, which Porfirio Díaz sliced from eastern Yucatán at the same time that he sliced

Campeche off in the west. Isla Mujeres is connected to Mérida by a road at the end of which there is a six-mile ferry hop from Puerto Juárez to the island. Cozumel is accessible only by air.

They call Isla Mujeres the Poor Man's Cozumel, which is to say that its visitors are for the most part Mexicans and its hotels reasonably priced. It has the better beaches but is poorer in Maya ruins. The town is a jerry-built sprawl of guest bungalows and fishermen's shacks on a shifting "main street" of sand. But what beaches! The sand is powder-fine and white, the water turquoise and transparent to great depths. There is no undertow except on the exposed side of the island, where there are many rocks. But how long Isla Mujeres will keep its beachcombers' informality is a question. At one of the little hotels in 1968 I watched an entertainment of colored slides: bathing beauties climaxed by a promoter's vision of the Isla Mujeres of the Future—every square foot checkerboarded with asphalt streets like Manhattan.

Cozumel, its jungles and coconut groves still sheltering crumbling temples (some unexplored), was an important shrine in pre-Columbian times. The fact that the most substantial of these Maya sites was destroyed in 1943 to make way for the airport indicates how recent and rapid has been the island's exploitation as a luxury resort. This was the temple visited by Grijalva, Alvarado, Cortés, and the Montejos, Grijalva having been the first to see it on May 3, 1518. The archaeologist Loring Hewen, who now lives in Mérida, says that the thirty sites located on Cozumel indicate a large population; some of the sites were continuously occupied for two thousand years. The principal shrine was to Ix Chel, a moon goddess responsible for childbirth and procreation. Bishop Landa mentions an Oracle at Cozumel—a priest inside a hollow statue who spoke to pilgrims from all over Mayaland. The Spaniards put an end to that, but they did not succeed in colonizing Cozumel, which became a haven for pirates like Henry Morgan and Jean Lafitte. It remained for the tourists to really restore Cozumel's ancient prosperity, with the ruined temples and sunken pirate galleons as much of an allure as its skin-diving reefs, beaches and excellent fishing.

Tulum

Tulum, to use a cliché in its literal sense, is out of this world. Unconnected by road to the rest of Mexico, the ruins are situated on a bluff overlooking the Atlantic, with magnificent beaches below running to the horizon as far as Cozumel in the north and Belize (British Honduras) in the south. Back of the ruins the wastes of

Quintana Roo stretch to the western horizon: a flat interminable jungle broken every hundred miles or so by a cenote like a lidless eye. An hour's flight by chartered Cessna from Mérida, Tulum will remain an utterly empty ruin—until a coastal highway from Puerto Juárez to Belize, which the government has in mind, knifes through it, and the hotels go up.

Grijalva, who saw Tulum from his vessel in 1518, was so astonished that he made an understandable exaggeration: He described it as a city as large as Seville. But he wasn't the first European to see it. Unknown to him two Spaniards, shipwrecked in 1511 on one of the voyages to Darien, were being held prisoner there. One was Gonzáles Guerrero, who married an Indian and went native; the other was Jerónimo de Aguilar, who later escaped and joined Cortés to become a key figure in the Conquest.

Tulum is a late Maya-Toltec walled city, later than Chichén Itzá —in fact, the only structure at Chichén Itzá contemporaneous with Tulum is the so-called Skull Rack. Chichén Itzá was abandoned some time before the Conquest, but Tulum was a vital unit in Hunac Ceel's League of Mayapan. After the Conquest, Tulum was abandoned too, and there is no further mention of it until Stephens' visit in 1842. Then it became a Maya strongpoint in the War of the Castes until Díaz crushed the last pockets of separatist rebellion at the turn of the century and divided the peninsula into its three present parts. In the twenties, Lothrop and Morley did the basic archaeological classification of the ruins. Two decades later, the primitive airstrip was built near the village of Tancah—the strip to which an ancient Jeep comes bumping, if signaled by the dipping wings of one's low-flying Cessna, to save visitors a fifteen-minute walk through the scrub.

Tulum's superb situation and its remoteness are its principal attractions. But two of the temples are of unusual interest. One contains black-and-white frescoes in a fair state of preservation; they are in a style remarkably close to the Mixtec codices from faraway Oaxaca. Another, with walls that slant inward toward the floor, has over the portal a so-called Diving God. Roys [20] says that this stucco figure is actually a glyph of Ah Muzencab, the Maya bee god.

It remains to be said that many other ruins, some merely identified on maps and others undiscovered, lurk in the jungles of Quintana Roo; and that the hunting for *tigrillos*, deer and pheasants is good— but not nearly as good as at Xpuhil in Campeche, where wild boar

[20] Roys (ed.), *op. cit.*

and the larger jaguar, ocelot, spider and howler monkeys, and even an occasional sluggish tapir, are still to be found.

Baja California

A finger of hot land eight hundred miles long, covered with desert and semiarid rugged mountains—what has Baja California got to offer? Nothing, for the average tourist, except a handful of posh beach resorts at the southern tip—but a great deal for fishermen, hunters, amateur explorers and adventurous nature lovers. The top half of the peninsula is a Mexican state. It includes the flourishing border cities of Tijuana and Mexicali, the Pacific resort Ensenada, all the arable land and good roads (in the first hundred miles) and nothing essentially Mexican. The bottom half of the peninsula, connected to the top only by a truck trail, is a territory, and includes all the points of historical interest and great beauty, as well as luxury hotels from La Paz to Cabo San Lucas. The body of water between the peninsula and the western coast of Mexico is the Gulf of California (Sea of Cortez), described without much exaggeration as the greatest fish trap in the world.

The thoroughly Americanized *state* is of interest only to southern Californians with claustrophobia. Tijuana and Mexicali can no longer be described as vice-ridden brothels, but the marks of their past are still upon them. Mexicali has become a progressive commercial city of ninety thousand. Slightly smaller Tijuana, with its duty-free shops, Frontón Stadium, race tracks, bullfighting, night clubs, bars and curio shops, is geared to rich American pocketbooks and poor American tastes. Ensenada has an adequate hard-sand beach for swimming (April through October), a dozen expensive hotels and motels, good yellowtail and deep-sea fishing, and a boom in California-type ranch houses for elderly retirees.

Before coming to the greater charms of the territory, a word about the peninsula's curious history. It was discovered in 1534 by Diego de Becerra, on orders from Cortés, who was looking for the "Seven Cities of Cibola," legendary source of Moctezuma's treasure. The Captain-General visited it himself the following year, landing near Las Cruces and finding pearls near the site of La Paz. The name "California" may derive from Cortés' description of one harbor as a "hot furnace" (*callida fornax*) or from a subsequent voyage by Francisco de Ulloa in 1539, when "Upper" California was first seen. The peninsula, with its scattering of Indian nomads, was left alone until the Jesuits built their first mission at Loreto in 1698, making this town the capital of both Californias for a time. After the expulsion of the Jesuits in 1768, Franciscans and Dominicans continued the pioneering religious work, but pirates and adventurers exercised more control over the coast than New Spain did. By the time the United States declared war on Mexico in 1847, the missionaries had virtually given up, and the peninsula seemed as ripe for plucking as Alta California, Arizona, New Mexico and Texas.

Why the empire builders from the north never plucked it is an interesting story. By the time the war had been won, Americans controlled all the strategic ports, and the natives were showing even less disposition to object than they had in the north. President Polk, however, made the mistake of sending secret supplemental instructions to Nicholas Trist, who was negotiating the Treaty of Guadalupe Hidalgo. These instructions stated that the United States must have the territories of New Mexico and Upper California—"and Baja California provided the Mexicans do not hold out too firmly." The courier died of fever in Veracruz, and his dispatch case was rifled; as a result, when Trist was shown the memorandum *by the Mexicans*, his stand for including the peninsula was so weakened that he was obliged to concede it to Mexico.[21]

Today the territory, though somewhat scanted on federal funds as compared with the state, is one of Mexico's most rapidly developing tourist enclaves. Through its capital, La Paz, it may be reached from the mainland both by automobile ferry from Mazatlán, and by jet from Guadalajara and the capital, as well as from Los Angeles. Small planes belonging to the resort hotels farther south, or available in La Paz by charter, make most of the other attractions of the territory accessible to those who can afford it.

The chief of these attractions, sooner or later, is likely to be the territory's northern sector between Santa Rosalia and Loreto. The deep inlet of Concepción Bay on the Gulf of California is one of the world's largest and most beautiful natural harbors. Just to the north of it is Mulegé, a luxuriant oasis of date palms and mangoes along a mile of fresh water. There is a territorial prison at Mulegé from which, they say, no prisoner has ever wanted to escape; the

---

[21] The story is told by Ralph Hancock in his *Baja California: Hunting, Fishing and Travel in Lower California, Mexico* (Los Angeles, Academy Publishers, 1953). This travelogue, and *The Sea of Cortez* by Ray Cannon (Menlo Park, California, Lane Magazine and Book Company, 1966) are the most informative accounts of the peninsula in all its aspects.

prisoners spend the day gardening for good wages or fishing for the six-foot snook that abound in the lagoon. No one guards them, and they are called back at night by their wives with conch-shell horns.

High in the mountains back of Loreto is the finest mission church on the peninsula, the only one, in fact, in mint condition. This is San Javier, its five-foot-thick walls of superbly cut stone still intact from 1757 (the date carved in stone in the Moorish arch over one doors). There is a gilded altar and some, but not all, of the original religious paintings are still in their ornate frames. The church is accessible by car on a bad road.

Another attraction, far to the northwest in the purple San Francisco Mountains bordering the Vizcaino Desert, is not accessible at all. Employing helicopters and mules, the novelist Erle Stanley Gardner discovered caves here with extraordinary paintings in red and black of animals and hunters with cow-horn headdresses. Carbon dating of wooden artifacts in the caves indicated an age of 530 years. Archaeologists are of the opinion that these paintings were made just prior to the Conquest by a nomadic tribe desperate over the diminishing supply of game and hoping to recall it by magic.[22]

La Paz, 150 miles south of Loreto on the large Bay of La Paz, did not become a permanent settlement until 1811. Its two occupations by the Americans—in 1847, and by the freebooter William Walker somewhat later—were brief. Its present prosperity as capital of the territory and base for all trips into the vacation wonderland to the south dates from 1953, when the Mexican airlines inaugurated regular service. But the American presence here is still felt. I was startled on my arrival in 1968, handing the taxi driver a hundred-peso note to pay my thirty-five-peso fare from the airport to the Los Cocos Hotel, to be given five crisp American greenbacks in change! There is an excellent beach (Corumuel) ten minutes out of the low-lying, nondescript city; and an even better one at Puerto Ballandra, a forty-five-minute drive away; and of course the best deep-sea fishing anywhere in season,[23] but the magnets for the well-

[22] See Erle Stanley Gardner, "The Case of the Baja Caves," in *Life International*, July 30, 1962.

[23] Nourished by the silt of the vast Colorado River watershed, by guano deposits from the birds, and plankton in its warm motionless waters, the Gulf of California swarms with ten-mile hordes of game fish feeding on bigger hordes of forage fish. Cannon says that when the waters "bloom" in the winter, "pile-ups" occur: "Huge manta rays, gigantic jewfish, and black sea bass with mouths large enough to gulp in a beer keg, come up from their fifty-fathom caves. All carnivores become as if insane, as they gorge, disgorge and gorge again. Maddened by the blood and by greed, they slash and rip and kill even their own kind. They gut creatures twice their size and behead the lesser.

heeled are the hotels spotted around the peninsula's tip. These include Rancho Las Cruces, Palmilla and Hacienda Cabo San Lucas, all owned, operated and sumptuously decorated by the pioneering Abelardo Rodríguez, son of former President Rodríguez; and Bud Parr's equally plush Hotel Cabo San Lucas, at the peninsula's tip. The cape itself is spectacular. Several hundred-foot-high granite rocks rise sheer out of the deep blue waters. The headland itself has caves and an arch wide and high enough to permit passage of a large dory. On both sides of it are small beaches of golden sand. The slopes behind them are covered (January–February) with tiny yellow *aceitilla* blossoms, a pink-flowering creeper, called *San Miguel* locally, and many varieties of flowering cactus. Split-tailed terns, pelicans and cormorants are as plentiful as flying fish.

How long will Mexico's Land's End be so wild and beautiful? Maybe always, say the disgruntled hotelmen in La Paz: "The highway from Ensenada will never be built. Why? Because the state of Baja is much more powerful politically than this territory. Tijuana would become a ghost town. Nobody would stop there, except for gas. They'd never let that happen." The hotelmen say it regretfully, shaking their heads, but visitors smile happily and keep their fingers crossed.

Even the playful dolphins pound sharks by ramming them in the belly, then leap high in the air to express their pleasure." Eight-foot eels, 300-pound totuavas (croakers) and sea bass up to 600 pounds have been taken in this astonishing trench, whose depth is two miles in places. Around Cerralvo Island 1,000-pound swordfish are not uncommon, and the other bills, marlin and sail, are plentiful where a drop-off to 300 fathoms at the north end of the island plunges down to 800 fathoms off the east side, providing a perfect swimway for the big game fish. Here are tuna, feeding on mackerel and spinner dolphin, black marlin up to 800 pounds and more, and rocket-shaped needle fish. In the forty-foot-deep tidal pools around Puerto Chileno at the cape, there is an abundance of blue crevallés, snappers, groupers, goatfish, gobies and blennies.

Amazingly, considering the dryness of the terrain with its scarcity of trees and water holes, wildlife is plentiful in many parts of the peninsula. There are pumas and bobcats, coyotes, foxes, squirrel, ringtail cats, raccoons, badgers, deer (up to 300 pounds on Tiburón Island) mountain goats and antelope, boar, wild asses, and rattlers.

MEXICAN CHRONOLOGY

Pre-Conquest

c. 9000 B.C.	First traces of man in Mexico.
c. 6000 B.C.	First traces of agriculture in Mexico.
c. 2000 B.C.	First traces of pottery making in Mexico.
c. 800 B.C.	First Horizon Culture (Olmec) emerges.
c. 300 B.C.	Second Horizon Culture (Teotihuacán) emerges; Monte Albán settled.
c. 500 A.D.	Teotihuacán begins decline; southern Zapotec (Monte Albán) and Maya cultures begin to flourish.
c. 900 A.D.	End of Classic Maya culture.
c. 980 A.D.	Toltecs consolidate power north of Mexico City by building Tula.
c. 1200 A.D.	Toltecs driven from Tula, migrate to Maya sites in Yucatán.
c. 1248 A.D.	Aztec tribes from north occupy site of Tenochtitlán (Mexico City).
c. 1428 A.D.	Aztec culture at apogee dominates Valley of Mexico; Mixtec Renaissance in South.
c. 1502 A.D.	Moctezuma II ascends to throne of Aztec Empire, controlling most of Mexico.

Conquest

1519	Cortés, after skirting coasts of Yucatán and Tabasco already visited by Córdoba and Grijalva, lands at Veracruz and conquers Totonacs at Cempoala. Tlaxcalans defeated. Cholula invested. Entry into Tenochtitlán.
1520	Defeat of Narváez at Cempoala. Death of Moctezuma II. *La Noche Triste* (June 30). Battle of Otumba. Cuauhtémoc becomes last Aztec emperor.

1521 Siege and destruction of Tenochtitlán.
1522 Alvarado, en route to Guatemala, subjugates Zapotecs and Mixtecs, founds Oaxaca. Tarascon Empire in western Mexico conquered.
1524 Entry of friars into Mexico City; Cortés permits himself to be publicly scourged by them as example to Indians. Expedition by Cortés to Guatemala and Honduras.
1525 Cuauhtémoc executed.
1531 Apparition of Virgin of Guadalupe to Juan Diego, "confirmed" by Bishop Zumárraga.
1540 Montejos found Mérida, enslave the Toltec-Mayas.
1547 Death of Cortés in Spain.

New Spain

1550 End of viceroyalty of Mendoza, first Viceroy of New Spain; succeeded by Velasco.
1551 University of Mexico founded.
1640 Work begun on Cathedral of Valladolid (Morelia).
1695 Death of Sor Juana Inés de la Cruz at age 34.
1757 Santa Prisca at Taxco built by order of José de la Borda.
1759 Birth of Francisco Eduardo Tresguerras.
1767 Expulsion of the Jesuit Order.
1771 Reformist Viceroy Bucareli tries to break *gachupín* monopoly.
1774 Reform fails with dismissal of liberal Viceroy Gigedo.

Independence

1810 Hidalgo sounds *Grito de Dolores*. Fall of the Alhóndiga at Guanajuato to Hidalgo and Allende. Valladolid (Morelia) captured by revolutionists. Battle of Las Cruces.
1811 Hidalgo defeated at Bridge of Calderón near Guadalajara.
1813 Morelos drafts radical constitution at Chilpancingo. Defeated by Iturbide at Valladolid (Morelia).
1821 Iturbide publishes Plan of Iguala. Independence from Spain proclaimed.
1822 Iturbide crowned Emperor.
1823 Iturbide overthrown, flees to Europe.

The War with the United States

1834 Dictatorship of Santa Anna begins.
1836 Fall of the Alamo. Santa Anna defeated at San Jacinto, Texas.

1837   Texas' independence recognized by United States, Great Britain, France, Belgium.

1845   Texas admitted as a state to the United States.

1846   United States declares war on Mexico. Doniphan conquers New Mexico and Zachary Taylor captures Monterrey.

1847   Kearny takes California. Santa Anna defeated by Taylor at Buena Vista. Winfield Scott takes Veracruz, and following his victory at Cerro Gordo, advances to Puebla and Mexico City. Santa Anna's armies, defeated at Contreras, Churubusco, and Chapultepec, capitulate and Scott becomes military Governor of Mexico.

1848   Treaty of Guadalupe Hidalgo. Mexico cedes New Mexico, Arizona and California to the United States, receiving $15 million, retaining Baja California.

1855   Santa Anna ousted from seventh and last presidency, flees abroad.

The Reform and the Dictatorship

1857   Juárez President.

1858   Juárez driven to Veracruz by clerical-landowner alliance.

1860   Porfirio Díaz and Marcos Pérez recapture Oaxaca for Juárez.

1861   Juárez, first civilian to rule Mexico, enters capital in black carriage. Civil War begins in the United States. European armies invade Mexico.

1862   General Zaragoza defeats French at Puebla (*Cinco de Mayo*).

1863   French take Mexico City, install Maximilian Hapsburg as Emperor.

1864   Maximilian crowned. Juárez flees to New Orleans, organizes resistance.

1867   Siege of Querétaro. Maximilian executed. Reform begins anew.

1872   Death of Juárez. Díaz plots revolt against his successor.

1876   Díaz' dictatorship begins.

1901   Victoriano Huerta completes subjugation of dissident Mayas in Yucatán and turns peninsula over to fifty henequen planters.

1909   The Creelman interview. Vasconcelos and others demand liberty. Madero arouses country on antireelection speaking tour.

1910   Madero, escaping Díaz' jail, publishes Plan of San Luis Potosí.

The Revolution

1910 Ciudad Juárez stormed by Francisco Villa and Pascual Orozco.

1911 Díaz flees into exile. Madero elected President in free election.

1913 The Ten Tragic Days. Madero murdered. Huerta dictator.

1914 Huerta defeated by armies of Villa and Obregón, acting in behalf of Constitutionalist "First Chief," Carranza. At Convention of Aguascalientes, Villa and Zapata join forces, breaking with Carranza and Obregón, and taking the capital.

1915 Villa defeated by Obregón at Celaya and León.

1917 Constitution of Carranza passed but not enforced.

1920 Carranza ousted by Obregón and Calles. Carranza assassinated. Obregón President.

1923 Vasconcelos gives Orozco and Rivera first major mural commissions.

1924 Calles succeeds Obregón, who is assassinated four years later.

Modern Mexico

1928 Calles becomes *jefe máximo*. Monolithic ruling party (PNR) created.

1931 Anticlerical campaign. Garrido Canabal's Red Shirts rule Tabasco.

1932 Caso begins excavation of Monte Albán.

1934 Cárdenas President. Calles in eclipse. Distribution of land to peasants begins.

1936 Orozco begins four years' mural work in Guadalajara.

1938 Cárdenas expropriates foreign oil properties. Cedillo rebellion suppressed.

1939 Siqueiros paints "Trial of Fascism" for Electrical Workers' Union.

1940 Ávila Camacho succeeds Cárdenas as President.

1946 Alemán President. Discovery of Bonampak murals by Giles G. Healey. Work on University City (O'Gorman Library, etc.) begins.

1952 Ruiz Cortines President. Ruz Lhuillier discovers King's Tomb at Palenque. Tamayo paints Bellas Artes murals.

1958 López Mateos President.

1964 Díaz Ordas President.

INDEX

INDEX

of persons mentioned in the text